On Democracy

On

A Veritas Paperback

Democracy

Robert A. Dahl

with a New Preface, an Introduction,
and Two Chapters by
Ian Shapiro

Yale UNIVERSITY PRESS   *New Haven & London*

Library of Congress Control Number: 2014957695
ISBN 978-0-300-25405-1 (paperback)

A catalogue record for this book is available from the British Library.

10 9 8 7 6 5 4 3 2 1

CONTENTS

Robert Dahl died in 2014 at the age of ninety-eight. He might well have been the most important political scientist of the twentieth century, and he was certainly one of its preeminent social scientists. He received strings of awards and honorary degrees, including the first Johan Skytte Prize, created in 1995 to remedy the lack of a Nobel Prize for Political Science. Citations to Dahl's work run to the tens of thousands, dwarfing those of his contemporaries. Numerous leaders of the profession today were his students.

Born in 1915 in Inwood, Iowa, Dahl grew up in Alaska, graduated from the University of Washington in 1936, finished his Ph.D. at Yale in 1940, and then joined the war effort. He served on the War Production Board and as a first lieutenant in the army, winning a Bronze Star with oak cluster for distinguished service. Following a brief stint in the Roosevelt administration he returned to Yale, this time as faculty, in 1946. He taught for forty years, retiring as Sterling Professor Emeritus in 1986. He remained an active scholar for another two decades.

In many ways, Dahl created the field of modern political science. To be sure, the scholarly study of politics goes back to at least the ancient Greeks. Dahl was no Plato, Aristotle, or Thomas Hobbes, but he added something new to the armchair reflection leavened by illuminating anecdote that had characterized the enterprise for millennia: the systematic use of evidence to evaluate rigorously stated theoretical claims. Generations of Dahl's successors developed both theories and empirical methods of many kinds since he produced his innovative works in the 1950s and 1960s, sometimes in ways that he found less than congenial. Few would deny that they stood on Dahl's shoulders.

Dahl is often considered the founder of the behavioral school of political science. That is because he emphasized observable conduct in his early theoretical work on power and the behavior of urban elites in *Who Governs?*, his study of decision-making in New Haven, Connecticut. But it misconstrues Dahl to identify him with that or any methodological school. Some of his work was conceptual, geared to enhancing our understanding of ideas like power and democracy. Some of it was institutional; he studied the feasibility and effectiveness of the separation of powers, whether democracy could survive without a market economy, and whether democratic firms could be efficient. Still other questions were normative, geared to determining which system of political representation is best, whether delegating political power to experts is a good idea, and how much inequality is desirable. He was a problem-driven scholar who addressed the major questions of his time and selected the methods appropriate to the task.

One illuminating window into Dahl's scholarship is to view him as having been engaged in a lifelong dialogue with James Madison. Dahl had great respect for the founding generation. Madison's contention in *Federalist* Number 10 that multiple factions could make democracy viable on a large scale might be the earliest statement of the logic of crosscutting cleavages on which Dahl would build his pluralist theory of democracy.

But the founders' institutional theories were another matter. In *A Preface to Democratic Theory*, published in 1956, he developed a trenchant critique of the separation of powers in general, of judicial review in particular, and of the system of representation that the founders devised as part of what turned out to be a vain attempt to head off civil war over slavery. Dahl maintained that the founders and legions of their followers were mistaken to think that the American constitutional order was responsible for the survival of American democracy. Rather, it was the pluralistic character of the society that permitted the constitutional order to survive.

In a seminal article in 1957, Dahl zeroed in on judicial review, arguing that the available data failed to support the conventional wisdom that the Supreme Court protects minority rights. Subsequent empirical scholarship has borne out Dahl's contention. Whether one looks at the United States over its own history, at comparisons among many countries, or at democracies that have gone from not having judicial review to having it, Dahl turns out to have been right that the heavy lifting is done by democracy, not constitutional courts. Authoritarian leaders ignore judges and courts with impunity, and adding courts to democracies has no appreciable effect on their protection of civic freedoms or minority rights. Yet curiously, we continue pressing for the creation of independent judiciaries to enforce bills of rights in new democracies.

Other major literatures have grown out of Dahl's critique of republican institutions in the *Preface* and elsewhere. One stream of scholarship focuses on the consequences of multiplying veto players through the structures of government. Scholars following Dahl have shown that doing so not only biases things toward the status quo but also biases things in favor of the well resourced. You need a lot of heft to move a recalcitrant elephant.

Dahl's work spawned another huge literature on representation. His skepticism of catering to intense minorities has stood up well. Critics of consociational democracy and other schemes designed to do this have shown that such catering tends to entrench them, producing the divisions and antipathies such schemes are intended to ameliorate. Dahl himself was especially troubled by the overrepresentation of small states in the U.S. Senate, one feature of the United States constitution that is virtually impossible to amend.

Dahl studied democracies all over the world, but usually with the United States in mind as a comparative benchmark. Although he disagreed strongly with Madison on many points, he thought that the bulk of the founders' mistakes derived from the challenge of creating a large-scale democracy for the first time—without our advantages of accumulated evidence and hindsight. Dahl was gratified to discover that Madison's post–*Federalist Papers* political experience led him to abandon his antipathy for political parties and, eventually, his hostility to majority rule as well. In Dahl's afterword to the fiftieth anniversary edition of the *Preface* published in 2006, he noted with appreciation that in 1833, three years before his death, Madison had declared that critics of majority rule "must either join the avowed disciples of aristocracy, oligarchy or monarchy, or look for a Utopia exhibiting a perfect homogeneousness of interests, opinions and feelings nowhere yet found in civilized communities."[1]

On Democracy was published in 1998. Dahl conceived of it as a guide to the democratic systems of the contemporary world and a sketch of the main challenges that they faced, a kind of *fin de siècle* stocktaking. The twentieth century had been one of major triumphs and shocking failures of democracy. The franchise had finally become universal. Exclusions based on race and gender were abolished in the older democracies, and architects of new democracies took universal adult suffrage for granted. But democracy suffered major setbacks in the middle third of the century with the rise and catastrophic consequences of fascism and communism.

The Second World War ended the European fascist interlude, though military authoritarianism returned to Greece between 1967 and 1974 and survived in Spain until General Franco's death the following year. Communism did not start collapsing until the mid-1980s. Democracy was quickly restored in much of Eastern Europe (with the notable exception of Yugoslavia) after the Berlin Wall fell in November of 1989, but things were less sanguine farther east. The former Asiatic republics of the USSR did not democratize. Democracy's hold on Russia was tenuous at best, as Dahl noted—a judgment he would surely reiterate today. The year 1989 saw brutal repression of democratic forces in China. Much of the rest of Asia, Africa, and Latin America remained authoritarian.

But, on balance, Dahl concluded that things looked good for democracy at the turn of the century. Whether measured in absolute numbers or as a proportion of the world's population, more people lived in democracies than ever before. And although nondemocratic regimes still outnumbered democracies (a ratio that would soon reverse itself), Dahl identified an unprecedented sixty-five democracies.

To be sure, Dahl was no teleologist. He noted that despite democracy's ancient lineage, it had vanished from the face of the earth for centuries. In principle that could happen again. But it seemed to him unlikely, given democracy's near-universal status as the font of political legitimacy in the contemporary world—reflected in the fact that most authoritarian leaders claim popular authorization and most authoritarian systems are portrayed as democracies or as peoples' republics of some sort. It is not surprising, therefore, that *On Democracy* devotes little space to the disappearance of democracy, a judgment that I suggest in my introduction to this new edition that he would likely revise if he were alive today. Dahl did identify three future challenges for democracy: whether more nondemocracies would democratize, whether new democracies would become consolidated, and whether the older ones would "perfect and deepen their democracy."

My additions at the end of this volume are organized around these three challenges. In Chapter 16, I take up the first two. There, I discuss newer democracies that have been struggling for life in the years since Dahl wrote in light of the evolving scholarship—much of it shaped by Dahl's original work on pluralism. Although there have been few advances in the study of transitions to democracy for reasons that I set out, we do know more about the conditions that make for successful consolidation of democracies. I explain why this knowledge supplies few grounds for optimism about the revolutions that spread across the Middle East in the second decade of the twenty-first century, or about other new democracies that lack diversified economies. Despite the widespread attention to the role of political institutions and Islamic political cultures in these countries, unless their economies develop and diversify, democracy is unlikely to be sustainable in any of them.

The challenges confronting established democracies are my subject in Chapter 17. Dahl wrote two books after the present one: *How Democratic Is the American Constitution?*, published in 2002, and *On Political Equality* four years later. In the first he expanded his long-standing critique of American institutions, arguing that they should be reformed in more democratic directions. In particular, he stressed that the Supreme Court's role should be limited to protecting "the fundamental rights that are necessary to the existence of a democratic political system." The more the Court strays from this democracy-reinforcing mandate, he argued, the more it becomes an unelected legislature that enacts laws and policies "in the guise of interpreting the Constitution—or, even more questionable, divining the obscure and often unknowable intentions of the Framers." Dahl confessed to a degree of "measured pessimism" over whether the Court could be reined in as he advocated, but he thought that it was not out of the question.[2]

On Political Equality offered a more somber assessment of the advanced democracies, and especially the United States, in light of the dramatic increases in inequality that had been in train for the better part of three decades by the time he wrote. In place of asking questions about "deepening" democracy by extending it to other spheres of life, notably the economy (which he had first proposed in *A Preface to Economic Democracy* in 1985), Dahl was now worried that inequality might contribute to democratic backsliding, a worry that he would surely reiterate today. Just as Madison had come to fear that the monied interests Alexander Hamilton championed in the early 1790s would destroy America's nascent democratic order, Dahl felt pressed to ask whether inequality might reach levels that would compromise democracy fundamentally. In Chapter 17 I argue that these concerns were well founded. Ironically, in view of Dahl's long-standing concerns about the Supreme Court, I conclude that, rather than protect the fundamental rights needed for the operation of democratic politics, the Court has aided and abetted democracy's subversion by monied interests.

I would like to thank, without implicating, Joseph LaPalombara, David Mayhew, and Douglas Rae for helpful comments on the Introduction.

Ian Shapiro

NOTES
1 Robert Dahl, *A Preface to Democratic Theory*, expanded ed. (Chicago, IL: University of Chicago Press, 2006), p. 167.
2 Robert Dahl, *How Democratic Is the American Constitution?* (New Haven, CT: Yale University Press, 2002), pp. 153–154, 156.

NOTE ON THE TEXT

Dahl's original text has not been altered. Apart from my new Introduction and the two additional chapters, which make up part V, I have added Appendix D "On Counting Democratic Countries II." This is adapted, modified, and updated from Robert Dahl, Ian Shapiro, and José Cheibub, *The Democracy Sourcebook* (Cambridge, MA: MIT Press, 2003). It summarizes current scholarship on different ways of measuring democracy and is reprinted with permission from Cheibub, its principal author, and MIT Press. I published parts of the Preface as "Democracy Man" in *Foreign Affairs* on February 12, 2014. That material is reproduced here with permission.

Ian Shapiro

Speculating about how someone who is no longer with us would view our present circumstances is always risky. It seems safe to say, however, that were he alive today Robert Dahl would be alarmed by the rise of populist political parties and extremist politics across much of the democratic world. In country after country, protectionist, anti-immigrant, and even anti-system parties have emerged and gained traction to a degree that would have surprised him as it has surprised many of us. Even traditional bastions of democracy have not been immune. Britain's establishment was upended by the Brexit referendum in June of 2016 that substantial majorities of both major parties in Parliament opposed. Later that year, Republicans in the United States found themselves powerless to stop Donald Trump's insurgency. Dahl would surely have sought to understand the factors that had produced this virulent politics and its baleful effects on political parties in so many democracies, and to consider what the best responses might be.

It is harder to say what Dahl would have concluded about this state of affairs. That is partly because, for all his voluminous writing about almost every aspect of democratic politics over more than half a century, Dahl had surprisingly little to say about the nature or operation of political parties. True, he affirmed their vital importance for the healthy operation of any democracy, and he noted with appreciation that within five years of the Constitutional Convention, James Madison had abandoned his antipathy for parties and come round to this view.[1] Whereas Madison previously had sought to design institutions so as to limit the "mischiefs of faction" that he had seen as embedded in parties, he now viewed parties not merely as inevitable but desirable. "In all political societies," he declared, "different interests and parties arise out of the nature of things, and the great art of politicians lies in making them checks and balances to each other."[2] Dahl had long been critical of the American founders' confidence in the separation of powers, noting that Madison's oft repeated phrase from *Federalist* Number 51 that "ambition must be made to counteract ambition" lacked a convincing account of how this might actually work.[3] It is scarcely surprising, therefore, that he found Madison's new focus on the idea of competing parties checking and balancing one another more congenial.

Dahl was skeptical, however, that this could be achieved in a constitutional system that had expressly been designed to frustrate the effective operation of parties. In 1950, a committee of the American Political Science Association investigating the state of America's parties had proposed reforms designed to make them more like the disciplined programmatic parties in the United Kingdom.[4] Dahl, then a young scholar four years into his career, did not participate in the APSA committee or comment on its report. But three years later, in *Politics, Economics, and Welfare,* he and his colleague Charles Lindblom registered skepticism toward proposals for stronger party government suggested by political scientists who had been inspired by the APSA report. Dahl and Lindblom identified major obstacles embedded in the constitution: the separation of powers that often produces divided-party government; the bicameral system that overrepresents small rural states in the Senate; an independently elected president who is often at odds with even with his own congressional party; staggered elections for the different branches that blunt the accountability for what the government does; and a strong federal system that further diffuses the national government's power and accountability.[5]

Even bracketing these institutional considerations, Dahl and Lindblom were doubtful that people in the United States would ever cleave to ideologically well-defined political parties. Rather, interest groups would look out for themselves. "In a country where social pluralism and disagreement are great relative to the amount of basic agreement, almost every group can make a rational calculation that its advantage lies in keeping open the opportunity to block action and insist on bargaining" for benefits for its members.[6] Accordingly, even though Dahl preferred parliamentary government to the American hybrid, as he would dub it in his *Preface to Democratic Theory* in 1956, he did not hold out much hope that the American system could meaningfully be reformed in that direction.[7]

Dahl's concerns about the U.S. system's hobbled capacity to govern in the public interest became more pronounced over time. By the time he published *How Democratic Is the American Constitution?* in 2002 (based on his Castle Lectures delivered at Yale two years earlier) he had concluded that some version for proportional representation (PR) and multiparty government would be better for the United States. Territorially based representation cannot be abolished without amending the constitution which guarantees each state two and only two Senators and at least one House seat with a minimum district size of 30,000. Accordingly, drawing on the example of mixed systems in such countries as New Zealand and Germany, Dahl proposed a 600-member house of representatives with half elected in single-member districts and the other half from statewide party lists, allocated in proportion to the share of the national vote.[8]

Dahl argued that the United States lacks the frequently touted advantages of single-member district systems that typically produce two parties.[9] One is better accountability: governments in two-party systems must implement the programs they run on or be held to account by voters at the next election, whereas coalition partners in multiparty systems can always blame one another, diffusing accountability. But Dahl noted that in the United States an independently elected president plus frequent divided party control in the legislature also diffuses accountability. On the other alleged advantage of two-party systems—that they are better at delivering what most voters need—Dahl followed his former student Arend Lijphart in contending that the evidence suggests otherwise. At least when compared to the United States, PR systems are more effective at providing social protection and ameliorating injustice. They are less unequal and they incarcerate fewer people. Add to this that PR systems are fairer and more representative than two-party systems in which the winning party might not have a plurality—never mind a majority—of the national popular vote, and the case for introducing a mixed system of the German sort seemed to him clear. There would be no loss of accountability, there would be gains in fairness, and there might be better policy as well.[10]

Would Dahl take the same view today? I am skeptical. At least he would have thought it a more difficult call. For one thing, the greater ability of PR systems to deliver social protection seems, in hindsight, to have depended at least partly on the presence of strong left-of-center parties like Germany's Social Democrats (SPD) that were frequently in government and indeed had often been the leading party in government when he wrote in 2002. This, in turn, reflected the existence of big industrial workforces and strong labor unions that could bargain with and balance business interests in the economy and political system. The combined effects of globalization and technology have diminished the industrial workforces in all the older democracies, and the shift to service sector economies that are much harder to organize has weakened the power of organized labor. The result is that left-of-center parties have diminished capacity to defend shrinking industrial workforces, and even less to defend others in their traditional constituencies. Unemployment actually increases when they are in office.[11]

It is not surprising in this context that left parties in multiparty systems have been fragmenting over the past two decades. Germany's SPD has been hemorrhaging voters to the neo-Marxist *Die Linke*, the Green Party, and some even to the far-right anti-immigrant *Alternative für Deutschland* (AfD). This pattern has been repeated in almost all the multiparty democracies, with center-left parties that routinely used to come in first or second now placing fourth or fifth in increasingly fragmented fields. And fragmentation on the left can precipitate fragmentation on the right, also illustrated in Germany. In the early 2010s, Angela Merkel moved toward the center partly in hopes of picking off disaffected SPD voters for her Christian Democrats (CDU), but this opened up space on her right for the AfD to emerge and grow to the point that, by 2017, it had become the third largest party in the Bundestag.

Fragmentation makes it harder to form governments because a greater number of parties is often needed to command a majority in the legislature. This means satisfying often mutually incompatible demands. After Germany's 2017 elections, Merkel spent many months in fruitless negotiations with the Greens and Germany's libertarian *Freie Demokratische Partei*. This was scarcely surprising since the Greens want enhanced environmental regulation whereas the Free Democrats' raison d'être is to reduce regulation. Her previous partner, the SPD, had refused to return to a grand coalition because they attributed their declining share of the vote to the compromises they had made to govern with her CDU. They relented following the collapse of her other negotiations only because by then polling revealed that the AfD would do even better were Germany to hold another election. That fear was validated by regional elections the following year, when both the CDU and the SPD again lost support to the extreme parties.[12]

These developments might well have prompted Dahl to rethink his tentative endorsement of the German model in *How Democratic Is the American Constitution?* and worry more about democratic backsliding. As he noted in *On Democracy,* there is nothing inevitable about democracy's survival, and it is hard not to think, today, about parallels with the 1920s and early 1930s. They were also an era of economic stagnation and stress for many voters living in the aftermath of World War One and the Depression. In Weimar Germany, parties in the Reichstag had fragmented, creating openings for Hitler's National Socialists to get a foothold and then expand—just as Benito Mussolini's fascist dominated National List had done in Italy after 1924. In Britain, by contrast, the two-party system made it impossible for Oswald Mosley's New Party and its successor British Union of Fascists to win seats at Westminster, despite the fact that at one point they boasted 50,000 members and in 1936 one commentator observed it to be more vibrant than Hitler's National Socialists had been in the run-up to their seizure of power three years earlier.[13]

To date in Germany, the mainstream parties have shunned the AfD as beyond the pale from the standpoint of forming coalitions. But how long can that continue if the AfD keeps growing while other parties shrink and fragment? Governments in countries like Austria and the Netherlands have been forced to depend on far-right parties, at least implicitly. Again, in the United Kingdom this problem does arise. Parties like the racist British National Party and the far-left Communist Party of Britain have no electoral presence at Westminster, and even the United Kingdom Independence Party (UKIP)—whose 3.8 million votes in the 2015 general election would have garnered close to a hundred seats in Parliament if Britain had proportional representation—secured only a single seat.[14] Putting proportional representation on the table for the United States must raise comparable questions, such as whether Nazi sympathizer Charles Lindbergh and his America First committee might have morphed into a significant congressional party in the 1940s or whether Joseph McCarthy might have gone the same route once ostracized by the Republicans after 1954. The two-party system blocks such possibilities.

Some will note that America's two-party system did not prevent Donald Trump's takeover of the Republicans in 2016. But the reason is that America's parties, always weak as Dahl and Lindblom noted in 1953, have been weakened further by reforms since the 1970s. In particular, the increased importance of low turnout primaries dominated by activists on the fringes of the parties magnifies their influence out of all proportion to their numbers. Trump was selected in the Republican primaries by some five percent of the U.S. electorate.[15] Similar dynamics play out in Congress. The United States has had congressional primaries since the Progressive era, but in recent decades the great increase in the number of safe seats has amplified their importance.[16] As with presidential primaries, congressional primaries are bedeviled by low turnout that empowers the activists on the fringes of the parties—contributing to polarized parties in Congress no less than at the presidential level.

It wasn't always so. In the early nineteenth century, congressional parties selected their presidential candidates. These "congressional caucuses" faced powerful incentives to pick candidates with whom they could govern while also winning in their own districts and states, in effect making the U.S. system operate more like a parliamentary one. In the run-up to the 1828 election, Andrew Jackson, furious at having been denied selection despite his good showing with voters four years earlier, mounted the first populist assault on this system which he lambasted as a bastion of corrupt elitism. It was replaced by party conventions starting in the 1830s. This was the first in the long series of reforms that have further weakened America's congenitally weak congressional parties, culminating in our current system. This weakening renders parties less able to govern effectively and more susceptible to influence—and even hostile takeovers—by fringe elements and well-funded outside groups.

Were Dahl alive today, I believe he would favor strengthening congressional parties. Despite the limitations inherent in this endeavor for the reasons he and Lindblom identified in 1953, he would have recognized the ways in which the situation has become worse and supported reforms to reverse the trend. As he said in 2002, "we can be pretty sure that a country wholly without competitive parties is a country without democracy."[17] With the United States perilously close to that threshold, and with the multiparty alternative no longer as appealing as it once appeared, Dahl would likely have favored reforms to de-emphasize the role of primaries in selecting candidates for Congress and the presidency, particularly when turnout is low as typically it is. He might well also have advocated redistricting reforms, particularly the move in a number of states to shift this responsibility from state legislatures, where the party in control predictably draws boundaries so as to buttress its partisan advantage, to independent commissions. I suspect that he would have argued that these commissions should deploy criteria to diversify districts so as to make them competitive between the parties, reducing the number of safe seats. Dahl might also have endorsed moves to push for statehood for Puerto Rico and Washington, D.C., as well as initiatives to break up large states like Texas and California. This would blunt the massively disproportionate power of small states in the Senate that troubled him.[18]

Dahl might also have rethought his antipathy for the Electoral College. He observed that it had never operated as the founders intended, but his main objection was twofold: as with the Senate, the Electoral College overrepresents small states and it can produce outcomes, like the ones he identified in 1876 and 2000 and which occurred again in 2016, where the winner of the popular vote fails to win the presidency.[19] Dahl noted that the smaller states would likely continue using their disproportionate Senate power to block efforts to repeal the Electoral College by constitutional amendment, so he endorsed the proposal that state legislatures require proportional allocation of their Electoral College votes. In a like spirit, he might have looked favorably on the National Popular Vote Interstate Compact, an agreement by states (adopted by sixteen of them and the District of Colombia as of March 2020) to award all their electoral College votes to whoever wins the popular vote nationally, once this proposal has been adopted by states controlling a majority of the Electoral College votes.[20]

Or would he? If our only consideration is fair representation in presidential elections, then exorcising the Electoral College's effects makes eminent sense. But it becomes a more difficult call if populist politics and weak parties in the legislature are major concerns. America's founders had anticipated a weak presidency. Their worry was that Congress, and particularly the House of Representatives, would be the most powerful branch due to its proximity to the people. In fact, power has migrated to the presidency seldom to be reclaimed by the other branches for long, partly because—as Dahl was one of the first scholars to observe—it is much harder for four-hundred-and-thirty-five Representatives and a hundred Senators to subordinate their own conflicts and coordinate to protect their institution than it is for a president to aggrandize the presidency at their expense.[21]

Direct popular election would strengthen the president's independent legitimacy, enhancing his or her ability to declare that no one else speaks for the American people. It would make the U.S. system more like Latin America's presidential systems that, as Dahl's longtime colleague Juan Linz established, are less stable and more susceptible to the appeals of populist demagogues than are parliamentary democracies.[22] The authors of West Germany's constitution after World War II avoided replicating the toxic combination of a weak legislature and a powerful executive that had helped wreak such havoc in Weimar during the early 1930s. It is hard to imagine Dahl wanting to push the United States in that direction from the vantage-point of 2020.

Dahl's criticisms of the American system that began in the 1950s and became more extensive in his last works make it clear that he would have preferred more far-reaching reforms than those discussed here. But Dahl was also a realist, disinclined to let the best become the enemy of the good. This is why he focused mainly on proposals that could be implemented without the laborious process of constitutional amendment. Like Madison, he was also keenly attuned to what could be learned from evidence and experience, and willing to revise his opinions in light of those lessons. For this reason, I have suggested here that he would have been less sanguine today than he was in 2002 about reforming the American system along the lines of Europe's multiparty systems. They no longer seem to offer the advantages that some scholars attributed to them in the 1980s and '90s, and the emergence and growth of extremist parties in many of them over the past decade surely would have given him pause. He would also have been alarmed by the rise of populist extremism in the United States, which is why, I have argued, he would likely have endorsed policies designed to strengthen America's parties within the constraints of a constitutional system that he regarded as flawed but unlikely to change.

Ian Shapiro

NOTES

1 Robert Dahl, *How Democratic Is the American Constitution?* (New Haven, CT: Yale University Press, 2003), p. 33; James Madison, "Parties," National Gazette, ca. January 23, 1792. https://founders.archives.gov/documents/Madison/01-14-02-0176 [04-12-2020].

2 For his subsequent ascription of that checking role to political parties, see James Madison, "Parties," *National Gazette*, ca. January 23, 1792. https://founders.archives.gov/documents/Madison/01-14-02-0176 [05-14-2020.

3 Madison's discussion of the separation of powers engendering a system in which ambition counteracts ambition occurs in Federalist Number 51. See Alexander Hamilton, James Madison, and John Jay, *The Federalist Papers*, ed. by Ian Shapiro (New Haven:Yale University Press, 2009), p. 264. For Dahl's critique, see *A Preface to Democratic Theory* (Chicago: University of Chicago Press, 1953), pp. 4-33.

4 "Toward a More Responsible Two-Party System: A Report of the Committee on Political Parties, American Political Science Association," *American Political Science Review*, supplement: Vol. 44, No. 3 (1950) part 2, pp. 1-97.

5 Robert Dahl and Charles Lindblom, *Politics, Economics, and Welfare* (New York: Routledge, Taylor & Francis, 1953), pp. 354-356.

6 Dahl and Lindblom, *Politics*, p. 355.

7 Dahl, *Preface, pp. 124-151*.

8 Dahl, *How Democratic?*, pp. 174-175.

9 This follows from Duverger's law, which holds that the number of parties is determined by district magnitude (the number of candidates elected per district) plus one. See Maurice Duverger, *Political Parties: Their Organization and Activity in the Modern State*, 2nd ed. (New York: Routledge & Kegan Paul, 1964). This will be true provided the districts are large and similarly diverse. If there is considerable regional variation, as in India, then there will be partly proliferation even with single member plurality districts.

10 Dahl, *How Democratic?*, pp. 91-120.

11 Christian Salas, Frances Rosenbluth, and Ian Shapiro, "Political Parties and Public Policy," *NOMOS LXIII: Democratic Failure,* edited by Melissa Schwartzberg and Daniel Viehoff (New York: NYU press, forthcoming 2020), manuscript p. 12.

12 Josie Le Blond, "Merkel Suffers Another Election Setback in Key German State of Hesse," *The Guardian,* October 29, 2018. https://www.theguardian .com/world/2018/oct/28/merkel-suffers-another-election-setback-key -german-state-of-hesse [05–15–2020].

13 Frances Rosenbluth and Ian Shapiro, *Responsible Parties: Saving Democracy from Itself* (New Haven: Yale University Press, 2018), p. 164.

14 Rosenbluth and Shapiro, *Responsible Parties,* pp. 16–17.

15 "Only 9 Percent of America Selected Trump and Clinton as the Nominees," https://www.nytimes.com/interactive/2016/08/01/us/elections/nine-percent -of-america-selected-trump-and-clinton.html.

16 Alan Abramowitz, Brad Alexander, and Matthew Gunning, "Incumbency, Redistricting, and the Decline of Competition in U.S. House Elections," *Journal of Politics,* Vol. 68, No. 1 (February 2006), pp. 75–88. See also David Wasserman and Ally Finn, "Introducing the 2017 Cook Political Report Partisan Voting Index," Cook Political Report April 7, 2017. https://www .dropbox.com/s/2bzk5lssu2iyir2/2017%20Cook%20Political%20Report%20 Partisan%20Voter%20Index.pdf?dl=0 [05–15–2020]

17 Dahl, *How Democratic?,* p. 30.

18 Dahl, *How Democratic?,* 13–18, 48–50, 144–148.

19 Dahl, *How Democratic?,* pp. 73–89.

20 Dahl, *How Democratic?,* pp. 86–87; "Status of National Popular Vote Bill in Each State," National Popular Vote, https://www.nationalpopularvote.com /state-status [05–16–2020].

21 See Ian Shapiro, *Politics Against Domination* (Cambridge, MA: Harvard University Press, 2016), pp. 68–70.

22 Juan Linz, "The Perils of Presidentialism," *The Journal of Democracy,* Vol. 1, No. 1 (Winter 1990), pp. 51–69

On Democracy

CHAPTER 1

Do We Really Need a Guide?

During the last half of the twentieth century the world witnessed an extraordinary and unprecedented political change. All of the main alternatives to democracy either disappeared, turned into eccentric survivals, or retreated from the field to hunker down in their last strongholds. Earlier in the century the premodern enemies of democracy—centralized monarchy, hereditary aristocracy, oligarchy based on narrow and exclusive suffrage—had lost their legitimacy in the eyes of much of humankind. The main antidemocratic regimes of the twentieth century—communist, fascist, Nazi—disappeared in the ruins of calamitous war or, as in the Soviet Union, collapsed from within. Military dictatorships had been pretty thoroughly discredited by their failures, particularly in Latin America; where they managed to survive they often adopted a pseudo-democratic façade.

So had democracy at last won the contest for the support of people throughout the world? Hardly. Antidemocratic beliefs and movements continued, frequently associated with fanatical nationalism or religious fundamentalism. Democratic governments (with varying degrees of "democracy") existed in fewer than half the countries of the world, which contained less than half the world's population. One-fifth of the world's people lived in China, which in its illustrious four thousand years of history had never experienced democratic government. In Russia, which had made the transition to democratic rule only in the last decade of the century, democracy was fragile and weakly supported. Even in countries where democracy had long been established and seemed secure, some observers held that democracy was in crisis, or at least severely strained by a decline in the confidence of citizens that their elected leaders, the political parties, and government officials could or would cope fairly or successfully with issues like persistent unemployment, poverty, crime, welfare programs, immigration, taxation, and corruption.

Suppose we divide the nearly two hundred countries of the world into those with nondemocratic governments, those with new democratic governments, and those with long and relatively well established democratic governments. Admittedly, each group contains an enormously diverse set of countries. Yet our threefold simplification helps us to see that viewed from a democratic perspective each group faces a different challenge. For the nondemocratic countries, the challenge is whether and how they can make the *transition* to democracy. For the newly democratized countries, the challenge is whether and how the new democratic practices and institutions can be strengthened or, as some political scientists would say, *consolidated,* so that they will withstand the tests of time, political conflict, and crisis. For the older democracies, the challenge is to perfect and *deepen* their democracy.

At this point, however, you might well ask: Just what do we mean by democracy? What distinguishes a democratic government from a nondemocratic government? If a nondemocratic country makes the transition to democracy, what is the transition *to?* When can we tell whether it has made the transition? As to consolidating democracy, what, exactly, is consolidated? And what can it mean to speak of deepening democracy in a democratic country? If a country is already a democracy, how can it become more democratic? And so on.

Democracy has been discussed off and on for about twenty-five hundred years, enough time to provide a tidy set of ideas about democracy on which everyone, or nearly everyone, could agree. For better or worse, that is not the case.

The twenty-five centuries during which democracy has been discussed, debated, supported, attacked, ignored, established, practiced, destroyed, and then sometimes reestablished have not, it seems, produced agreement on some of the most fundamental questions about democracy.

Ironically, the very fact that democracy has such a lengthy history has actually contributed to confusion and disagreement, for "democracy" has meant different things to different people at different times and places. Indeed, during long periods in human history democracy disappeared in practice, remaining barely alive as an idea or a memory among a precious few. Until only two centuries ago—let's say ten generations—history was very short on actual examples of democracies. Democracy was more a subject for philosophers to theorize about than an actual political system for people to adopt and practice. And even in the rare cases where a "democracy" or a "republic" actually existed, most adults were not entitled to participate in political life.

Although in its most general sense democracy is ancient, the form of democracy I shall be mainly discussing in this book is a product of the twentieth century. Today we have come to assume that democracy must guarantee virtually every adult citizen the right to vote. Yet until about four generations ago—around 1918, or the end of the First World War—in every independent democracy or republic that had ever existed up to then, a good half of all adults had always been excluded from the full rights of citizenship. These were, of course, women.

Here, then, is an arresting thought: if we accept universal adult suffrage as a requirement of democracy, there would be some persons in practically every democratic country who would be older than their democratic system of government. Democracy in our modern sense may not be exactly youthful, but it is hardly ancient.

You might object at once: Wasn't the United States a democracy from the American Revolution onward—a "democracy in a republic," as Abraham Lincoln called it? Didn't the illustrious French writer Alexis de Tocqueville, after visiting the United States in the 1830s, call his famous work *Democracy in America?* And didn't the Athenians call their system a democracy in the fifth century B.C.E.? What was the Roman republic, if not some kind of democracy? If "democracy" has meant different things at different times, how can we possibly agree on what it means today?

Once started, you might persist: Why is democracy desirable anyway? And just how democratic is "democracy" in countries that we call democracies today: the United States, Britain, France, Norway, Australia, and many others? Further, is it possible to explain why these countries are "democratic" and many others are not? The questions could go on and on.

The answer to the question in the title of this chapter, then, is pretty clear. If you are interested in searching for answers to some of the most basic questions about democracy, a guide can help.

Of course, during this short tour you won't find answers to all the questions you might like to ask. To keep our journey relatively brief and manageable, we shall have to bypass innumerable paths that you might feel should be explored. They probably should be, and I hope that by the end of our tour you will undertake to explore them on your own. To help you do so, at the end of the book I'll provide a brief list of relevant works for further reading on your part.

Our journey begins at the beginning: the origins of democracy.

PART I *The Beginning*

CHAPTER 2

Where and How Did Democracy Develop?

A BRIEF HISTORY

I started, you remember, by saying that democracy has been discussed off and on for twenty-five hundred years. Is democracy really that old, you might wonder? Many Americans, and probably others as well, might believe that democracy began two hundred years ago in the United States. Others, aware of its classical roots, would claim ancient Greece or Rome. Just where did it begin and how did it evolve?

It might please us to see democracy as more or less continuously advancing from its invention, so to speak, in ancient Greece twenty-five hundred years ago and spreading gradually outward from that tiny beginning to the present day, when it has reached every continent and a substantial portion of humanity.

A pretty picture but false for at least two reasons.

First, as everyone acquainted with European history knows, after its early centuries in Greece and Rome the rise of popular government turned into its decline and disappearance. Even if we were to allow ourselves considerable latitude in deciding what governments we would count as "popular," "democratic," or "republican," their rise and decline could not be portrayed as a steady upward climb to the distant summit, punctuated only by brief descents here and there. Instead the course of democratic history would look like the path of a traveler crossing a flat and almost endless desert broken by

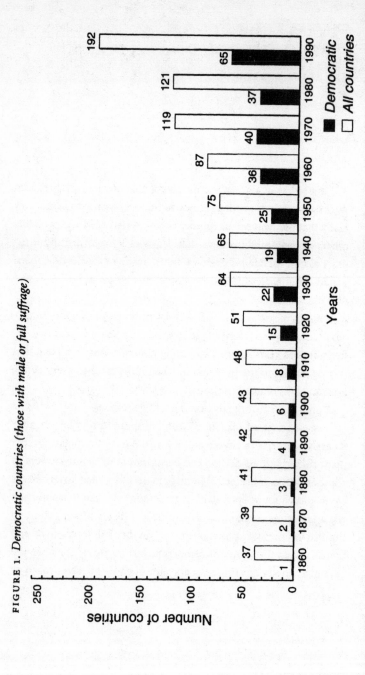

FIGURE 1. Democratic countries (those with male or full suffrage)

■ Democratic
□ All countries

Years

Number of countries

only a few hills, until the path finally begins the long climb to its present heights (fig. 1).

In the second place, it would be a mistake to assume that democracy was just invented once and for all, as, for example, the steam engine was invented. When anthropologists and historians find that similar tools or practices have appeared in different times and places, they generally want to know how these separate appearances came about. Did the tools or practices spread by means of diffusion from its original inventors to the other groups, or instead were they independently invented by different groups? Finding an answer is often difficult, perhaps impossible. So too with the development of democracy in the world. How much of its spread is to be explained simply by its diffusion from its early sources and how much, if any, by its having been independently invented in different times and places?

Although with democracy the answer is surrounded by a good deal of uncertainty, my reading of the historical record is in essence this: some of the expansion of democracy—perhaps a good deal of it—can be accounted for mainly by the diffusion of democratic ideas and practices, but diffusion cannot provide the whole explanation. Like fire, or painting or writing, democracy seems to have been invented more than once, and in more than one place. After all, if the conditions were favorable for the invention of democracy at one time and place (in Athens, say, about 500 B.C.E.), might not similar favorable conditions have existed elsewhere?

I assume that democracy can be independently invented and reinvented whenever the appropriate conditions exist. And the appropriate conditions have existed, I believe, at different times and in different places. Just as a supply of tillable land and adequate rainfall have generally encouraged the development of agriculture, so certain favorable conditions have always supported a tendency toward the development of a democratic government. For example, because of favorable conditions some form of democracy probably existed for tribal governments long before recorded history.

Consider this possibility: Certain people, we'll assume, make up a fairly well-bounded group—"we" and "they," ourselves and others, my people and their people, my tribe and other tribes. In addition, let's assume that the group—the tribe, let's say—is fairly independent of control by outsiders; the members of tribe can, so to speak, more or less run their own show without interference by outsiders. Finally, let's assume that a substantial number of the members of the group, perhaps the tribal elders, see themselves as about equal in being well qualified to have a say in governing the group. In these circumstances, democratic tendencies are, I believe, likely to arise. A push toward democratic participation develops out of what we might call *the logic of equality*.

Over the long period when human beings lived together in small groups and survived by hunting game and collecting roots, fruits, berries, and other offerings of nature, they would no doubt have sometimes, perhaps usually, developed a system in which a good many of the members animated by the logic of equality—the older or more experienced ones, anyway—participated in whatever decisions they needed to make as a group. That such was indeed the case is strongly suggested by studies of nonliterate tribal societies. For many thousands of years, then, some form of primitive democracy may well have been the most "natural" political system.

We know, however, that this lengthy period came to an end. When human beings began to settle down for long stretches of time in fixed communities, primarily for agriculture and trade, the kinds of circumstances favorable to popular participation in government that I just mentioned—group identity, little outside interference, an assumption of equality—seem to have become rare. Forms of hierarchy and domination came to be more "natural." As a result, popular governments vanished among settled people for thousands of years. They were replaced by monarchies, despotisms, aristocracies, or oligarchies, all based on some form of ranking or hierarchy.

Then around 500 B.C.E. in several places favorable conditions seem to have reappeared and a few small groups of people began to develop systems of government that provided fairly extensive opportunities to participate in group decisions. Primitive democracy, one might say, was reinvented in a more advanced form. The most crucial developments occurred in Europe, three along the Mediterranean coast, others in Northern Europe.

THE MEDITERRANEAN

It was in classical Greece and Rome around 500 B.C.E. that systems of government providing for popular participation by a substantial number of citizens were first established on foundations so solid that, with occasional changes, they endured for centuries.

Greece. Classical Greece was not a country in our modern sense, a place in which all Greeks lived within a single state with a single government. Instead, Greece was composed of several hundred independent cities, each with its surrounding countryside. Unlike the United States, France, Japan, and other modern countries, the so-called nation-states or national states that have *largely* dominated the modern world, the sovereign states of Greece were city-states. The most famous city-state, in classical times and after, was Athens. In 507 B.C.E. the Athenians adopted a system of popular government that lasted nearly two centuries, until the city was subjugated by its more powerful neighbor to the north, Macedonia. (After 321 B.C.E. the Athenian government limped along under Macedonian control for generations; then the city was subjugated again, this time by the Romans.)

It was the Greeks—probably the Athenians—who coined the term *democracy,* or *demokratia,* from the Greek words *demos,* the people, and *kratos,* to rule. It is interesting, by the way, that while in

Athens the word *demos* usually referred to the entire Athenian people, sometimes it meant only the common people or even just the poor. The word *democracy*, it appears, was sometimes used by its aristocratic critics as a kind of epithet, to show their disdain for the common people who had wrested away the aristocrats' previous control over the government. In any case, *democratia* was applied specifically by Athenians and other Greeks to the government of Athens and of many other cities in Greece as well.[1]

Among the Greek democracies, that of Athens was far and away the most important, the best known then and today, of incomparable influence on political philosophy, and often held up later as a prime example of citizen participation or, as some would say, participatory democracy.

The government of Athens was complex, too complex to describe adequately here. At its heart and center was an *assembly* in which all citizens were entitled to participate. The assembly elected a few key officials—generals, for example, odd as that may seem to us. But the main method for selecting citizens for the other public duties was by a lottery in which eligible citizens stood an equal chance of being selected. According to some estimates, an ordinary citizen stood a fair chance of being chosen by lot once in his lifetime to serve as the most important presiding officer in the government.

Although some Greek cities joined in forming rudimentary representative governments for their alliances, leagues, and confederacies (primarily for common defense), little is known about these representative systems. They left virtually no impress on democratic ideas and practices and none, certainly, on the later form of representative democracy. Nor did the Athenian system of selecting citizens for public duties by lot ever become an acceptable alternative to elections as a way of choosing representatives.

Thus the *political institutions* of Greek democracy, innovative though they had been, in their time, were ignored or even rejected outright during the development of modern representative democracy.

Rome. About the time that popular government was introduced in Greece, it also made its appearance on the Italian peninsula in the city of Rome. The Romans, however, chose to call their system a republic, from *res*, meaning thing or affair in Latin, and *publicus*, public: loosely rendered, a republic was the thing that belonged to the people. (I'll come back to these two words, democracy and republic.)

The right to participate in governing the Republic was at first restricted to the patricians, or aristocrats. But in a development that we shall encounter again, after much struggle the common people (the *plebs*, or plebeians) also gained entry. As in Athens, the right to participate was restricted to men, just as it was also in all later democracies and republics until the twentieth century.

From its beginnings as a city of quite modest size, the Roman Republic expanded by means of annexation and conquest far beyond the old city's boundaries. As a result, the Republic came to rule over all of Italy and far beyond. What is more, the Republic often conferred Roman citizenship, which was highly valued, on the conquered peoples, who thus became not mere subjects but Roman citizens fully entitled to a citizen's rights and privileges.

Wise and generous as this gift was, if we judge Rome from today's perspective we discover an enormous defect: Rome never adequately adapted its institutions of popular government to the huge increase in the number of its citizens and their great geographical distances from Rome. Oddly, from our present point of view, the assemblies in which Roman citizens were entitled to participate continued meeting, as before, within the city of Rome—in the very Forum that tourists still see today, in ruins. But for most Roman citizens living in the far-flung territory of the Republic, the city was too far away to attend, at least without extraordinary effort and expense. Consequently, an increasing and ultimately overwhelming number of citizens were, as a practical matter, denied the opportunity to participate in the citizen assemblies at the center of the Roman system of government. It was rather as if American citizenship had been conferred on the people in the various states as the country expanded, even though the people in the new states could only exercise their right to vote in national elections by showing up in Washington, D.C.

Although the Romans were a highly creative and practical people, from their practice of electing certain important officials in citizen assemblies they never developed a workable system of *representative* government based on *democratically elected* representatives.

Before we jump to the conclusion that the Romans were less creative or capable than we are, let us remind ourselves that innovations and inventions to which we have grown accustomed often seem so obvious to us that we wonder why our predecessors did not introduce them earlier. Most of us readily take things for granted that at an earlier time remained to be discovered. So, too, later generations may wonder how *we* could have overlooked certain innovations that they will take for granted. Because of what *we* take for granted might not we, like the Romans, be insufficiently creative in reshaping our political institutions?

Although the Roman Republic endured considerably longer than the Athenian democracy and longer than any modern democracy has yet endured, it was undermined after about 130 B.C.E. by civil unrest, war, militarization, corruption, and a decline in the sturdy civic spirit that had previously existed among its citizens. What little remained of authentic republican practices perished with the dictatorship of Julius Caesar. After his assassination in 44 B.C.E., a republic once governed by its citizens became an empire ruled by its emperors.

With the fall of the Republic, popular rule entirely disappeared in southern Europe. Except for the political systems of small, scattered tribes it vanished from the face of the earth for nearly a thousand years.

Italy. Like an extinct species reemerging after a massive climatic change, popular rule began to reappear in many of the cities of northern Italy around 1100 C.E. Once again it was in relatively small city-states that popular governments developed, not in large regions or countries. In a pattern familiar in Rome and later repeated during the emergence of modern representative governments, participation in the governing bodies of the city-states was at first restricted to members of upper-class families: nobles, large landowners, and the like. But in time, urban residents who were lower in the socioeconomic scale began to demand the right to participate. Members of what we today would call the middle classes—the newly rich, the smaller merchants and bankers, the skilled craftsmen organized in guilds, the footsoldiers commanded by the knights—were not only more numerous than the dominant upper classes but also capable of organizing themselves. What is more, they could threaten violent uprisings, and if need be carry them out. As a result, in many cities people like these—the *popolo,* as they were sometimes called— gained the right to participate in the government of the city.

For two centuries and more these republics flourished in a number of Italian cities. A good many republics were, like Florence and Venice, centers of extraordinary prosperity, exquisite craftsmanship, superb art and architecture, unexcelled urban design, magnificent poetry and music, and an enthusiastic rediscovery of the ancient world of Greece and Rome. What later generations were to call the Middle Ages came to a close, and that incredible outburst of brilliant creativity, the Renaissance, arrived.

Unhappily for the development of democracy, however, after about the mid-1300s the republican governments of some of the major cities increasingly gave way to the perennial enemies of popular government: economic decline, corruption, oligarchy, war, conquest, and seizure of power by authoritarian rulers, whether princes, monarchs, or soldiers. Nor was that all. Viewed in the longer sweep of historical trends, the city-state was doomed as a foundation for popular government by the emergence of a rival with overwhelmingly superior forces: the national state or country. Towns and cities were destined to be incorporated into this larger and more powerful entity, thus becoming, at most, subordinate units of government.

Glorious as it had been, the city-state was obsolete.

Words About Words

You may have noticed that I have referred to "popular governments" in Greece, Rome, and Italy. To designate their popular governments, the Greeks, as we saw, invented the term *democracy*. The Romans drew on their native Latin and called their government a "republic," and later the Italians gave that name to the popular governments of some of their city-states. You might well wonder whether *democracy* and *republic* refer to fundamentally different types of constitutional systems. Or instead do the two words just reflect differences in the languages from which they originally came?

The correct answer was obfuscated by James Madison in 1787 in an influential paper he wrote to win support for the newly proposed American constitution. One of the principal architects of that constitution and a statesman exceptionally well informed in the political science of his time, Madison distinguished between "a pure democracy, by which I mean a society consisting of a small number of citizens, who assemble and administer the government in person," and a "republic, by which I mean a government in which the scheme of representation takes place."

This distinction had no basis in prior history: neither in Rome nor, for example, in Venice was there "a scheme of representation." Indeed, the earlier republics all pretty much fit into Madison's definition of a "democracy." What is more, the two terms were used interchangeably in the United States during the eighteenth century. Nor is Madison's distinction found in a work by the well-known French political philosopher Montesquieu, whom Madison greatly admired and frequently praised. Madison himself would have known that his proposed distinction had no firm historical basis, and so we must conclude that he made it to discredit critics who contended that the proposed constitution was not sufficiently "democratic."

However that may be (the matter is unclear), the plain fact is that the words *democracy* and *republic* did not (despite Madison) designate differences in types of popular government. What they reflected, at the cost of later confusion, was a difference between Greek and Latin, the languages from which they came.

NORTHERN EUROPE

Whether called democracies or republics, the systems of popular government in Greece, Rome, and Italy all lacked several of the crucial characteristics of modern representative government. Classical Greece as well as medieval and Renaissance Italy were composed of popular local governments but lacked an effective national government. Rome had, so to speak, just one local government based on popular participation but no national parliament of elected representatives.

From today's perspective, conspicuously absent from all these systems were at least three basic political institutions: *a national parliament* composed of *elected representatives,* and *popularly chosen local governments* that were ultimately subordinate to the national government. A system combining democracy at local levels with a popularly elected parliament at the top level had yet to be invented.

This combination of political institutions originated in Britain, Scandinavia, the Lowlands, Switzerland, and elsewhere north of the Mediterranean.

Although the patterns of political development diverged widely among these regions, a highly simplified version would look something like this. In various localities freemen and nobles would begin to participate directly in local assemblies. To these were added regional and national assemblies consisting of representatives, some or all of whom would come to be *elected*.

Local assemblies. I begin with the Vikings, not only from sentiment, but also because their experience is little known though highly relevant. I have sometimes visited the Norwegian farm about 80 miles northeast of Trondheim from which my paternal grandfather emigrated (and which to my delight is still known as Dahl Vestre, or West Dahl). In the nearby town of Steinkjer you can still see a boat-shaped ring of large stones where Viking freemen regularly met from about 600 C.E. to 1000 C.E. to hold an adjudicative assembly called in Norse a *Ting*. (Incidentally, the English word *thing* is derived from an Old English word meaning both thing and assembly.) Similar places, some even older, can be found elsewhere in the vicinity.

By 900 C.E., assemblies of free Vikings were meeting not just in the Trondheim region but in many other areas of Scandinavia as well. As in Steinkjer the Ting was typically held in an open field marked off by large vertical stones. At the meeting of the Ting the freemen settled disputes; discussed, accepted, and rejected laws; adopted or turned down a proposed change of religion (as they did when they accepted Christianity in place of the old Norse religion); and even elected or gave their approval to a king—who was often required to swear his faithfulness to the laws approved by the Ting.

The Vikings knew little or nothing, and would have cared less, about the democratic and republican political practices a thousand years earlier in Greece and Rome. Operating from the logic of equality that they applied to free men, they seem to have created assemblies on their own. That the idea of equality was alive and well among Viking freemen in the tenth century is attested to by the answer given by some Danish Vikings when, while traveling up a river in France, they were asked by a messenger calling out from the riverbank, "What is the name of your master?" "None," they replied, "we are all equals."[3]

But we must resist the temptation to exaggerate. The equality that Vikings boasted about applied only among free men, and even they varied in wealth and status. Beneath the freemen were the slaves. Like the Greeks and Romans, or for that matter Europeans and Americans centuries later, the Vikings possessed slaves: enemies captured in battle, or the hapless victims of raids on neighboring peoples, or simply persons bought in the ancient and ubiquitous commerce in slaves. And unlike the men free by birth, when slaves were freed they remained dependent on their previous owners. If slaves were a caste below the free men, above them was an aristocracy of families with wealth, usually in land, and hereditary status. At the apex stood a king whose power was limited by his election, his obligation to obey the laws, and his need to retain the loyalty of the nobles and the support of the free men.

In spite of these severe limits on equality, the class of free men—free peasants, smallholders, farmers—was large enough to impose a lasting democratic influence on political institutions and traditions.

In several other parts of Europe, local conditions also sometimes favored the emergence of popular participation in government. The high mountain valleys of the Alps, for example, provided a measure of protection and autonomy to free men engaged in pastoral activities. As a modern writer describes Raetia (later the Swiss canton of Graubünden) around 800 C.E.: "Free peasants . . . found themselves in a uniquely egalitarian situation. Bound together by their common status . . . and by their common rights of usage over [mountain pastures], they developed a sense of equality wholly at odds with the hierarchical, status-conscious thrust of medieval feudalism. This distinctive spirit was to dominate the later emergence of democracy in the Raetian Republic."[4]

From assemblies to parliaments. When the Vikings ventured westward to Iceland, they transplanted their political practices and in several localities re-created a Ting. But they did more: foreshadowing the later appearance of national parliaments elsewhere, in 930 C.E. they created a sort of supra-Ting, the *Althing,* or National Assembly, which remained the source of Icelandic law for three centuries, until the Icelanders were finally subjugated by Norway.[5]

Meanwhile in Norway, Denmark, and Sweden regional assemblies developed and then, as in Iceland, national assemblies. Although the subsequent growth in the power of the king and the centralized bureaucracies under his control reduced the importance of these national assemblies, they left their mark on later developments.

In Sweden, for example, the tradition of popular participation in the assemblies of the Viking period led in the fifteenth century to a precursor of a modern representative parliament when the king began to summon meetings of representatives from different sectors of Swedish society: nobility, clergy, burghers, and common people. These meetings eventually evolved into the Swedish *riksdag,* or parliament.[6]

In the radically different environment of the Netherlands and Flanders, the expansion of manufacturing, commerce, and finance helped to create urban middle classes composed of persons who commanded sizable economic resources. Rulers perpetually starved for revenues could neither ignore this rich lode nor tax it without gaining the consent of its owners. To obtain consent, rulers summoned meetings of representatives drawn from the towns and the most important social classes. Although these assemblies, parliaments, or "estates," as they were often called, did not evolve directly into the national legislatures of today, they established traditions, practices, and ideas that strongly favored such a development.

Meanwhile, from obscure beginnings a representative parliament was gradually coming into existence that in the centuries to come would exert far and away the greatest influence on the idea and practice of representative government. This was the parliament of medieval England. A product less of intention and design than of blind evolution, Parliament grew out of assemblies summoned sporadically, and under the pressure of need, during the reign of Edward I from 1272 to 1307.

How Parliament evolved from these beginnings is too lengthy and complex a story to be summarized here. By the eighteenth century, however, that evolution had led to a constitutional system in which the king and Parliament were each limited by the authority of the other; within Parliament the power of the hereditary aristocracy in the House of Lords was offset by the power of the people in the House of Commons; and the laws enacted by king and Parliament were interpreted by judges who were mostly, though by no means always, independent of king and Parliament alike.

In the 1700s this seemingly marvelous system of checks and balances among the country's major social forces and the separation of the powers within the government was widely admired in Europe. It was lauded by the famous French political philosopher Montesquieu, among others, and admired in America by the Framers of the Constitution, many of whom hoped to create in America a republic that would retain the virtues of the English system without the vices of a monarchy. The republic they helped to form would in due time provide something of a model for many other republics.

DEMOCRATIZATION:
ON THE WAY, BUT ONLY ON THE WAY

Looking back with all the advantages of hindsight, we can easily see that by the early eighteenth century political ideas and practices had appeared in Europe that were to become important elements in later democratic beliefs and institutions. Using language that is more modern and abstract than people of the time would have employed, let me summarize what these elements were.

Favored by local conditions and opportunities in several areas of Europe—notably Scandinavia, Flanders, the Netherlands, Switzerland, and Britain—the logic of equality stimulated the creation of *local assemblies* in which free men could participate in governing, at least to an extent. The idea that governments needed the *consent of the governed,* initially a claim primarily about raising taxes, was gradually growing into a claim about laws in general. Over an area too large for primary assemblies of free men, as in a large town, city, region, or country, consent required *representation* in the body that raised taxes and made laws. In sharp contrast to Athenian practice, representation was to be secured not by lot or random selection but by *election.* To secure the consent of free citizens in a country, nation, or nation-state would require elected representative legislatures, or parliaments, at several levels: local, national, and perhaps provincial, regional, or other intermediate levels as well.

These European political ideas and practices provided a base from which democratization could proceed. Among proponents of further democratization, accounts of popular governments in classical Greece, Rome, and the Italian cities sometimes lent greater plausibility to their advocacy. Those historical experiences had demonstrated that governments subject to the will of the people were more than illusory hopes. Once upon a time they had actually existed, and had lasted for centuries to boot.

What hadn't been achieved. If the ideas, traditions, history, and practices just described held a promise of democratization, it was, at best, only a promise. Crucial pieces were still missing.

First, even in countries with the most auspicious beginnings, gross inequalities posed enormous obstacles to democracy: differences between the rights, duties, influence, and power of slaves and free men, rich and poor, landed and landless, master and servant, men and women, day laborers and apprentices, skilled craftworkers and owners, burghers and bankers, feudal lords and tenants, nobles and commoners, monarchs and their subjects, the king's officials and those they ordered about. Even free men were highly unequal in status, wealth, work, obligations, knowledge, freedom, influence, and power. And in many places the wife of a free man was regarded by law, custom, and practice as his property. Then as always and everywhere the logic of equality ran head-on into the brute facts of inequality.

Second, even where assemblies and parliaments existed they were a long way from meeting minimal democratic standards. Parliaments were often no match for a monarch; it would be centuries before control over the king's ministers would shift from monarch to parliament or a president would take the place of a king. Parliaments themselves were bastions of privilege, particularly in chambers reserved for the aristocracy and higher clergy. Representatives elected by "the people" had at best only a partial say in lawmaking.

Third, the representatives of "the people" did not really represent the whole people. For one thing, free men were, after all, men. Except for the occasional female monarch, half the adult population was excluded from political life. But so were many adult males—most adult males, in fact. As late as 1832 in Great Britain the right to vote extended to only 5 percent of the population over age twenty. In that year it took a tempestuous struggle to expand the suffrage to slightly more than 7 percent (fig. 2)! In Norway, despite

FIGURE 2. *Great Britain's electorate, 1831–1931 (data from* Encyclopedia Britannica *[1970], s.v. "Parliament")*

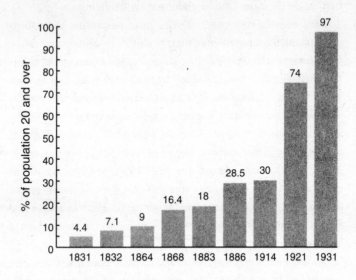

the promising appearance of popular participation in the Tings of Viking times, the percentage was little better.[7]

Fourth, until the eighteenth century and later, democratic ideas and beliefs were not widely shared or even well understood. In all countries the logic of equality was effective only among a few and a rather privileged few at that. Even an understanding of what a democratic republic would require in the way of political institutions was all but nonexistent. In speech and press freedom of expression was seriously restricted, particularly if it was exercised to criticize the king. Political opposition lacked legitimacy and legality. "His Majesty's Loyal Opposition" was an idea whose time had not yet come. Political parties were widely condemned as dangerous and undesirable. Elections were notoriously corrupted by agents of the Crown.

The advance of democratic ideas and practices depended on the existence of certain favorable conditions that did not yet exist. As long as only a few people believed in democracy and were prepared to fight for it, existing privilege would maintain itself with the aid of undemocratic governments. Even if many more people came to believe in democratic ideas and goals, other conditions would still be required if further democratization were to be achieved. Later on, in Part IV, I'll describe some of most important of these conditions.

Meanwhile, we need to recall that after the promising beginnings sketched out in this chapter, democratization did not proceed on an ascending path to the present. There were ups and downs, resistance movements, rebellions, civil wars, revolutions. For several centuries the rise of centralized monarchies reversed some of the earlier advances—even though, ironically, these very monarchies may have helped to create some conditions that were favorable to democratization in the longer run.

Looking back on the rise and decline of democracy, it is clear that we cannot count on historical forces to insure that democracy will always advance—or even survive, as the long intervals in which popular governments vanished from the earth remind us.

Democracy, it appears, is a bit chancy. But its chances also depend on what we do ourselves. Even if we cannot count on benign historical forces to favor democracy, we are not mere victims of blind forces over which we have no control. With adequate understanding of what democracy requires and the will to meet its requirements, we can act to preserve and, what is more, to advance democratic ideas and practices.

CHAPTER 3

What Lies Ahead?

When we discuss democracy perhaps nothing gives rise to more confusion than the simple fact that "democracy" refers to both an ideal and an actuality. We often fail to make the distinction clear. For example:

Alan says, "I think democracy is the best possible form of government."

Beth replies, "You must be crazy to believe that the so-called democratic government in this country is the best we can have! Why, I don't even think it's much of a democracy."

Alan is of course speaking of democracy as an ideal, whereas Beth is referring to an actual government usually called a democracy. Until Alan and Beth make clear which meaning each has in mind, they may flounder about, talking right past each other. From extensive experience I know how easily this can happen—even, I regret to add, among scholars who are deeply knowledgeable about democratic ideas and practices.

We can usually avoid this kind of confusion just by making clear which meaning we intend:

Alan continues, "Oh, I didn't mean our actual government. As to that, I'd be inclined to agree with you."

Beth replies, "Well, if you're talking about ideal governments, then I think you're dead right. I do believe that as an ideal, democracy is the best form of government. That's why I'd like our own government to be a lot more democratic than it really is."

Philosophers have engaged in endless debates about the differences between our judgments about goals, ends, values, and so on and our judgments about reality, actuality, and so on. We make judgments of the first kind in response to questions like "What *ought* I to do? What is the right thing for me to do?" We make judgments of the second kind in response to such questions as "What *can* I do? What options are open to me? What are the likely consequences of my choosing to do X rather than Y?" A convenient label for the first is value judgments (or moral judgments), for the second, empirical judgments.

Words About Words

Although philosophers have engaged in endless debates about the nature of value judgments and empirical judgments and differences between one kind of judgment and the other, we need not concern ourselves here with these philosophical issues, for in everyday life we are fairly accustomed to distinguishing between real things and ideal things. However, we need to bear in mind that the distinction between value judgments and empirical judgments is useful, provided that we don't push it too far. If we assert, "A government ought to give equal consideration to the good and interests of every person bound by its decisions," or "Happiness is the highest good," we are as close to making "pure" value judgments as we can get. An example at the opposite extreme, a strictly empirical proposition, is Newton's famous law of universal gravitation, asserting that the force between any two bodies is directly proportional to the product of their masses and inversely proportional to the square of the distance between them. In practice, many assertions contain or imply elements of both kinds of judgments. This is nearly always the case with judgments about public policy. For example, someone who says, "The government should establish a program of universal health insurance" is asserting in effect that (1) health is a good end, (2) the government should strive to achieve that end, and (3) universal health insurance is the best means of attaining that end. Moreover, we make an enormous number of empirical judgments like (3) that represent the best judgment we can make in the face of great uncertainties. These are not "scientific" conclusions in a strict sense. They are often based on a mixture of hard evidence, soft evidence, no evidence, and uncertainty. Judgments like these are sometimes called "practical" or "prudential." Finally, one important kind of practical judgment is to balance gains to one value, person, or group against costs to another value, person, or group. To describe situations of this kind I'll sometimes borrow an expression often used by economists and say that we have to choose among various possible "trade-offs" among our ends. As we move along we'll encounter all these variants of value judgments and empirical judgments.

DEMOCRATIC GOALS AND ACTUALITIES

Although it is helpful to distinguish between ideals and actualities, we also need to understand how democratic ideals or goals and democratic actualities are connected. I am going to spell out these connections more fully in later chapters. Meanwhile, let me use the chart as a rough guide to what lies ahead.

Each of the four items under Ideal and Actual is a fundamental question:

What is democracy? What does democracy mean? Put another way, what standards should we use to determine whether, and to what extent, a government is democratic?

FIGURE 3. *The main elements*

IDEAL		ACTUAL	
Goals and Ideals		Actual Democratic Governments	
What is democracy?	Why democracy?	What political institutions does democracy require?	What conditions favor democracy?
Chapter 4	Chapters 5–7	Part III	Part IV

I believe that such a system would have to meet five criteria and that a system meeting these criteria would be fully democratic. In Chapter 4, I describe four of these criteria, and in Chapters 6 and 7, I show why we need a fifth. Remember, however, that the criteria describe an ideal or perfect democratic system. None of us, I imagine, believes that we could actually attain a perfectly democratic system, given the many limits imposed on us in the real world. The criteria do provide us, though, with standards against which we can compare the achievements and the remaining imperfections of actual political systems and their institutions, and they can guide us toward solutions that would bring us closer to the ideal.

Why democracy? What reasons can we give for believing that democracy is the best political system? What values are best served by democracy?

In answering these questions it is essential to keep in mind that we are *not* just asking why people now support democracy, or why they have supported it in the past, or how democratic systems have come about. People may favor democracy for many reasons. Some, for example, may favor democracy without thinking much about why they do; in their time and place, giving lip service to democracy may just be the conventional or traditional thing to do. Some might endorse democracy because they believe that with a democratic government they will stand a better chance of getting rich, or because they think democratic politics would open up a promising political career for them, or because someone they admire tells them to, and so on.

Are there reasons for supporting democracy of more general and perhaps even universal relevance? I believe there are. These will be discussed in Chapters 5 through 7.

In order to meet the ideal standards as best we can, given the limits and possibilities in the real world, what political institutions are necessary?

As we shall see in the next chapter, in varying times and places political systems with significantly different political institutions have been called democracies or republics. In the last chapter we encountered one reason why democratic institutions differ: they have been adapted to huge differences in the size or scale of political units—in population, territory, or both. Some political units, such as an English village, are tiny in area and population; others, like China, Brazil, or the United States, are gigantic in both. A small city or town might meet democratic criteria reasonably well without some of the institutions that would be required in, say, a large country.

Since the eighteenth century, however, the idea of democracy has been applied to entire countries: the United States, France, Great Britain, Norway, Japan, India . . . . Political institutions that seemed necessary or desirable for democracy on the small scale of a town or city proved to be wholly inadequate on the far larger scale of a modern country. The political institutions suitable for a town would be wholly inadequate even for countries that would be small on a global scale, such as Denmark or the Netherlands. As a result, in the nineteenth and twentieth centuries a new set of institutions developed that in part resemble political institutions in earlier democracies and republics but, viewed in their entirety, constitute a wholly new political system.

Chapter 2 provided a brief sketch of this historical development. In Part III, I describe more fully the political institutions of actual democracies and how they vary in important ways.

A word of caution: to say that certain institutions are necessary is not to say that they are enough to achieve perfect democracy. In every democratic country a substantial gap exists between actual and ideal democracy. That gap offers us a challenge: can we find ways to make "democratic" countries more democratic?

If even "democratic" countries are not fully democratic, what can we say about countries that lack some or all of the major political institutions of modern democracy—the nondemocratic countries? How if at all can they be made more democratic? Indeed, just why is it that some countries have become relatively more democratic than others? These questions lead us to still others. What conditions in a country (or any other political unit) favor the development and stability of democratic institutions? And, conversely, what conditions are likely to prevent or impede their development and stability?

In today's world these questions are of extraordinary importance. Fortunately, at the end of the twentieth century we have much better answers than could be obtained only a few generations ago and far better answers than at any earlier time in recorded history. In Part IV, I indicate what we know about answers to these crucial question as the twentieth century draws to a close.

To be sure, the answers we have are by no means free from uncertainty. Yet they do provide a firmer starting point for seeking solutions than we have ever had before.

FROM VALUE JUDGMENTS TO
EMPIRICAL JUDGMENTS

Before leaving the chart I want to call attention to an important shift as we move from left to right. In answering "What is democracy?" we make judgments that depend almost exclusively on our values, or what we believe is good, right, or a desirable goal. When we move on to the question "Why democracy?" our judgments still strongly depend on ideal values, but they also depend on our beliefs about causal connections, limits, and possibilities in the actual world around us—that is, on empirical judgments. Here we begin to rely more heavily on interpretations of evidence, facts, and purported facts. When we try to decide what political institutions democracy actually requires, we rely even more on evidence and empirical judgments. Yet here, too, what matters to us depends in part on our previous judgments about the meaning and value of democracy. Indeed, the reason we may be concerned with the shape of political institutions in the actual world is that the values of democracy and its criteria are important to us.

When we reach the right side of the chart and undertake to determine what conditions favor the development and stability of democratic institutions, our judgments are straightforwardly empirical; they depend entirely on how we interpret the evidence available to us. For example, do or do not democratic beliefs contribute significantly to the survival of democratic political institutions? Yet here again the reason these empirical judgments are important and relevant to us is that we care about democracy and its values.

Our path, then, will take us from the exploration of ideals, goals, and values in Part II to the much more empirical descriptions of democratic political institutions in Part III. We'll then be in a position to move on in Part IV to a description of the conditions that are favorable or unfavorable for democratic political institutions, where our judgments will be almost exclusively empirical in nature. Finally, in the last chapter I'll describe some of the challenges that democracies face in the years ahead.

PART II

Ideal Democracy

CHAPTER 4

What Is Democracy?

All of us have goals that we cannot attain by ourselves. Yet we might attain some of these by cooperating with others who share similar aims.

Let us suppose, then, that in order to achieve certain common ends, you and several hundred other persons agree to form an association. What the specific goals of the association are, we can put aside so as to focus strictly on the question that forms the title of this chapter: What is democracy?

At the first meeting, let us further assume, several members suggest that your association will need a constitution. Their view is favorably received. Because you are thought to possess some skills on matters like these, a member proposes that you be invited to draft a constitution, which you would then bring to a later meeting for consideration by the members. This proposal is adopted by acclamation.

In accepting this task you say something like the following:

"I believe I understand the goals we share, but I'm not sure how we should go about making our decisions. For example, do we want a constitution that entrusts to several of the ablest and best informed among us the authority to make all our important decisions? That arrangement might not only insure wiser decisions but spare the rest of us a lot of time and effort."

The members overwhelmingly reject a solution along these lines. One member, whom I am going to call the Main Speaker, argues:

"On the most important matters that this association will deal with, no one among us is so much wiser than the rest that his or her views should automatically prevail. Even if some members may know more about an issue at any given moment, we're all capable of learning what we need to know. Of course, we'll need to discuss matters and deliberate among ourselves before reaching our decisions. To deliberate and discuss and then decide on policies is one reason why we're forming this association. But we're all equally qualified to participate in discussing the issues and then deciding on the policies our association should follow. Consequently, our constitution should be based on that assumption. It should guarantee all of us the right to participate in the decisions of the association. To put it plainly, because we are all equally qualified we should govern ourselves democratically."

Further discussion reveals that the views set forth by the Main Speaker accord with the prevailing view. You then agree to draft a constitution in conformity with these assumptions.

As you begin your task you quickly discover, however, that various associations and organization calling themselves "democratic" have adopted many different constitutions. Even among "democratic" countries, you find, constitutions differ in important ways. As one example, the Constitution of the United States provides for a powerful chief executive in the presidency and at the same time for a powerful legislature in the Congress; and each of these is rather independent of the other. By contrast, most European countries have preferred a parliamentary system in which the chief executive, a prime minister, is chosen by the parliament. One could easily point to many other important differences. There is, it appears, no single "democratic" constitution (a matter I shall return to in Chapter 10).

You now begin to wonder whether these different constitutions have something in common that justifies their claim to being "democratic." And are some perhaps *more* "democratic" than others? What does *democracy* mean? Alas, you soon learn that the term is used in a staggering number of ways. Wisely, you decide to ignore this hopeless variety of definitions, for your task is more specific: to design a set of rules and principles, a constitution, that will determine how the association's decisions are to be made. And your constitution must be in conformity with one elementary principle: that all the members are to be treated (under the constitution) as if they were equally qualified to participate in the process of making decisions about the policies the association will pursue. Whatever may be the case on other matters, then, in governing this association all members are to be considered as *politically equal.*

CRITERIA FOR A DEMOCRATIC PROCESS

Within the enormous and often impenetrable thicket of ideas about democracy, is it possible to identify some criteria that a process for governing an association would have to meet in order to satisfy the requirement that all the members are equally entitled to participate in the association's decisions about its policies? There are, I believe, at least five such standards (fig. 4).

Effective participation. Before a policy is adopted by the association, all the members must have equal and effective opportunities for making their views known to the other members as to what the policy should be.

Voting equality. When the moment arrives at which the decision about policy will finally be made, every member must have an equal and effective opportunity to vote, and all votes must be counted as equal.

Enlightened understanding. Within reasonable limits as to time, each member must have equal and effective opportunities for learning about the relevant alternative policies and their likely consequences.

Control of the agenda. The members must have the exclusive opportunity to decide how and, if they choose, what matters are to be placed on the agenda. Thus the democratic process required by the three preceding criteria is never closed. The policies of the association are always open to change by the members, if they so choose.

Inclusion of adults. All, or at any rate most, adult permanent residents should have the full rights of citizens that are implied by the first four criteria. Before the twentieth century this criterion was unacceptable to most advocates of democracy. To justify it will require us to examine why we should treat others as our political equals. After we've explored that question in Chapters 6 and 7, I'll return to the criterion of inclusion.

FIGURE 4. *What is democracy?*

Democracy provides opportunities for:
1. Effective participation
2. Equality in voting
3. Gaining enlightened understanding
4. Exercising final control over the agenda
5. Inclusion of adults

Meanwhile, you might begin to wonder whether the first four criteria are just rather arbitrary selections from many possibilities. Do we have good reasons for adopting these particular standards for a democratic process?

WHY THESE CRITERIA?

The short answer is simply this: each is necessary if the members (however limited their numbers may be) are to be politically equal in determining the policies of the association. To put it in another way, to the extent that any of the requirements is violated, the members will not be politically equal.

For example, if some members are given greater opportunities than others for expressing their views, their policies are more likely to prevail. In the extreme case, by curtailing opportunities for discussing the proposals on the agenda, a tiny minority of members might, in effect, determine the policies of the association. The criterion of effective participation is meant to insure against this result.

Or suppose that the votes of different members are counted unequally. For example, let's assume that votes are assigned a weight in proportion to the amount of property a member owns, and members possess greatly differing amounts of property. If we believe that all the members are equally well qualified to participate in the association's decisions, why should the votes of some be counted for more than the votes of others?

Although the first two criteria seem nearly self-evident, you might question whether the criterion of enlightened understanding is necessary or appropriate. If the members are equally qualified, why is this criterion necessary? And if the members are not equally qualified, then why design a constitution on the assumption that they are?

However, as the Main Speaker said, the principle of political equality assumes that the members are all equally well qualified to participate in decisions *provided* they have adequate opportunities to learn about the matters before the association by inquiry, discussion, and deliberation. The third criterion is meant to insure that these opportunities exist for every member. Its essence was set forth in 431 B.C.E. by the Athenian leader Pericles in a famous oration commemorating the city's war dead. "Our ordinary citizens, though occupied with the pursuits of industry, are still fair judges of public matters; . . . and instead of looking on discussion as a stumbling-block in the way of action, we think it an indispensable preliminary to any wise action at all."[1]

Taken together the first three criteria might seem sufficient. But suppose a few members are secretly opposed to the idea that all should be treated as political equals in governing the affairs of the association. The interests of the largest property owners, they say to you, are really more important than the interests of the others. Although it would be best, they contend, if the votes of the largest property owners were given such extra weight that they could always win, this seems to be out of the question. Consequently, what is needed is a provision that would allow them to prevail no matter what a majority of members might adopt in a free and fair vote.

Coming up with an ingenious solution, they propose a constitution that would nicely meet the first three criteria and to that extent would appear to be fully democratic. But to nullify those criteria they propose to require that at the general meetings the members can only discuss and vote on matters that have already been placed on the agenda by an executive committee; and membership on the executive committee will be open only to the largest property holders. By controlling the agenda, this tiny cabal can be fairly confident that the association will never act contrary to its interests, because it will never allow any proposal to be brought forward that would do so.

On reflection, you reject their proposal because it violates the principle of political equality that you have been charged to uphold. You are led instead to a search for constitutional arrangements that will satisfy the fourth criterion and thus insure that final control rests with the members as a whole.

In order for the members to be political equals in governing the affairs of the association, then, it would have to meet all four criteria. We have, it seems, discovered the criteria that must be met by an association if it is to be governed by a democratic process.

SOME CRUCIAL QUESTIONS

Have we now answered the question "What is democracy?"? Would that the question were so easy to answer! Although the answer I have just offered is a good place to start, it suggests a good many more questions.

To begin with, even if the criteria might be usefully applied to the government of a very small, voluntary association, are they really applicable to the government of a *state*?

Words About Words

Because the term *state* is often used loosely and ambiguously, let me say briefly what I mean by it. By *state* I mean a very special type of association that is distinguishable by the extent to which it can secure compliance with its rules, among all those over whom it claims jurisdiction, by its superior means of coercion. When people talk about "the government," ordinarily they mean the government of the state under whose jurisdiction they live. Throughout history, with rare exceptions, states have exercised their jurisdiction over people occupying a certain (or in some cases, uncertain or contested) territory. Thus we can think of a state as a territorial entity. Although in some times and places the territory of a state has been no larger than a city, in recent centuries states have generally claimed jurisdiction over entire countries.

One could find much to quibble with in my brief attempt to convey the meaning of the word *state*. Writings about the state by political and legal philosophers would probably require enough paper to use up a small forest. But what I have said will, I believe, serve our purposes.[2]

Back, then, to our question. Can we apply the criteria to the government of a state? Of course we can! Indeed, the primary focus of democratic ideas has long been the state. Though other kinds of associations, particularly some religious organizations, played a part in the later history of democratic ideas and practices, from the beginnings of democracy in ancient Greece and Rome the political institutions we usually think of as characteristic of democracy were developed primarily as means for democratizing the government of states.

Perhaps it bears repeating that as with other associations no state has ever possessed a government that fully measured up to the criteria of a democratic process. None is likely to. Yet as I hope to show, the criteria provide highly serviceable standards for measuring the achievements and possibilities of democratic government.

A second question: Is it realistic to think that an association could ever fully meet these criteria? To put the question in another way, can any actual association ever be fully democratic? In the real world is it likely that every member of an association will truly have equal opportunities to participate, to gain an informed understanding of the issues, and to influence the agenda?

Probably not. But if so, are these criteria useful? Or are they just pie-in-the-sky, utopian hopes for the impossible? The answer, simply stated, is that they are as useful as ideal standards can ever be, and they are more relevant and useful than many. They do provide standards against which to measure the performance of actual associations that claim to be democratic. They can serve as guides for shaping and reshaping concrete arrangements, constitutions, practices, and political institutions. For all those who aspire to democracy, they can also generate relevant questions and help in the search for answers.

Because the proof of the pudding is in the eating, in the remaining chapters I hope to show how the criteria can help guide us toward solutions for some of the central problems of democratic theory and practice.

A third question: Granting that the criteria may serve as useful guides, are they all we would need for designing democratic political institutions? If, as I imagined above, you were charged with the task of designing a democratic constitution and proposing the actual institutions of a democratic government, could you move straightforwardly from the criteria to the design? Obviously not. An architect armed only with the criteria provided by the client—as to location, size, general style, number and types of rooms, cost, timing, and so on—could then draw up plans only after taking into account a great many specific factors. So, too, with political institutions.

How we may best interpret our democratic standards, apply them to a specific association, and create the political practices and institutions they require is, of course, no simple task. To do so we must plunge headlong into political realities, where our choices will require innumerable theoretical and practical judgments. Among other difficulties, when we try to apply several criteria—in this case at least four—we are likely to discover that they sometimes conflict with one another and we'll have to make judgments about trade-offs among conflicting values, as we shall discover in our examination of democratic constitutions in Chapter 10.

Finally, an even more fundamental question: the views of the Main Speaker were accepted, it seems, without challenge. But why should they be? Why should we believe that democracy is desirable, particularly in governing an association as important as the state? And if the desirability of democracy presupposes the desirability of political equality, why should we believe in something that, on the face of it, looks rather preposterous? Yet if we don't believe in political equality, how can we support democracy? If, however, we do believe in political equality among the citizens of a state, won't that require us to adopt something like the fifth criterion—inclusive citizenship?

To these challenging questions we now turn.

CHAPTER 5

Why Democracy?

Why should we support democracy? More specifically, why should we support democracy in governing the state? The state, remember, is a unique association whose government possesses an extraordinary capacity for obtaining compliance with its rules by (among other means) force, coercion, and violence. Are there no better ways of governing a state? Would a nondemocratic system of government be better?

Words About Words

Throughout this chapter I'll use the term *democracy* loosely to refer to actual governments, not ideal ones, that meet the criteria set out in the last chapter to a significant extent but by no means fully. Sometimes I'll also use *popular government* as a comprehensive term that includes not only twentieth-century democratic systems but also systems that are otherwise democratic but in which substantial parts of the adult population are excluded from the suffrage or other forms of political participation.

Until the twentieth century, most of the world proclaimed the superiority of nondemocratic systems both in theory and in practice. Until very recently, a preponderant majority of human beings—at times, all—have been subject to nondemocratic rulers. And the

FIGURE 5. *Why democracy?*

Democracy produces desirable consequences:
1. Avoiding tyranny
2. Essential rights
3. General freedom
4. Self determination
5. Moral autonomy
6. Human development
7. Protecting essential personal interests
8. Political equality

In addition, modern democracies produce:

9. Peace-seeking
10. Prosperity

heads of nondemocratic regimes have usually tried to justify their rule by invoking the ancient and persistent claim that most people are just not competent to participate in governing a state. Most people would be better off, this argument goes, if they would only leave the complicated business of governing to those wiser than they—a minority at most, perhaps only one person. In practice, these rationalizations were never quite enough, so where argument left off coercion took over. Most people never explicitly consented to be ruled by their self-assigned superiors; they were forced to do so. This older view—and practice—is by no means dead even today. In one form or another the contest over government by "the one, the few, or the many" is still with us.

In the face of so much history, why should we believe that democracy is a better way of governing the state than any nondemocratic alternative? Let me count the reasons.

In comparison with any feasible alternative to it, democracy has at least ten advantages (fig. 5).

1. *Democracy helps to prevent government by cruel and vicious autocrats.*

Perhaps the most fundamental and persistent problem in politics is to avoid autocratic rule. Throughout all recorded history, including our own times, leaders driven by megalomania, paranoia, self-interest, ideology, nationalism, religious belief, convictions of innate superiority, or sheer emotion and impulse have exploited the state's exceptional capacities for coercion and violence to serve their own ends. The human costs of despotic rule rival those of disease, famine, and war.

Consider a few examples from the twentieth century. Under Joseph Stalin's rule in the Soviet Union (1929–1953), many millions of persons were jailed for political reasons, often because of Stalin's paranoid fear of conspiracies against him. An estimated twenty million people died in labor camps, were executed for political reasons, or died from the famine (1932–33) that resulted when Stalin compelled peasants to join state-run farms. Though another twenty million victims of Stalin's rule may have managed to survive, they suffered cruelly.[1] Or consider Adolph Hitler, the autocratic ruler of Nazi Germany (1933–1945). Not counting tens of millions of military and civilian casualties resulting from World War II, Hitler was directly responsible for the death of six million Jews in concentration camps as well as innumerable opponents, Poles, gypsies, homosexuals, and members of other groups he wished to exterminate. Under the despotic leadership of Pol Pot in Cambodia (1975–1979), the Khmer Rouge killed a quarter of the Cambodian population: an instance, one might say, of self-inflicted genocide. So great was Pol Pot's fear of the educated classes that they were almost exterminated: wearing spectacles or having uncalloused hands was quite literally a death warrant.

To be sure, the history of popular rule is not without its own serious blemishes. Like all governments, popular governments have sometimes acted unjustly or cruelly toward people outside their borders, people living in other states—foreigners, colonials, and so on. In this respect popular governments have behaved no worse toward outsiders than nondemocratic governments, and often they have behaved better. In some cases, as in India, the colonial power has contributed inadvertently or intentionally to the creation of democratic beliefs and institutions. Yet we should not condone the injustices often shown by democratic countries toward outsiders, for in so acting they contradict a fundamental moral principle that, as we shall see in the next chapter, helps to justify political equality among the citizens of a democracy. The only solution to this contradiction may be a universal code of human rights that is effectively enforced throughout the world. Important as this problem and its solution are, however, they are beyond scope of this small book.

More directly challenging to democratic ideas and practices is the harm inflicted by popular governments on persons who live within their jurisdiction and are compelled to obey its laws but who are deprived of rights to participate in governing. Although these people are governed, they do not govern. Fortunately, the solution to this problem is obvious, if not always easy to carry out: democratic rights should be extended to members of the excluded groups. This solution was in fact widely adopted in the nineteenth and early twentieth centuries when previous limits on the suffrage were abolished and universal adult suffrage became a standard aspect of democratic government.[2]

But wait! you might say. Can't democratic governments also inflict harm on a minority of citizens who do possess voting rights but are outvoted by majorities? Isn't this what we mean by "the tyranny of the majority"?

I wish the answer were simple. Alas! it is much more complicated than you might suppose. The complications arise because virtually every law or public policy, whether adopted by a democratic majority, an oligarchic minority, or a benign dictator, is bound to inflict some harm on some persons. Simply put, the issue is not whether a government can design all its laws so that none ever injures the interests of any citizen. No government, not even a democratic government, could uphold such a claim. The issue is whether in the long run a democratic process is likely to do less harm to the fundamental rights and interests of its citizens than any nondemocratic alternative. If only because democratic governments prevent abusive autocracies from ruling, they meet this requirement better than nondemocratic governments.

Yet just because democracies are far less tyrannical than nondemocratic regimes, democratic citizens can hardly afford to be complacent. We cannot reasonably justify the commission of a lesser crime because others commit larger crimes. Even when a democratic country, following democratic procedures, inflicts an injustice the result is still . . . an injustice. Majority might does not make majority right.[3]

However, there are other reasons for believing that democracies are likely to be more just and more respectful of basic human interests than nondemocracies.

2. *Democracy guarantees its citizens a number of fundamental rights that nondemocratic systems do not, and cannot, grant.*

Democracy is not only a process of governing. Because rights are necessary elements in democratic political institutions, democracy is inherently also a system of rights. Rights are among the essential building blocks of a democratic process of government.

Consider, for a moment, the democratic standards described in the last chapter. Is it not self-evident that in order to satisfy these standards a political system would necessarily have to insure its citizens certain rights? Take effective participation: to meet that standard, would not its citizens necessarily possess a *right* to participate and a *right* to express their views on political matters, to hear what other citizens have to say, to discuss political matters with other citizens? Or consider what the criterion of voting equality requires: citizens must have a *right* to vote and to have their votes counted fairly. So with the other democratic standards: clearly citizens must have a *right* to investigate alternatives, a *right* to participate in deciding how and what should go on the agenda, and so on.

By definition, no nondemocratic system allows its citizens (or subjects) this broad array of political rights. If any political system were to do so, it would, by definition, become a democracy!

Yet the difference is not just a trivial matter of definitions. To satisfy the requirements of democracy, the rights inherent in it must actually be available to citizens. To promise democratic rights in writing, in law, or even in a constitutional document is not enough. The rights must be effectively enforced and effectively available to citizens in practice. If they are not, then to that extent the political system is not democratic, despite what its rulers claim, and the trappings of "democracy" are merely a façade for nondemocratic rule.

Because of the appeal of democratic ideas, in the twentieth century despotic rulers have often cloaked their rule with a show of "democracy" and "elections." Imagine, however, that in such a country all the rights necessary to democracy somehow become, realistically speaking, available to citizens. Then the country has made a transition to democracy—as happened with great frequency during the last half of the twentieth century.

At this point you might want to object that freedom of speech, let us say, won't exist just because it is a part of the very definition of democracy. Who cares about definitions? Surely, you will say, the connection must be something more than definitional. And you are, of course, correct. Institutions that provide for and protect basic democratic rights and opportunities are necessary to democracy: not simply as a logically necessary condition but as an empirically necessary condition in order for democracy to exist.

Even so, you might ask, isn't this just theory, abstractions, the game of theorists, philosophers, and other intellectuals? Surely, you may add, it would be foolish to think that the support of a few philosophers is enough to create and maintain democracy. And you would, of course, be right. In Part IV we'll examine some of the conditions that increase the chances that democracy will be maintained. Among these is the existence of fairly widespread democratic beliefs among citizens and leaders, including beliefs in the rights and opportunities necessary to democracy.

Fortunately, the need for these rights and opportunities is not so obscure that it lies beyond the comprehension of ordinary citizens and their political leaders. To quite ordinary Americans in the late eighteenth century, for example, it was fairly obvious that they could not have a democratic republic without freedom of expression. One of the first actions of Thomas Jefferson after he was elected to the presidency in 1800 was to bring an end to the infamous Alien and Sedition Acts enacted under his predecessor, John Adams, which would have stifled political expression. In doing so Jefferson responded not only to his own convictions but, it appears, to views widely held among ordinary American citizens in his time. If and when many citizens fail to understand that democracy requires certain fundamental rights, or fail to support the political, administrative, and judicial institutions that protect those rights, then their democracy is in danger.

Fortunately, this danger is somewhat reduced by a third benefit of democratic systems.

3. *Democracy insures its citizens a broader range of personal freedom than any feasible alternative to it.*

In addition to all the rights, freedoms, and opportunities that are strictly necessary in order for a government to be democratic, citizens in a democracy are certain to enjoy an even more extensive array of freedoms. A belief in the desirability of democracy does not exist in isolation from other beliefs. For most people it is a part of a cluster of beliefs. Included in this cluster is the belief that freedom of expression, for example, is desirable in itself. In the universe of values or goods, democracy has a crucial place. But it is not the only good. Like the other rights essential to a democratic process, free expression has its own value because it is instrumental to moral autonomy, moral judgment, and a good life.

What is more, democracy could not long exist unless its citizens manage to create and maintain a supportive political culture, indeed a general culture supportive of these ideals and practices. The relation between a democratic system of government and the democratic culture that supports it is complex and we'll come back to it in Chapter 12. Suffice it to say here that a democratic culture is almost certain to emphasize the value of personal freedom and thus to provide support for additional rights and liberties. What the Greek statesman Pericles said of Athenian democracy in 431 B.C.E. applies equally to modern democracy: "The freedom we enjoy in our government extends also to our ordinary life."[4]

To be sure, the assertion that a democratic state provides a broader range of freedom than any feasible alternative would be challenged by one who believed that we would all gain greater freedom if the state were abolished entirely: the audacious claim of anarchists.[5] But if you try to imagine a world with no state at all, where every person respects the fundamental rights of every other and all matters requiring collective decisions are settled peacefully by unanimous agreement, you will surely conclude, as most people do, that it is impossible. Coercion of some persons by other persons, groups, or organizations would be all too likely: for example, by persons, groups, or organizations intending to rob others of the fruits of their labor, to enslave or dominate those weaker than themselves, to impose their own rule on others, or, indeed, to re-create a coercive state in order to secure their own domination. But if the abolition of the state would produce unbearable violence and disorder—"anarchy" in its popular meaning—then a good state would be superior to the bad state that is likely to follow upon the heels of anarchy.

If we reject anarchism and assume the need for a state, then a state with a democratic government will provide a broader range of freedom than any other.

4. *Democracy helps people to protect their own fundamental interests.*

Everyone, or nearly everyone, wants certain things: survival, food, shelter, health, love, respect, security, family, friends, satisfying work, leisure, and others. The specific pattern of your wants will probably differ from the specific pattern of another's. Like most people, you will surely want to exercise some control over the factors that determine whether and to what extent you can satisfy your wants—some freedom of choice, an opportunity to shape your life in accordance with your own goals, preferences, tastes, values, commitments, beliefs. Democracy protects this freedom and opportunity better than any alternative political system that has ever been devised. No one has put the argument more forcefully than John Stuart Mill.

A principle "of as universal truth and applicability as any general propositions which can be laid down respecting human affairs," he wrote, ". . . is that the rights and interests of every or any person are secure from being disregarded when the person is himself able, and habitually disposed, to stand up for them. . . . Human beings are only secure from evil at the hands of others in proportion as they have the power of being, and are, self-*protecting*." You can protect your rights and interests from abuse by government, and by those who influence or control government, he went on to say, only if you can participate fully in determining the conduct of the government. Therefore, he concluded, "nothing less can be ultimately desirable than the admission of all to a share in the sovereign power of the state," that is, a democratic government.[6]

Mill was surely right. To be sure, even if you are included in the electorate of a democratic state you cannot be certain that all your interests will be adequately protected; but if you are excluded you can be pretty sure that your interests will be seriously injured by neglect or outright damage. Better inclusion than exclusion!

Democracy is uniquely related to freedom in still another way.

5. Only a democratic government can provide a maximum opportunity for persons to exercise the freedom of self-determination—that is, to live under laws of their own choosing.

No normal human being can enjoy a satisfactory life except by living in association with other persons. But living in association with others has a price: you cannot always do just what you like. As you left your childhood behind, you learned a basic fact of life: what you would like to do sometimes conflicts with what others would like to do. You have also learned that the group or groups to which you want to belong follow certain rules or practices that as a member you, too, will have to obey. Consequently, if you cannot simply impose your wishes by force, then you must find a way to resolve your differences peacefully, perhaps by agreement.

Thus a question arises that has proved deeply perplexing in both theory and practice. How can you choose the rules that you are obliged by your group to obey? Because of the state's exceptional capacity to enforce its laws by coercion, the question is particularly relevant to your position as a citizen (or subject) of a state. How can you both be free to choose the laws that are to be enforced by the state and yet, having chosen them, not be free to disobey them?

If you and your fellow citizens always agreed, the solution would be easy: you would all simply agree unanimously on the laws. Indeed, in these circumstances you might have no need for laws, except perhaps to serve as a reminder; in obeying the rules you would be obeying yourself. In effect the problem would vanish, and the complete harmony between you and your fellows would make the dream of anarchism come true. Alas! Experience shows that genuine, unforced, lasting unanimity is rare in human affairs; enduring and perfect consensus is an unattainable goal. So our difficult question remains.

If we can't reasonably expect to live in perfect harmony with all our fellow human beings, we might try instead to create a process for arriving at decisions about rules and laws that would satisfy certain reasonable criteria.

- The process would insure that before a law is enacted you and all other citizens will have an opportunity to make your views known.
- You will be guaranteed opportunities for discussion, deliberation, negotiation, and compromise that in the best circumstances might lead to a law that everyone will find satisfactory.
- In the more likely event that unanimity cannot be achieved, the proposed law that has the greatest number of supporters will be enacted.

These criteria, you will notice, are parts of the ideal democratic process described in the previous chapter. Although that process cannot guarantee that all the members will literally live under laws of their own choosing, it expands self-determination to its maximum feasible limits. Even when you are among the outvoted members whose preferred option is rejected by the majority of your fellow citizens, you may nonetheless decide that the process is fairer than any other that you can reasonably hope to achieve. To that extent you are exercising your freedom of self-determination by freely choosing to live under a democratic constitution rather than a nondemocratic alternative.

6. *Only a democratic government can provide a maximum opportunity for exercising moral responsibility.*

What does it mean to say that you exercise moral responsibility? It means, I believe, that you adopt your moral principles and make decisions that depend on these principles only after you have engaged in a thoughtful process of reflection, deliberation, scrutiny, and consideration of the alternatives and their consequences. For you to be morally responsible is for you to be self-governing in the domain of morally relevant choices.

This is more demanding than most of us can hope to meet most of the time. Yet to the extent that your opportunity to live under the laws of your own choosing is limited, the scope for your moral responsibility is also limited. How can you be responsible for decisions that you cannot control? If you cannot influence the conduct of government officials, how can you be responsible for their conduct? If you are subject to collective decisions, as certainly you are, and if the democratic process maximizes your opportunity to live under laws of your own choosing, then—to an extent that no nondemocratic alternative can achieve—it also enables you to act as a morally responsible person.

7. *Democracy fosters human development more fully than any feasible alternative.*

This is a bold claim and considerably more controversial than any of the others. It is, you will notice, an empirical assertion, a claim as to facts. In principle, we should be able to test the claim by devising an appropriate way of measuring "human development" and comparing human development among people who live in democratic and nondemocratic regimes. But the task is of staggering difficulty. As a consequence, though such evidence as exists supports the proposition, we probably should regard it as an assertion that is highly plausible but unproved.

Just about everyone has views about the human qualities they think are desirable or undesirable, qualities that should be developed if they are desirable and deterred if they are undesirable. Among the desirable qualities that most of us would want to foster are honesty, fairness, courage, and love. Many of us also believe that fully developed adult persons should possess the capacity for looking after themselves, for acting to take care of their interests and not simply counting on others to do so. It is desirable, many of us think, that adults should act responsibly, should weigh alternative courses of action as best they can, should consider consequences, and should take into account the rights and obligations of others as well as themselves. And they should possess the ability to engage in free and open discussions with others about the problems they face together.

At birth, most human beings possess the potentiality for developing these qualities. Whether and how much they actually develop them depends on many circumstances, among which is the nature of the political system in which a person lives. Only democratic systems provide the conditions under which the qualities I have mentioned are likely to develop fully. All other regimes reduce, often drastically, the scope within which adults can act to protect their own interests, consider the interests of others, take responsibility for important decisions, and engage freely with others in a search for the best decision. A democratic government is not enough to insure that people develop these qualities, but it is essential.

8. *Only a democratic government can foster a relatively high degree of political equality.*

One of the most important reasons for preferring a democratic government is that it can achieve political equality among citizens to a much greater extent than any feasible alternative. But why should we place a value on political equality? Because the answer is far from self-evident, in the two following chapters I shall explain why political equality is desirable, why, indeed, it necessarily follows if we accept several reasonable assumptions that probably most of us do believe in. I shall also show that if we accept political equality then we must add the fifth democratic criterion in figure 4.

The advantages of democracy that I have discussed so far would tend to apply to democracies past and present. But as we saw in Chapter 2, some of the political institutions of the democratic systems with which we are familiar today are a product of recent centuries; indeed, one of them, universal adult suffrage, is mainly a product of the twentieth century. These modern representative systems with full adult suffrage appear to have two additional advantages that could not necessarily be claimed for all earlier democracies and republics.

9. *Modern representative democracies do not fight wars with one another.*

This extraordinary advantage of democratic governments was largely unpredicted and unexpected. Yet by the last decade of the twentieth century the evidence had become overwhelming. Of thirty-four international wars between 1945 and 1989 none occurred among democratic countries. What is more, "there has been little expectation of or preparation for war among them either."[7] The observation even holds true before 1945. Well back into the nineteenth century, countries with representative governments and other democratic institutions, where a substantial part of the male population was enfranchised, did not fight wars with one another.

Of course modern democratic governments have fought wars with nondemocratic countries, as they did in World Wars I and II. They have also imposed colonial rule by military force on conquered peoples. They have sometimes interfered in the political life of other countries, even weakening or helping in the overthrow of a weak government. Until the 1980s, for example, the United States had an abysmal record of giving support to military dictatorships in

Latin America; in 1954 it was instrumental in the military coup that overthrew the newly elected government of Guatemala.

Nonetheless, the remarkable fact is that modern representative democracies do not engage in war with *one another*. The reasons are not entirely clear. Probably the high levels of international trade among modern democracies predisposes them to friendliness rather than war.[8] But it is also true that democratic citizens and leaders learn the arts of compromise. In addition, they are inclined to see people in other democratic countries as less threatening, more like themselves, more trustworthy. Finally, the practice and history of peaceful negotiations, treaties, alliances, and common defense against nondemocratic enemies reinforce the predisposition to seek peace rather than fight wars.

Thus a more democratic world promises also to be a more peaceful world.

10. *Countries with democratic governments tend to be more prosperous than countries with nondemocratic governments.*

Until about two centuries ago, a common assumption among political philosophers was that democracy was best suited to a frugal people: affluence, it was thought, was a hallmark of aristocracies, oligarchies, and monarchies, but not democracy. Yet the experience of the nineteenth and twentieth centuries demonstrated precisely the opposite. Democracies were affluent, and by comparison nondemocracies were, on the whole, poor.

The relation between affluence and democracy was particularly striking in the last half of the twentieth century. The explanation is partly to be found in the affinity between representative democracy and a market economy, in which markets are for the most part not highly regulated, workers are free to move from one place or job to another, privately owned firms compete for sales and resources, and consumers can choose among goods and services offered by competing suppliers. By the end of the twentieth century, although not all countries with market economies were democratic, all countries with democratic political systems also had market economies.

In the past two centuries a market economy has generally produced more affluence than any alternative to it. Thus the ancient wisdom has been turned on its head. Because all modern democratic countries have market economies, and a country with a market economy is likely to prosper, a modern democratic country is likely also to be a rich country.

Democracies typically possess other economic advantages over most nondemocratic systems. For one thing, democratic countries foster the education of their people; and an educated workforce is helpful to innovation and economic growth. In addition, the rule of law is usually sustained more strongly in democratic countries; courts are more independent; property rights are more secure; contractual agreements are more effectively enforced; and arbitrary intervention in economic life by government and politicians is less likely. Finally, modern economies depend on communication, and in democratic countries the barriers to communication are much lower. Seeking and exchanging information is easier, and far less dangerous than it is in most nondemocratic regimes.

In sum, despite some notable exceptions on both sides, modern democratic countries have generally tended to provide a more hospitable environment in which to achieve the advantages of market economies and economic growth than have the governments of nondemocratic regimes.

Yet if the affiliation between modern democracy and market economies has advantages for both, we cannot overlook an important cost that market economies impose on a democracy. Because a market economy generates economic inequality, it can also diminish the prospects for attaining full political equality among the citizens of a democratic country. We return to this problem in Chapter 14.

It would be a grievous error to ask too much of any government, including a democratic government. Democracy cannot guarantee that its citizens will be happy, prosperous, healthy, wise, peaceful, or just. To attain these ends is beyond the capacity of any government, including a democratic government. What is more, in practice democracy has always fallen far short of its ideals. Like all previous attempts to achieve a more democratic government, modern democracies also suffer from many defects.

In spite of its flaws, however, we must never lose sight of the benefits that make democracy more desirable than any feasible alternative to it:

1. Democracy helps to prevent government by cruel and vicious autocrats.
2. Democracy guarantees its citizens a number of fundamental rights that nondemocratic systems do not, and cannot, grant.
3. Democracy insures its citizens a broader range of personal freedom than any feasible alternative to it.
4. Democracy helps people to protect their own fundamental interests.
5. Only a democratic government can provide a maximum opportunity for persons to exercise the freedom of self-determination—that is, to live under laws of their own choosing.
6. Only a democratic government can provide a maximum opportunity for exercising moral responsibility.
7. Democracy fosters human development more fully than any feasible alternative.
8. Only a democratic government can foster a relatively high degree of political equality.

9. Modern representative democracies do not fight wars with one another.
10. Countries with democratic governments tend to be more prosperous than countries with nondemocratic governments.

With all these advantages, democracy is, for most of us, a far better gamble than any attainable alternative to it.

CHAPTER 6

Why Political Equality 1?

INTRINSIC EQUALITY

Many people will conclude that the advantages of democracy discussed in the last chapter may be enough—perhaps more than enough—to justify their belief that democratic government is superior to any alternatives that are realistically attainable. And yet, you just might wonder whether it is reasonable for you to assume, as a belief in democracy seems to presuppose, that citizens ought to be treated as political *equals* when they participate in governing. Why should the rights necessary to a democratic process of governing be extended *equally* to citizens?

The answer, though crucial to a belief in democracy, is very far from obvious.

IS EQUALITY SELF-EVIDENT?

In words that were to become famous throughout the world, in 1776 the authors of the American Declaration of Independence announced: "We hold these truths to be self-evident, that all men are created equal, that they are endowed by their Creator with certain inalienable Rights, that among these are Life, Liberty, and the pursuit of happiness." If equality is self-evident then no further justification is needed. None can be found in the Declaration. Yet for most of us it is very far from self-evident that all men—and women—are created equal. If the assumption is not self-evidently true, can we reasonably justify adopting it? And if we cannot, how can we defend a process for governing that seems to assume it to be true?

Critics have often dismissed assertions about equality like that in the Declaration of Independence as nothing more than empty rhetoric. If a claim like that is supposed to state a fact about human beings, they insist, it is self-evidently false.

To the charge of falsity, critics sometimes add hypocrisy. As an example they point out that the authors of the Declaration ignored the inconvenient fact that in the new states they were now declaring independent, a preponderant majority of persons were excluded from enjoying the inalienable rights with which they were supposedly endowed by no less than their Creator. Then and long thereafter women, slaves, free Negroes, and native peoples were deprived not only of political rights but of many other "inalienable rights" essential to life, liberty, and the pursuit of happiness. Indeed, property was also an "inalienable" right, and slaves were the property of their owners. Thomas Jefferson, the principal author of the Declaration, himself owned slaves. In important respects women, too, were the property of their husbands. And a substantial number of free men—on some estimates about 40 percent—were denied the right to vote; in all the new American states the right to vote was restricted to property holders into the nineteenth century.

Neither then nor later was inequality at all peculiar to the United States. On the contrary. In the 1830s the French writer Alexis de Tocqueville concluded that in comparison with Europe one of the distinctive characteristics of the United States was the extraordinary degree of social equality among that country's citizens.

Although many inequalities have diminished since 1776, many remain. We need only look around us to see inequalities everywhere. Inequality, not equality, appears to be the natural condition of humankind.

Thomas Jefferson was too experienced in human affairs to be

unaware of the self-evident fact that in many important respects human capacities, advantages, and opportunities are not distributed equally at birth, much less after nurture, circumstance, and luck have compounded initial differences. The fifty-five men who signed the Declaration of Independence—men of practical experience, lawyers, merchants, planters—were hardly naive in their understanding of human beings. If we grant that they were neither ignorant of reality nor simply hypocritical, what could they possibly have meant by the audacious assertion that all men are created equal?

Despite so much evidence to the contrary, the idea that human beings are fundamentally equal made a great deal of sense to Jefferson, as it had to others before him like the English philosophers Thomas Hobbes and John Locke.[1] Since Jefferson's time many more persons throughout the world have come to accept, in some form, the idea of human equality. To many, equality is simply a fact. Thus to Alexis de Tocqueville in 1835 the increasing "equality of conditions" he observed in Europe as well as America was so striking that it was "a providential fact, and it possesses all the characteristics of a Divine decree: it is universal, it is durable, it constantly eludes all human interference, and all events as well as all men contribute to its progress."[2]

INTRINSIC EQUALITY: A MORAL JUDGMENT

Equalities and inequalities can take an almost infinite variety of forms. Inequality in the ability to win a marathon race or a spelling bee is one thing. Inequality in opportunities to vote, speak, and participate in governing in other ways is quite another.

To understand why it is reasonable to commit ourselves to political equality among citizens of a democratic state, we need to recognize that sometimes when we talk about equality we do not mean to express a factual judgment. We do not intend to describe what we believe is or will be true, as we do when we make statements about winners of marathon races or spelling bees. Instead we mean to express a moral judgment about human beings; we intend to say something about what we believe *ought* to be. One such moral judgment might be put this way: "We ought to regard the good of every human being as *intrinsically* equal to that of any other." Employing the words of the Declaration, as a *moral* judgment we insist that one person's life, liberty, and happiness is not intrinsically superior or inferior to the life, liberty, and happiness of any other. Consequently, we say, we ought to treat all persons as if they possess equal claims to life, liberty, happiness, and other fundamental goods and interests. Let me call this moral judgment the principle of *intrinsic equality*.

The principle does not take us very far, and in order to apply it to the government of a state, it helps to add a supplementary principle that it seems to imply: "In arriving at decisions, the government must give equal consideration to the good and interests of every person bound by those decisions." But why should we apply the principle of intrinsic equality to the government of a state and obligate it to give equal consideration to the interests of all? Unlike the authors of the Declaration, the claim that the truth of intrinsic equality is self-evident strikes me, and no doubt many others, as highly implausible. Yet intrinsic equality embodies so fundamental a view about the worth of human beings that it lies close to the limits of further rational justification. As with factual judgments, so, too, with moral judgments: if you pursue any assertion far enough down toward its foundations you finally reach limits beyond which reasonable argument takes you no further. In Martin Luther's memorable words of 1521: "It is neither safe nor prudent to do aught against conscience. Here I stand—I cannot do otherwise. God help me. Amen."

Although the principle of intrinsic equality lies close to these ultimate limits, we have not quite reached them. For several reasons, intrinsic equality is, I believe, a reasonable principle on which to base the government of a state.

WHY WE SHOULD ADOPT THE PRINCIPLE

Ethical and religious grounds. First, for a great many people throughout the world it is consistent with their most fundamental ethical beliefs and principles. That we are all equally God's children is a tenet of Judaism, Christianity, and Islam; Buddhism incorporates a somewhat similar view. (Among the world's major religions, Hinduism may be an exception.) Most moral reasoning, most systems of ethics, explicitly or implicitly assume some such principle.

The weakness of an alternative principle. Second, whatever might be the case with other associations, for governing a state many of us find every general alternative to intrinsic equality implausible and unconvincing. Suppose Citizen Jones were to propose the following alternative as a principle for governing the state: "In making decisions the government must always treat my good and my interests as superior to those of everyone else." Implicitly rejecting the principle of intrinsic equality, Jones asserts what might be called a principle of intrinsic superiority—or at least Jones's intrinsic superiority. The claim to intrinsic superiority could be made more inclusive, of course, and it usually is: "The good and interests of my group [Jones's family, class, caste, race, or whatever] are superior to those of all others."

It will come as no shock to acknowledge at this point that we human beings have more than a trace of egoism: in varying degrees we tend to be more concerned with our own interests than those of others. Consequently, many of us might be strongly tempted make just such a claim for ourselves and those to whom we are most attached. But unless we ourselves can count confidently on controlling the government of the state, why should we accept the intrinsic superiority of certain others as a fundamental political principle?

To be sure, a person or a group with enough power could enforce a claim to their intrinsic superiority over your objections—literally over your dead body. Throughout human history many individuals and groups have used—or rather, abused—their power in just that way. But because naked force has its limits, those who have laid a claim to being the embodiment of an intrinsic superiority to others have invariably cloaked their otherwise transparently feeble claim with myth, mystery, religion, tradition, ideology, and pomp and circumstance.

Yet if you were not a member of the privileged group and could safely reject their claim to intrinsic superiority, would you freely and knowingly consent to such a preposterous principle? I strongly doubt it.

Prudence. The two preceding reasons for adopting a principle of intrinsic equality as a basis for governing a state suggest a third: prudence. Because the government of a state not only confers great benefits but also can inflict great harm, prudence dictates a cautious concern for the manner in which its unusual capacities will be employed. A governing process that definitely and permanently privileged your own good and interests over those of others might be appealing if you were confident that you or your group would always prevail. But for many people that outcome is so unlikely, or at least so uncertain, that it is safer to insist that your interests will be given equal consideration with those of others.

Acceptability. A principle you find prudent to adopt, many others will also. Thus a process that guarantees equal consideration for all, you may reasonably conclude, is more likely to secure the assent of all the others whose cooperation you need to achieve your ends.

Seen in this perspective, the principle of intrinsic equality makes a great deal of sense.

Yes, despite the claim to the contrary in the Declaration of Independence, it is indeed far from obvious why we should hold to the principle of intrinsic equality and give equal consideration to the interests of all in governing the state.

But if we interpret intrinsic equality as a principle of government that is justified on grounds of morality, prudence, and acceptability, it appears to me to make more sense than any alternative to it.

CHAPTER 7

Why Political Equality II?

CIVIC COMPETENCE

It may now come as an unpleasant surprise to learn that even if we accept intrinsic equality and the equal consideration of interests as sound moral judgments, we are not necessarily bound to endorse democracy as the best process for governing a state.

THE COUNTERCLAIM OF GUARDIANSHIP

To see why this is so, let us imagine that a member of a small group of fellow citizens says to you and others: "Like you, we also strongly believe in intrinsic equality. But we are not only deeply devoted to the common good; we also know better than most how to achieve it. As a result we are much better fitted than the great majority of people to rule. So if you will only grant us exclusive authority over the government, we will devote our wisdom and our labors to serving the general good; and in doing so we will give equal consideration to the good and interests of all."

The claim that government should be turned over to experts deeply committed to rule for the general good and superior to others in their knowledge of the means to achieve it—Guardians, Plato called them—has always been the major rival to democratic ideas. Advocates of Guardianship attack democracy at a seemingly vulnerable point: they simply deny that ordinary people are competent to govern themselves. They do not necessarily deny that human beings are intrinsically equal in the sense that we explored earlier. As in Plato's ideal Republic, the Guardians might be committed to serving the good of all and, at least by implication, might hold that all those under their guardianship are intrinsically equal in their good or interests. Advocates of Guardianship in Plato's sense do not claim that the interests of the persons chosen as guardians are intrinsically superior to the interests of others. They contend that experts in governing, the Guardians, would be superior in their *knowledge* of the general good and the best means to achieve it.

The argument for political guardianship makes a persuasive use of analogies, particularly analogies involving expert knowledge and competence: a physician's superior knowledge on matters of sickness and health, for example, or a pilot's superior competence to guide us safely to our destination. Why not therefore allow those with superior competence in governing to make crucial decisions about the health of the state? To pilot the government toward its proper destination, the public good? Surely we can't assume that all persons are invariably the best judges of their own interests. Children obviously are not; others, usually parents, must serve as their guardians until they are competent to take care of themselves. That adults can also be mistaken about their interests, about the best means to attain their goals, is demonstrated by common experience: most of us come to regret some of our past decisions. We were, we admit, mistaken. What is more, almost all of us do rely on experts to make crucial decisions that bear strongly and directly on our well-being, happiness, health, future, even our survival, not just physicians, surgeons, and pilots but in our increasingly complex society a myriad others. So if we let experts make decisions on important matters like these, why shouldn't we turn *government* over to experts?

Attractive as it may seem at times, the argument for Guardianship rather than democracy fails to take sufficient account of some crucial defects in the analogy.

To delegate certain subordinate decisions to experts is not equivalent to ceding final control over major decisions. As an old adage has it, experts should be kept on tap, not on top. Experts may possess knowledge that is superior to yours in some important respects. A good physician may know better than you how to diagnose your illness, what course it is likely to run, how severe it will be, how best to treat it, and whether it is in fact treatable. You may reasonably choose to follow your physician's recommendations. But that does not mean that you should cede to your physician the power to decide whether you should undertake the course of treatment she or he recommends. Likewise, it is one thing for government officials to seek the aid of experts; but it is quite another for a political elite to possess the power to decide on the laws and policies you will be compelled to obey.

Personal decisions made by individuals are not equivalent to decisions made and enforced by the government of a state. The fundamental issue in the debate over guardianship versus democracy is not whether as individuals we must sometimes put our trust in experts. The issue is who or what group should have the final say in decisions made by the government of a state. You might reasonably wish to turn certain personal decisions over to someone more expert on those matters than you, like your doctor, accountant, lawyer, airplane pilot, or others. But it does not follow automatically that it would be reasonable for you to turn over to a political elite the authority to control the major decisions of the government of the state, decisions that would be enforced if need be by coercion, imprisonment, perhaps even death.

To govern a state well requires much more than strictly scientific knowledge. Governing is not a science in the sense that physics or chemistry or even, in some respects, medicine is a science. This is true for several reasons. For one thing, virtually all important decisions about policies, whether personal or governmental, require ethical judgments. To make a decision about the ends that government policies should be designed to achieve (justice, equity, fairness, happiness, health, survival, security, well-being, equality, or whatnot) is to make an ethical judgment. Ethical judgments are not "scientific" judgments in the usual sense.[1]

Then, too, good ends often conflict with one another and resources are limited. Consequently, decisions about policies, whether personal or governmental, almost always require judgments about trade-offs, a balancing of different ends. For example, achieving economic equality may impair economic incentives; the costs of benefits for the elderly may be imposed on the young; expenditures on generations now living may impose costs on generations to come; preserving a wilderness area may come at the price of jobs for miners and timber-workers. Judgments about trade-offs among different ends are not "scientific." Empirical evidence is important and necessary, but it is never sufficient. In deciding how much we should sacrifice one end, good, or goal in order to attain some measure of another, we necessarily move well beyond anything that strictly scientific knowledge can provide.

There is another reason why decisions about policies require judgments that are not strictly "scientific." Even if the ends of policy decisions can be agreed on in a general way, there is almost always considerable uncertainty and conflict over the means: how the end may best be achieved, the desirability, feasibility, acceptability, and likely consequences of alternative means. What are the best means of taking care of the poor, the jobless, the homeless? How are the interests of children best protected and advanced? How large a budget is needed for military defense, and for what purposes? It is impossible to demonstrate, I believe, that a group exists, or could be created, who possess "scientific" or "expert" knowledge that provides definite answers to questions like these. Would we rather entrust the repair of our car to a theoretical physicist—or to a good automobile mechanic?

To govern a state well takes more than knowledge. It also requires incorruptibility, a firm resistance to all the enormous temptations of power, a continuing and inflexible dedication to the public good rather than benefits for oneself or one's group.

Because experts may be qualified to serve as your agents does not mean that they are qualified to serve as your rulers. Advocates of guardianship make not just one claim but two. A ruling elite can be created, they contend, whose members are both definitely superior to others in their knowledge of the ends a good government should seek and the best means to achieve those ends; *and* so deeply dedicated to pursuing the public good that they can safely be entrusted with the sovereign authority to govern the state.

As we have just seen, the first claim is highly dubious. But even if it could be shown to be justified, that would not by itself support the second claim. Knowledge is one thing; power is another. The likely effects of power on those who wield it were succinctly summed up in 1887 by an English baron, Lord Acton, in a famous statement: "Power tends to corrupt; absolute power corrupts absolutely." A century earlier William Pitt, a British statesman of vast experience in political life, had made a similar observation: "Unlimited power," he said in a speech in Parliament, "is apt to corrupt the minds of those who possess it."

This was also the general view among the members of the American Constitutional Convention in 1787, who were not lacking in experience on this question. "Sir, there are two passions which have a powerful influence on the affairs of men," said the oldest delegate, Benjamin Franklin. "These are ambition and avarice; the love of power and the love of money." One of the youngest delegates, Alexander Hamilton, concurred: "Men love power." And one of the most experienced and influential delegates, George Mason, concurred: "From the nature of man, we may be sure that those who have power in their hands . . . will always, when they can, . . . increase it."[2]

However wise and worthy the members of a ruling elite entrusted with the power to govern a state may be when they first take power, in a few years or a few generations they are likely to abuse it. If human history provides any lessons, one surely is that through corruption, nepotism, the advancement of individual and group interests, and abuse of their monopoly over the state's coercive power to suppress criticism, extract wealth from their subjects, and insure their obedience by coercion, the Guardians of a state are likely to turn into despots.

Finally, to design a utopia is one thing; to bring it about is quite another. An advocate of Guardianship confronts a host of formidable practical problems: How is the Guardianship to be inaugurated? Who will draw up the constitution, so to speak, and who will put it into action? How will the first Guardians be chosen? If Guardianship is to depend in some way on the consent of the governed and not outright coercion, how will consent be obtained? In whatever way the Guardians are first selected, will they then choose their successors, like the members of a club? If so, won't the system run a high risk of degenerating from an aristocracy of talent into an oligarchy of birth? Yet if the existing Guardians do not choose their successors, who will? How will abusive and exploitative Guardians be discharged? And so on.

THE COMPETENCE OF CITIZENS TO GOVERN

Unless advocates of Guardianship can provide convincing solutions to the problems in their prescription that I have just described, prudence and reason require, in my judgment, that we reject their case. In rejecting the case for Guardianship, in effect we conclude:

Among adults no persons are so definitely better qualified than others to govern that they should be entrusted with complete and final authority over the government of the state.

But if we should not be governed by Guardians, by whom should we be governed? By ourselves.

On most matters we tend to believe that unless a highly convincing case can be made to the contrary, every adult should be allowed to judge what is best for his or her own good or interests. We apply this presumption in favor of personal autonomy only to adults, however, and not to children. From experience we assume instead that parents must act as guardians to protect the interests of their children. If the parents fail, others, perhaps the government, may need to step in.

Sometimes we also reject the presumption for persons of adult age who are judged to lack a normal capacity to look out for themselves. Like children, they, too, may need guardians. Yet unlike children, for whom the presumption has been overruled by law and convention, with adults the presumption cannot be lightly overridden. The potential for abuse is all too obvious. Consequently, we require an independent finding, a judicial process of some kind.

If we assume that with few exceptions adults should be entrusted with the right to make personal decisions about what is in their best interest, why should we reject this view in governing the state? The key question here is no longer whether adults are generally competent to make the personal decisions they face daily. The question now is whether most adults are sufficiently competent to participate in governing the state. Are they?

To arrive at the answer, consider again some conclusions we reached in the last several chapters:

Democracy confers many advantages on its citizens. Citizens are strongly protected against despotic rulers; they possess fundamental political rights; in addition, they also enjoy a wider sphere of freedom; as citizens they acquire means for protecting and advancing their most important personal interests; they can also participate in deciding on the laws under which they will live; they can exercise a wide range of moral autonomy; and they possess unusual opportunities for personal development.

If we conclude that democracy provides these advantages over nondemocratic systems of government, several fundamental questions arise: Why should the advantages of democracy be restricted to some persons and not others? Why shouldn't they be available to all adults?

If a government ought to give equal consideration to the good of each person, should not all adults have the right to participate in deciding what laws and policies would best achieve the ends they seek, whether their ends are restricted narrowly to their own good or include the good of all?

If no persons are so definitely better qualified to govern that they should be entrusted with complete and final authority over the government of the state, then who is better qualified to participate than all the adults who are subject to the laws?

From the conclusions implied by these questions, another follows that I would put this way: *Except on a very strong showing to the contrary in rare circumstances, protected by law, every adult subject to the laws of the state should be considered to be sufficiently well qualified to participate in the democratic process of governing that state.*

A FIFTH DEMOCRATIC STANDARD: INCLUSION

The conclusion to which the argument of this chapter now points is that if you are deprived of an equal voice in the government of a state, the chances are quite high that your interests will not be given the same attention as the interests of those who do have a voice. If you have no voice, who will speak up for you? Who will defend your interests if you cannot? And not just your interests as an individual. If you happen to be a member of an entire group excluded from participation, how will the fundamental interests of that group be protected?

The answer is clear. The fundamental interests of adults who are denied opportunities to participate in governing will *not* be adequately protected and advanced by those who govern. The historical evidence on this point is overwhelming. As we saw in our brief survey of the evolution of democracy, nobles and burghers in England, discontented with the arbitrary way monarchs imposed burdens on them without their consent, demanded and gained the right to participate in governing. Centuries later the middle classes, believing that their fundamental interests were ignored, in turn demanded and gained that right. There and elsewhere the continuing legal or de facto exclusion of women, slaves, poor persons, and manual workers, among others, left the members of these groups poorly protected against exploitation and abuse even in countries like Great Britain and the United States where the government was otherwise largely democratic.

In 1861 John Stuart Mill contended that because the working classes were denied suffrage, no one in government spoke up for their interests. Although he did not believe, he said, that those who participated in the government deliberately intended to sacrifice the interests of the working classes to their own, nonetheless, he asked, "Does Parliament, or almost any of the members composing it, ever for an instant look at any question with the eyes of a workingman? When a subject arises in which the laborers as such have an interest, is it regarded from any point of view but that of employers of labor?"[3] The same question could have been asked about slaves in ancient and modern republics; about women throughout history until the twentieth century; about many persons nominally free but effectively deprived of democratic rights, such as blacks in the southern United States until the 1960s and in South Africa until the 1990s, and elsewhere.

Yes, individuals and groups may sometimes be mistaken about their own good. Certainly they may sometimes misperceive what is in their own best interests. But the preponderant weight of human experience informs us that no group of adults can safely grant to others the power to govern over them. Which leads us to a conclusion of crucial importance.

You may recall that when I discussed the criteria for democracy in Chapter 4, I postponed a discussion of the fifth: inclusion of adults (see figure 4, p. 38). This chapter and the last provide us, I believe, with ample reasons for concluding that to be democratic the government of a state must satisfy that standard. Let me now put it this way: *Full inclusion. The citizen body in a democratically governed state must include all persons subject to the laws of that state except transients and persons proved to be incapable of caring for themselves.*

UNSETTLED PROBLEMS

To reject the argument for Guardianship and adopt political equality as an ideal still leaves some difficult questions.

Don't citizens and government officials need help from experts? Indeed they do! The importance of experts and specialized knowledge for democratic governments to function well is undeniable.

Public policy is often so complex (and may be growing steadily more so) that no government could make satisfactory decisions without the help of highly informed specialists. Just as each of us in our personal decisions must sometimes depend on experts for guidance and must delegate important decisions to them, so, too, must governments, including democratic governments. How best to satisfy democratic criteria, maintain a satisfactory degree of political equality, and yet rely on experts and expert knowledge in making public decisions presents a serious problem, one that it would be foolish for advocates of democratic government to ignore. But I shall have to ignore it here.

If citizens are to be competent, won't they need political and social institutions to help make them so? Unquestionably. Opportunities to gain an enlightened understanding of public matters are not just part of the definition of democracy. They are a requirement for democracy.

Nothing I have said is meant to imply that a majority of citizens may not make mistakes. They can and do. This is precisely why advocates of democracy have always placed a high value on education. And civic education requires not only formal schooling but public discussion, deliberation, debate, controversy, the ready availability of reliable information, and other institutions of a free society.

But suppose the institutions for developing competent citizens are weak and many citizens don't know enough to protect their fundamental values and interests? What are we to do? In searching for an answer it is helpful to review the conclusions we have reached up to this point.

We have adopted the principle of intrinsic equality: We ought to regard the good of every human being as intrinsically equal to that of any other.

We have applied that principle to the government of a state: In arriving at decisions, the government must give equal consideration to the good and interests of every person bound by those decisions.

We have rejected Guardianship as a satisfactory way of applying the principle: Among adults no persons are so definitely better qualified than others to govern that they should be entrusted with complete and final authority over the government of the state.

Instead, we have accepted full inclusion: The citizen body in a democratically governed state must include all persons subject to the laws of the state except transients and persons proved to be incapable of caring for themselves.

Therefore, if the institutions for civic education are weak, only one satisfactory solution remains. They must be strengthened. We who believe in democratic goals are obliged to search for ways by which citizens can acquire the competence they need.

Perhaps the institutions for civic education that were created in democratic countries during the nineteenth and twentieth centuries are no longer adequate. If this is so, then democratic countries will need to create new institutions to supplement the old ones.

CONCLUDING COMMENTS AND PREVIEW

We have now explored about half the territory laid out in figure 3 (p. 29). Yet we have barely peeked into the other half: the basic institutions that are necessary for advancing the goal of democracy, and the conditions, social, economic, and other, that favor the development and maintenance of these democratic political institutions. We'll explore these in the following chapters.

We turn, then, from goals to actualities.

PART III *Actual Democracy*

CHAPTER 8

What Political Institutions Does
Large-Scale Democracy Require?

What does it mean to say that a country is governed democratically? In this chapter we'll focus on the political institutions of *democracy on a large scale,* that is, the political institutions necessary for a *democratic country.* We're not concerned here, then, with what democracy in a very small group might require, as in a committee. We also need to keep our standard warning in mind: every actual democracy has always fallen short of the democratic criteria described in Part II and shown in figure 4 (p. 38). Finally, we should be aware in this chapter as elsewhere that in ordinary language we use the word *democracy* to refer both to a goal or ideal and to an actuality that is only a partial attainment of the goal. For the time being, therefore, I'll count on the reader to make the necessary distinctions when I use the words *democracy, democratically, democratic government, democratic country,* and so on.

If a *country* is to be governed democratically, what would be required? At a minimum, it would need to possess certain political arrangements, practices, or institutions that would go a long way, even if not all the way, toward meeting ideal democratic criteria.

Words About Words

Political *arrangements* sound as if they might be rather provisional, which they could well be in a country that has just moved away from nondemocratic rule. We tend to think of *practices* as more habitual and therefore more durable. We usually think of *institutions* as having settled in for the long haul, passed on from one generation to the next. As a country moves from a non-democratic to a democratic government, the early democratic *arrangements* gradually become *practices*, which in due time turn into settled *institutions*. Helpful though these distinctions may be, however, for our purposes it will be more convenient if we put them aside and settle for *institutions*.

HOW CAN WE KNOW?

How can we reasonably determine what political institutions are necessary for large-scale democracy? We might examine the history of countries that have changed their political institutions in response, at least in part, to demands for broader popular inclusion and effective participation in government and political life. Although in earlier times those who sought to gain inclusion and participation were not necessarily inspired by democratic ideas, from about the eighteenth century onward they tended to justify their demands by appealing to democratic and republican ideas. What political institutions did they seek, and what were actually adopted in these countries?

Alternatively, we could examine countries where the government is generally referred to as democratic by most of the people in that country, by many persons in other countries, and by scholars, journalists, and the like. In other words, in ordinary speech and scholarly discussion the country is called a democracy.

Third, we could reflect on a specific country or group of countries, or perhaps even a hypothetical country, in order to imagine, as realistically as possible, what political institutions would be required in order to achieve democratic goals to a substantial degree. We would undertake a mental experiment, so to speak, in which we

FIGURE 6. *What political institutions does large-scale democracy require?*

Large-scale democracy requires:
1. Elected officials
2. Free, fair, and frequent elections
3. Freedom of expression
4. Alternative sources of information
5. Associational autonomy
6. Inclusive citizenship

would reflect carefully on human experiences, tendencies, possibilities, and limitations and design a set of political institutions that would be necessary for large-scale democracy to exist and yet feasible and attainable within the limits of human capacities.

Fortunately, all three methods converge on the same set of democratic political institutions. These, then, are minimal requirements for a democratic country (fig. 6).

THE POLITICAL INSTITUTIONS OF
MODERN REPRESENTATIVE DEMOCRACY

Briefly, the political institutions of modern representative democratic government are:

1. *Elected officials.* Control over government decisions about policy is constitutionally vested in officials elected by citizens. Thus modern, large-scale democratic governments are *representative*.
2. *Free, fair, and frequent elections.* Elected officials are chosen in frequent and fairly conducted elections in which coercion is comparatively uncommon.
3. *Freedom of expression.* Citizens have a right to express themselves without danger of severe punishment on political

matters broadly defined, including criticism of officials, the government, the regime, the socioeconomic order, and the prevailing ideology.

4. *Access to alternative sources of information.* Citizens have a right to seek out alternative and independent sources of information from other citizens, experts, newspapers, magazines, books, telecommunications, and the like. Moreover, alternative sources of information actually exist that are not under the control of the government or any other single political group attempting to influence public political beliefs and attitudes, and these alternative sources are effectively protected by law.

5. *Associational autonomy.* To achieve their various rights, including those required for the effective operation of democratic political institutions, citizens also have a right to form relatively independent associations or organizations, including independent political parties and interest groups.

6. *Inclusive citizenship.* No adult permanently residing in the country and subject to its laws can be denied the rights that are available to others and are necessary to the five political institutions just listed. These include the rights to vote in the election of officials in free and fair elections; to run for elective office; to free expression; to form and participate in independent political organizations; to have access to independent sources of information; and rights to other liberties and opportunities that may be necessary to the effective operation of the political institutions of large-scale democracy.

THE POLITICAL INSTITUTIONS IN PERSPECTIVE

Ordinarily these institutions do not arrive in a country all at once. As we saw in our brief history of democracy (Chapter 2), the last two are distinctly latecomers. Until the twentieth century universal suffrage was denied in both the theory and practice of democratic and republican government. More than any other single feature, universal suffrage distinguishes modern representative democracy from all earlier forms of democracy.

The time of arrival and the sequence in which the institutions have been introduced have varied tremendously. In countries where the full set of democratic institutions arrived earliest and have endured to the present day, the "older" democracies, elements of a common pattern emerge. Elections to a legislature arrived early on—in Britain as early as the thirteenth century, in the United States during its colonial period in the seventeenth and eighteenth centuries. The practice of electing higher lawmaking officials was followed by a gradual expansion of the rights of citizens to express themselves on political matters and to seek out and exchange information. The right to form associations with explicit political goals tended to follow still later. Political "factions" and partisan organization were generally viewed as dangerous, divisive, subversive of political order and stability, and injurious to the public good. Yet because political associations could not be suppressed without a degree of coercion that an increasingly large and influential number of citizens regarded as intolerable, they were often able to exist as more or less clandestine associations until they emerged from the shadows into the full light of day. In the legislative bodies what once were "factions" became political parties. The "ins" who served in the government of the day were opposed by the "outs," or what in Britain came to be officially styled His (or Her) Majesty's Loyal Opposition. In eighteenth-century Britain, the faction supporting the monarch and the opposing faction supported by the much of the gentry in the "country" were gradually transformed into Tories and Whigs. During that same century in Sweden, partisan adversaries in parliament somewhat facetiously called themselves the Hats and the Caps.[1]

During the final years of the eighteenth century in the newly formed republic of the United States, Thomas Jefferson, the vice president, and James Madison, leader of the House of Representatives, organized their followers in Congress to oppose the policies of the Federalist president, John Adams, and his secretary of the Treasury, Alexander Hamilton. To succeed in their opposition, they soon realized that they would have to do more than oppose the Federalists in the Congress and the cabinet: they would need to remove their opponents from office. To do that, they had to win national elections, and to win national elections they had to organize their followers throughout the country. In less than a decade, Jefferson, Madison, and others sympathetic with their views created a political party that was organized all the way down to the smallest voting precincts, districts, and municipalities, an organization that would reinforce the loyalty of their followers between and during election campaigns and make sure they came to the polls. Their Republican Party (soon renamed Democratic Republican and a generation later Democratic) became the first popularly based *electoral* party in the world. As a result, one of the most fundamental and distinctive political institutions of modern democracy, the political party, had burst beyond its confines in parliaments and legislatures in order to organize the citizens themselves and mobilize party supporters in national elections.

By the time the young French aristocrat Alexis de Tocqueville visited the United States in the 1830s, the first five democratic political institutions described above had already arrived in America. The institutions seemed to him so deeply planted and pervasive that he had no hesitation in referring to the United States as a democracy. In that country, he said, the people were sovereign, "society governs itself for itself," and the power of the majority was unlimited.[2] He was astounded by the multiplicity of associations into which Americans organized themselves, for every purpose, it seemed. And towering among these associations were the two major political parties. In the United States, it appeared to Tocqueville, democracy was about as complete as one could imagine it ever becoming.

During the century that followed all five of the basic democratic institutions Tocqueville observed during his visit to America were consolidated in more than a dozen other countries. Many observers in Europe and the United States concluded that any country that aspired to be civilized and progressive would necessarily have to adopt a democratic form of government.

Yet everywhere the sixth fundamental institution—inclusive citizenship—was missing. Although Tocqueville affirmed that "the state of Maryland, which had been founded by men of rank, was the first to proclaim universal suffrage," like almost all other men (and many women) of his time he tacitly assumed that "universal" did not include women.[3] Nor, indeed, some men. Maryland's "universal suffrage," it so happened, also excluded most African Americans. Elsewhere, in countries that were otherwise more or less democratic, as in America a full half of all adults were completely excluded from national political life simply because they were women; in addition large numbers of men were denied the suffrage because they could not meet literacy or property requirements, an exclusion supported by many people who considered themselves advocates of democratic or republican government. Although New Zealand extended suffrage to women in national elections in 1893 and Australia in 1902, in countries otherwise democratic women did not gain suffrage in national elections until about 1920; in Belgium, France, and Switzerland, countries that most people would have called highly democratic, women could not vote until after World War II.

Because it is difficult for many today to grasp what "democracy" meant to our predecessors, let me reemphasize the difference: in all democracies and republics throughout twenty-five centuries the rights to engage fully in political life were restricted to a minority of adults. "Democratic" government was government by males only—and not all of them. It was not until the twentieth century that in both theory and practice democracy came to require that the rights to engage fully in political life must be extended, with very few if any exceptions, to the entire population of adults permanently residing in a country.

Taken in their entirety, then, these six political institutions constitute not only a new type of political system but a new kind of popular government, a type of "democracy" that had never existed throughout the twenty-five centuries of experience since the inauguration of "democracy" in Athens and a "republic" in Rome. Because the institutions of modern representative democratic government, taken in their entirety, are historically unique, it is convenient to give them their own name. This modern type of large-scale democratic government is sometimes called *polyarchal* democracy.

Words About Words

Polyarchy is derived from Greek words meaning "many" and "rule," thus "rule by the many," as distinguished from rule by the one, or monarchy, and rule by the few, oligarchy or aristocracy. Although the term had been rarely used, a colleague and I introduced it in 1953 as a handy way of referring to a modern representative democracy with universal suffrage. Hereafter I shall use it in that sense. More precisely, a polyarchal democracy is a political system with the six democratic institutions listed above. Polyarchal democracy, then, is different from representative democracy with restricted suffrage, as in the nineteenth century. It is also different from older democracies and republics that not only had a restricted suffrage but lacked many of the other crucial characteristics of polyarchal democracy, such as political parties, rights to form political organizations to influence or oppose the existing government, organized interest groups, and so on. It is different, too, from the democratic practices in units so small that members can assemble directly and make (or recommend) policies or laws. (I return to this difference in a moment.)

Although other factors were often at work, the six political institutions of polyarchal democracy came about, in part at least, in response to demands for inclusion and participation in political life. In countries that are widely referred to as democracies today, all six exist. Yet you might well ask: Are some of these institutions no more than past products of historical struggles? Are they no longer necessary for democratic government? And if they are still necessary today, why?

THE FACTOR OF SIZE

Before answering these questions, I need to call attention to an important qualification. As I warned at the beginning of this chapter, we are considering institutions necessary for the government of a democratic *country*. Why "country"? *Because all the institutions necessary for a democratic country would not always be required for a unit much smaller than a country.*

Consider a democratically governed committee, or a club, or a very small town. Although equality in voting would seem to be necessary, small units like these might manage without many elected officials: perhaps a moderator to preside over meetings, a secretary-treasurer to keep minutes and accounts. The participants themselves could decide just about everything directly during their meetings, leaving details to the secretary-treasurer. Governments of small organizations would not have to be full-fledged *representative* governments in which citizens elect representatives charged with enacting laws and policies. Yet these governments could be democratic, perhaps highly democratic. So, too, even though they lacked

FIGURE 7. *Why the institutions are necessary*

In a unit as large as a country, these political institutions of polyarchal democracy . . .	are necessary to satisfy the following democratic criteria:
1. Elected representatives . . .	Effective participation
	Control of the agenda
2. Free, fair, and frequent elections . . .	Voting equality
	Control of the agenda
3. Freedom of expression . . .	Effective participation
	Enlightened understanding
	Control of the agenda
4. Alternative information . . .	Effective participation
	Enlightened understanding
	Control of the agenda
5. Associational autonomy . . .	Effective participation
	Enlightened understanding
	Control of the agenda
6. Inclusive citizenship . . .	Full inclusion

political parties or other independent political associations, they might be highly democratic. In fact, we might concur with the classical democratic and republican view that in small associations organized "factions" are not only unnecessary but downright harmful. Instead of conflicts exacerbated by factionalism, caucuses, political parties, and so on, we might prefer unity, consensus, agreement achieved by discussion and mutual respect.

The political institutions strictly required for democratic government depend, then, on the size of the unit. The six institutions listed above developed because they are necessary for governing *countries,* not smaller units. Polyarchal democracy is democratic government on the large scale of the nation-state or country.

To return to our questions: Are the political institutions of poly-archal democracy actually necessary for democracy on the large scale of a country? If so, why? To answer these twin questions, let us recall what a democratic process requires (fig. 7).

WHY (AND WHEN) DOES DEMOCRACY REQUIRE ELECTED REPRESENTATIVES?

As the focus of democratic government shifted to large-scale units like nations or countries, the question arose: How can citizens *participate effectively* when the number of citizens becomes too numerous or too widely dispersed geographically (or both, as in the case of a country) for them to participate conveniently in making laws by assembling in one place? And how can they make sure that matters with which they are most concerned are adequately considered by officials—that is, how can citizens *control the agenda of* government decisions?

How best to meet these democratic requirements in a political unit as large as a country is, of course, enormously difficult, indeed to some extent unachievable. Yet just as with the other highly demanding democratic criteria, this, too, can serve as a standard for evaluating alternative possibilities and solutions. Clearly the requirements could not be met if the top officials of the government could set the agenda and adopt policies independently of the wishes of citizens. The only feasible solution, though it is highly imperfect, is for citizens to elect their top officials and hold them more or less accountable through elections by dismissing them, so to speak, in subsequent elections.

To us that solution seems obvious. But what may appear self-evident to us was not at all obvious to our predecessors.

As we saw in Chapter 2, until fairly recently the possibility that citizens could, by means of elections, choose and reject representatives with the authority to make laws remained largely foreign to both the theory and practice of democracy. As we saw, too, the election of representatives mainly developed during the Middle Ages, when monarchs realized that in order to impose taxes, raise armies, and make laws they needed to win the consent of the nobility, the higher clergy, and a few not-so-common commoners in the larger town and cities.

Until the eighteenth century, then, the standard view was that democratic or republican government meant rule by the people, and if the people were to rule they had to assemble in one place and vote on decrees, laws, or policies. Democracy would have to be town meeting democracy; representative democracy was a contradiction in terms. By implication, whether explicit or implicit, a republic or a democracy could actually exist only in a small unit, like a town or city. Writers who held this view, such as Montesquieu and Jean-Jacques Rousseau, were perfectly aware of the disadvantages of a small state, particularly when it confronted the military superiority of a much larger state and were therefore extremely pessimistic about the future prospects for genuine democracy.

Yet the standard view was swiftly overpowered and swept aside by the onrushing force of the national state. Rousseau himself clearly understood that for a government of a country as large as Poland (for which he proposed a constitution), representation would be necessary. And shortly thereafter the standard view was driven off the stage of history by the arrival of democracy in America.

As late as 1787, when the Constitutional Convention met in Philadelphia to design a constitution appropriate for a large country with an ever-increasing population, the delegates were acutely aware of the historical tradition. Could a republic possibly exist on the huge scale the United States had already attained, not to mention the even grander scale the delegates foresaw?* Yet no one ques-

---

*A few delegates daringly forecast that the United States might ultimately have as many as one hundred million inhabitants. This number was reached in 1915.

tioned that if a republic were to exist in America it would have to take the form of a *representative* republic. Because of the lengthy experience with representation in colonial and state legislatures and in the Continental Congress, the feasibility of representative government was practically beyond debate.

By the middle of the nineteenth century, the traditional view was ignored, forgotten, or, if remembered at all, treated as irrelevant. "It is evident," John Stuart Mill wrote in 1861,

> that the only government which can fully satisfy all the exigencies of the social state is one in which the whole people participate; that any participation, even in the smallest public function, is useful; that the participation should everywhere be as great as the general degree of improvement of the community will allow; and that nothing less can be ultimately desirable than the admission of all to a share in the sovereign power of the state. But since all cannot, in a community exceeding a single small town, participate personally in any but some very minor portions of the public business, it follows that the ideal type of a perfect government must be representative.[4]

WHY DOES DEMOCRACY REQUIRE FREE, FAIR, AND FREQUENT ELECTIONS?

As we have seen, if we accept the desirability of political equality, then every citizen must have an *equal and effective opportunity to vote, and all votes must be counted as equal*. If equality in voting is to be implemented, then clearly elections must be free and fair. To be free means that citizens can go to the polls without fear of reprisal; and if they are to be fair, then all votes must be counted as equal. Yet free and fair elections are not enough. Imagine electing representatives for a term of, say, twenty years! If citizens are to retain *final control over the agenda*, then elections must also be frequent.

How best to implement free and fair elections is not obvious. In the late nineteenth century the secret ballot began to replace a public show of hands. Although open voting still has a few defenders, secrecy has become the general standard; a country in which it is widely violated would be judged as lacking free and fair elections. But debate continues as to the kind of voting system that best meets standards of fairness. Is a system of proportional representation (PR), like that employed in most democratic countries, fairer than the First-Past-the-Post system used in Great Britain and the United States? Reasonable arguments can be made for both, as we'll see when we return to this question in Chapter 10. In discussions about different voting systems, however, the need for a fair system is assumed; how best to achieve fairness and other reasonable objectives is simply a technical question.

How frequent should elections be? Judging from twentieth-century practices in democratic countries, a rough answer might be that annual elections for legislative representatives would be a bit too frequent and anything more than about five years would be too long. Obviously, however, democrats can reasonably disagree about the specific interval and how it might vary with different offices and different traditional practices. The point is that without frequent elections citizens would lose a substantial degree of control over their elected officials.

WHY DOES DEMOCRACY REQUIRE FREE EXPRESSION?

To begin with, freedom of expression is required in order for citizens to *participate* effectively in political life. How can citizens make their views known and persuade their fellow citizens and representatives to adopt them unless they can express themselves freely about all matters bearing on the conduct of the government? And if they are to take the views of others into account, they must be able to hear what others have to say. Free expression means not just that you have a right to be heard. It also means that you have a right to hear what others have to say.

To acquire an *enlightened understanding* of possible government actions and policies also requires freedom of expression. To acquire civic competence, citizens need opportunities to express their own views; learn from one another; engage in discussion and deliberation; read, hear, and question experts, political candidates, and persons whose judgments they trust; and learn in other ways that depend on freedom of expression.

Finally, without freedom of expression citizens would soon lose their capacity to influence *the agenda* of government decisions. Silent citizens may be perfect subjects for an authoritarian ruler; they would be a disaster for a democracy.

WHY DOES DEMOCRACY REQUIRE THE AVAILABILITY OF ALTERNATIVE AND INDEPENDENT SOURCES OF INFORMATION?

Like freedom of expression, the availability of alternative and relatively independent sources of information is required by several of the basic democratic criteria. Consider the need for *enlightened understanding*. How can citizens acquire the information they need in order to understand the issues if the government controls all the important sources of information? Or, for that matter, if any single group enjoys a monopoly in providing information? Citizens must have access, then, to alternative sources of information that are not under the control of the government or dominated by any other group or point of view.

Or think about *effective participation* and influencing the *public agenda*. How could citizens participate effectively in political life if all the information they could acquire was provided by a single source, say the government, or, for that matter, a single party, faction, or interest?

WHY DOES DEMOCRACY REQUIRE INDEPENDENT ASSOCIATIONS?

As we saw earlier, it took a radical turnabout in ways of thinking to accept the need for political associations—interest groups, lobbying organizations, political parties. Yet if a large republic requires that representatives be elected, then how are elections to be contested? Forming an organization, such as a political party, gives a group an obvious electoral advantage. And if one group seeks to gain that advantage, will not others who disagree with their policies? And why should political activity cease between elections? Legislators can be influenced; causes can be advanced, policies promoted, appointments sought. So, unlike a small city or town, the large scale of democracy in a country makes political associations both necessary and desirable. In any case, how can they be prevented without impairing the fundamental right of citizens to participate effectively in governing? In a large republic, then, they are not only necessary and desirable but inevitable. Independent associations are also a source of *civic education and enlightenment*. They provide citizens not only with information but also with opportunities for discussion, deliberation, and the acquisition of political skills.

WHY DOES DEMOCRACY REQUIRE INCLUSIVE CITIZENSHIP?

The answer is to be found, of course, in the reasons that brought us to the conclusion of the last chapter. We hardly need to repeat them here.

We can view the political institutions described in this chapter and summarized in figure 6 in several ways. For a country that lacks one or more of the institutions, and is to that extent not yet sufficiently democratized, knowledge of the basic political institutions can help us to design a strategy for making a full *transition* to modern representative democracy. For a country that has only recently made the transition, that knowledge can help inform us about the crucial institutions that need to be *strengthened, deepened, and consolidated*. Because they are all necessary for modern representative democracy (polyarchal democracy), we can also view them as establishing a *minimum level for democratization*.

Those of us who live in the older democracies, where the transition to democracy occurred some generations ago and the political institutions listed in figure 6 are by now solidly established, face a different and equally difficult challenge. For even if the institutions are necessary to democratization, they are definitely not *sufficient* for achieving fully the democratic criteria listed in figure 6 and described in Chapter 4. Are we not then at liberty, and indeed obligated, to appraise our democratic institutions against these criteria? It seems obvious to me, as to many others, that judged against democratic criteria our existing political institutions display many shortcomings.

Consequently, just as we need strategies for bringing about a transition to democracy in nondemocratic countries and for consolidating democratic institutions in newly democratized countries, so in the older democratic countries we need to consider whether and how to move beyond our existing level of democracy.

Let me put it this way. In many countries the task is to achieve democratization up to the level of polyarchal democracy. But the challenge to citizens in the older democracies is to discover how they might achieve a level of democratization *beyond* polyarchal democracy.

CHAPTER 9

Varieties 1

DEMOCRACY ON DIFFERENT SCALES

Are there different varieties of democracy? If so, what are they? Because the words *democracy* and *democratic* are bandied about indiscriminately, it is tempting to adopt the view of Humpty Dumpty in *Through the Looking Glass:*

> "When *I* use a word," Humpty Dumpty said, in rather a scornful tone, "it means just what I choose it to mean—neither more nor less."
>
> "The question is," said Alice, "whether you *can* make words mean so many different things."
>
> "The question is," said Humpty Dumpty, "which is to be the master—that's all."

BUT WORDS DO MATTER

In Humpty Dumpty's view, everyone is free to call any government a democracy—even a despotic government. That happens more often than you might suppose. Authoritarian leaders sometimes claim that their regime is really a special type of "democracy" that is superior to other sorts. For example, V. I. Lenin once asserted: "Proletarian democracy is a million times more democratic than any bourgeois democracy; Soviet government is a million times more democratic than the most democratic bourgeois republic."[1] This from the man who was the major architect in constructing the foundations of the totalitarian regime that ruled the Soviet Union for more than sixty years.

Fictions like these were also created by leaders and propagandists in the highly authoritarian "people's democracies" created in Central and Eastern Europe in countries that fell under Soviet domination during and after World War II.

But why should we cravenly accept the claims of despots that they really are democrats? A cobra does not become a dove because its owner says so. No matter what a country's leaders and propagandist may claim, we are entitled to judge a country to be a democracy only if it possesses *all* of the political institutions that are necessary to democracy.

Yet does this mean that democratic criteria can be satisfied only by the full set of political institutions of polyarchal democracy described in the last chapter? Not necessarily.

- The institutions of polyarchal democracy are necessary for democratizing the government of the state in a large-scale system, specifically a country. But they might be unnecessary or downright unsuitable for democracy in units on a smaller (or larger?) scale, or in smaller associations that are independent of the state and help to make up civil society. (More on this in a moment.)
- The institutions of polyarchal democracy were described in the preceding chapter in general terms. But might not democratic countries vary a great deal, and in important ways, in their specific political institutions: electoral arrangements, party systems, and the like? We'll consider some of these variations in the next two chapters.
- Because the institutions of polyarchal democracy are necessary does not imply that they are sufficient for democracy. Yes, a political system with these institutions will

meet the democratic criteria described in Chapter 4 more or less satisfactorily. But is it not possible that other, perhaps additional, institutions might enable a country to achieve one or more of those criteria more fully?

DEMOCRACY: GREEK VERSUS MODERN

If the political institutions required for democracy must include elected representatives, what are we to say about the Greeks, who first applied the word *democracy* to the governments of their city-states? Wouldn't we be pushing our present perspective to the point of anachronistic absurdity if we were to conclude that, like Lenin, Mussolini, and other twentieth-century antidemocrats, the Greeks simply misused the term? After all, it was they, not us, who first created and used the word *democracy*. To deny that Athens was a democracy would be rather like saying that what the Wright brothers invented was not an airplane because their early machine so little resembled ours today.

By proceeding with due respect for past usage, perhaps we can learn something about democracy from the people who not only gave us the word but provided concrete examples of what they meant by it. If we examine the best known example of Greek democracy, that of Athens, we soon notice two important differences from our present version. For reasons we've explored, most democrats today would insist that an acceptable democratic system must meet a democratic criterion that would have been unacceptable to the Greeks: inclusion. We have also added a political institution that the Greeks saw not only as unnecessary for their democracies but downright undesirable: the election of representatives with the authority to enact laws. We might say that the political system they created was a primary democracy, an assembly democracy, or a town meeting democracy. But they definitely did not create representative democracy as we understand it today.[2]

ASSEMBLY DEMOCRACY VERSUS
REPRESENTATIVE DEMOCRACY

Accustomed as we are to accepting the legitimacy of representative democracy we may find it difficult to understand why the Greeks were so passionately attached to assembly democracy. Yet until recently most other advocates of democracy felt as they did, all the way down to Jean-Jacques Rousseau in 1762, when *On the Social Contract* was published. Or beyond, to the Anti-Federalists who opposed the new American Constitution because they believed that under a *federal* government they would no longer be able to govern themselves; and to the citizens of cantons in Switzerland and towns in Vermont who to the present day have jealously preserved their town meetings; and to American students in the 1960s and 1970s who fervently demanded that "participatory democracy" should replace representative systems; and to many others who continue to stress the virtues of democratic government by citizen assemblies.

Advocates of assembly democracy who know their history are aware that as a democratic device representation has a shady past. As we saw in Chapter 2, representative government originated not as a democratic practice but as a device by which nondemocratic governments—monarchs, mainly—could lay their hands on precious revenues and other resources they wanted, particularly for fighting wars. In origin, then, representation was not democratic; it was a nondemocratic institution later grafted on to democratic theory and practice.

Beyond their well-founded suspicion of this institution lacking democratic credentials, the critics of representation had an even more basic point. In a small political unit, such as a town, assembly democracy allows citizens desirable opportunities for engaging in the process of governing themselves that a representative government in a large unit simply cannot provide.

Consider one of the ideal criteria for democracy described in Chapter 4: opportunities for participating effectively in decisions. In a small unit governed by its citizens gathered in a popular assembly, participants can discuss and debate the questions they think important; after hearing the pros and cons, they can make up their minds; they can vote directly on the matters before them; and as a consequence they do not have to delegate crucial decisions to representatives, who may well be influenced by their own aims and interests rather than those of their constituents.

Given these clear advantages, why was the older understanding of democracy reconfigured in order to accommodate a political institution that was nondemocratic in its origins?

REPRESENTATION ALREADY EXISTED

As usual, history provides part of the answer. In countries where the practice of electing representatives already existed, democratic reformers saw a dazzling opportunity. They saw no need to discard the representative system, despite its dubious origins and the narrow, exclusionary suffrage on which it rested. They believed that by broadening the electoral base the legislature or parliament could be converted into a more truly representative body that would serve democratic purposes. Some of them saw in representation a profound and dazzling alteration in the prospects for democracy. An eighteenth-century French thinker, Destutt de Tracy, whose criticisms of his predecessor, Montesquieu, greatly influenced Thomas Jefferson, observed triumphantly: "Representation, or representative government, may be considered as a new invention, unknown in Montesquieu's time. . . . Representative democracy . . . is democracy rendered practicable for a long time and over a great extent of territory."[3]

In 1820, James Mill described "the system of representation" as "the grand discovery of modern times."[4] New invention, grand discovery—the words help us to recapture some of the excitement that democratic reformers felt when they threw off the blinders of traditional democratic thought and saw that a new species of democracy could be created by grafting the medieval practice of representation to the ancient tree of democracy.

They were right. In essence the broadening process eventually led to a representative government based on an inclusive demos, thus helping to achieve our modern conception of democracy.

Still, given representation's comparative disadvantages, why didn't democratic reformers reject it altogether and opt instead for direct democracy in the form, say, of a Greek-style people's assembly? Although this possibility had some advocates, most advocates of democracy concluded, like the framers of the U.S. Constitution, that the political unit they wanted to democratize was too large for assembly democracy.

ONCE MORE: ON SIZE AND DEMOCRACY

Size matters. Both the number of persons in a political unit and the extent of its territory have consequences for the form of democracy. Imagine for a moment that you're a democratic reformer in a country with a nondemocratic government that you hope to democratize. You don't want your country to dissolve into dozens or perhaps hundreds of ministates, even though each might be small enough for its citizens to gather frequently to exercise their sovereignty in an assembly. The citizens of your country are too numerous to assemble, and what's more they extend over a territory too large for all of you to meet without daunting difficulties. What are you to do?

Perhaps today and increasingly in the future you might be able to solve the territorial problem by employing electronic means of communication that would enable citizens spread out over a large area to "meet," discuss issues, and vote. But it is one thing to enable citizens to "meet" electronically and quite another to solve the problem posed by large numbers of citizens. Beyond some limit, an attempt to arrange for them all to meet and engage in a fruitful discussion, even electronically, becomes ridiculous.

How big is too big for assembly democracy? How small is small enough? According to recent scholarly estimates, in Greek city-states the citizen body of adult males typically numbered between two thousand and ten thousand—about the right number, in the view of some Greek political theorists, for a good *polis,* or self-governing city-state. In Athens, however, the citizen body was much larger than that—perhaps around *sixty thousand* at the height to Athenian democracy in 450 B.C.E. "The result," as one scholar has written, "was that Athens simply had too many citizens to function properly as a *polis.*" A century later, as a result of emigration, deaths from war and disease, and additional restrictions on citizenship, the number may have been reduced by half, which was still too many for its assembly to accommodate more than a small fraction of Athenian male citizens.[5]

A bit of simple arithmetic soon reveals the inexorable consequences of time and numbers. Suppose we begin with a very tiny unit, a committee, let us say, of just ten members. We think it might be reasonable to allow each member at least ten minutes for discussing the matter at hand. So we shall need about an hour and forty minutes for our meeting, certainly not an exorbitant amount of time for our committee members to spend in meeting. But suppose the subject is so complicated that each committee member might require a half-hour. Then we'll need to plan on a five-hour meeting, or perhaps two meetings—still an acceptable amount of time.

But even a fairly large committee would prove to be a small citizen assembly. Consider, for example, a village of two hundred persons where the entire adult population consists of, say, one hundred persons, all of whom attend the meetings of an assembly. Suppose each

TABLE 1. *The high price of participatory democracy*

Number of Persons	Total time required if each person has					
	10 minutes			30 minutes		
	minutes	hours	8-hour days	minutes	hours	8-hour days
10	100	2		300	5	
20	200	3		600	10	1
50	500	8	1	1,500	25	3
500	5,000	83	10	15,000	250	31
1,000	10,000	167	21	30,000	500	63
5,000	50,000	833	104	150,000	2,500	313
10,000	100,000	1,667	208	300,000	5,000	625

is entitled to a total of ten minutes. That modest amount would require two eight-hour days—not impossible but surely not easy to bring about! Let's stay for a moment with our assumption of just ten minutes for each citizen's participation. As the numbers go up the situation becomes more and more absurd. In an "ideal polis" of ten thousand full citizens, the time required is far beyond all tolerable limits. Ten minutes allotted to each citizen would require more than two hundred eight-hour working days. A half-hour allotment hour would require almost two years of steady meetings (table 1)!

To assume that every citizen would want to speak is, of course, absurd, as anyone with the slightest familiarity with town meetings knows. Typically a few persons do most of the talking. The rest may refrain for any one of many reasons: because what they intended to say has already been covered adequately; or they have already made up their minds; or they suffer from stage fright, a sense of inadequacy, lack of a pressing interest in the subject at hand, incomplete knowledge, and so on. While a few carry on the discussion, then, the rest listen (or not), and when the time comes for a vote they vote (or don't).

In addition, lots of discussion and inquiry may take place elsewhere. Many of the hours required in table 1 may actually be used in discussing public matters in informal settings of many kinds. So we should not read table 1 in too simple-minded a way. Yet in spite of all reasonable qualifications, assembly democracy has some severe problems:

- Opportunities for participation rapidly diminish with the size of the citizen body.
- Although many more can participate by listening to speakers, the maximum number of participants in a single meeting who are likely to be able to express themselves in speech is very small—probably considerably less than a hundred.
- These fully participant members become, in effect, representatives of the others, except in voting. (This exception is, however, important, and I'll return to it in a moment.)
- Thus even in a unit governed by assembly democracy, a kind of de facto representative system is likely to exist.
- Yet nothing insures that the fully participating members are representative of the rest.
- To provide a satisfactory system for selecting representatives, citizens may reasonably prefer to elect their representatives in free and fair elections.

THE DEMOCRATIC LIMITS OF
REPRESENTATIVE GOVERNMENT

So representation, it appears, has the advantage. Or does it? The irony of the combination of time and numbers is that it impartially cuts both ways: it swiftly reveals a great democratic defect in representative government. Returning to table 1 and our arithmetical exercises, suppose we now calculate the time that would be required if each citizen were to meet briefly with his or her representative. Table 1 provides a devastating case against the participatory possibilities of representative government. Let's imagine that an elected representative wishes to set aside ten minutes for discussing matters with each adult citizen in the representative's district. We'll ignore travel time and other practicalities. Suppose the district contains ten thousand adult citizens, the largest number shown in table 1. Q.E.D.: The representative would have to allow more than half the days of the year just for meetings with constituents! In the United States, representatives to the U.S. Congress are elected from districts that on average contain more than four hundred thousand adult citizens. A member of the U.S. House of Representatives who wished to devote just ten minutes to each citizen in the district would have no time for anything else. If he or she were to spend eight hours a day at the task, every day of the year, she or he would need more than twenty years, or ten terms, longer than most representatives ever remain in Congress.

Assembly democracy or representative democracy? Small-scale democracy or large-scale democracy? Which is better? Which is more democratic? Each has its passionate advocates. As we have just seen, a strong case can be made for the advantages of each. Yet our rather artificial and even absurd arithmetic exercises have revealed inexorable limits on civic participation that apply with cruel indifference to both. For neither can escape the impassable bounds set by the interaction of the time required for an act of participation and the number of citizens entitled to participate.

The law of time and numbers: The more citizens a democratic unit contains, the less that citizens can participate directly in government decisions and the more that they must delegate authority to others.

A FUNDAMENTAL DEMOCRATIC DILEMMA

Lurking in the background is a fundamental democratic dilemma. If our goal is to establish a democratic system of government that provides maximum opportunities for citizens to participate in political decisions, then the advantage clearly lies with assembly democracy in a small-scale political system. But if our goal is to establish a democratic system of government that provides maximum scope for it to deal effectively with the problems of greatest concern to citizens, then the advantage will often lie with a unit so large that a representative system will be necessary. This is the dilemma of citizen participation versus system effectiveness:

The smaller a democratic unit, the greater its potential for citizen participation and the less the need for citizens to delegate government decisions to representatives. The larger the unit, the greater its capacity for dealing with problems important to its citizens and the greater the need for citizens to delegate decisions to representatives.

I do not see how we can escape this dilemma. But even if we cannot escape it, we can confront it.

SMALL IS BEAUTIFUL, SOMETIMES

As with all other human activities, political systems don't necessarily realize their possibilities. A book title captures the essence of one perspective: *Small Is Beautiful.*[6] Unquestionably, it is possible in theory for very small political systems to attain a very high level of citizen participation that large systems can never match. Yet they often, perhaps usually, fall far short of achieving their potential.

The town meetings in some of the smaller towns of New England provide good examples of limits and possibilities. Although in most of New England the traditional town meeting has been mainly or entirely replaced as a legislative body by elected representatives, it is alive and well in the mainly rural state of Vermont.

A sympathetic observer and participant who studied town meetings in Vermont found that 1,215 town meetings were held between

1970 and 1994 in 210 Vermont towns of fewer than forty-five hundred residents. From the records of 1,129 of these town meetings he concluded that

> the average number of people in attendance when the attendance count was the highest at each meeting was 139. An average of 45 of these participated at least once. . . . [O]n average 19 percent of a town's eligible voters will be present at town meeting and 7 percent of a town's eligible voters (37 percent of the attenders) will speak out at least once. . . . The great majority of people that speak will do so more than once. . . . The average meeting takes almost four hours . . . of deliberative time. It lasts long enough to give each of its attenders two minutes and 14 seconds of time to talk. Since many fewer speak than attend, of course, the average time available for each speaker is almost exactly five minutes. . . . Conversely, since there are about four times as many participations as there are participators, the average town meeting allows for only one minute and 20 seconds for each act of participation.[7]

Town meetings, it appears, are not exactly paragons of participatory democracy. Yet that is not the whole story. When citizens know the issues to be dealt with are trivial or uncontroversial, they choose to stay home—and why not? But controversial issues bring them out. Although my own town in Connecticut has largely abandoned its traditional town meeting, I can recall questions on which citizens were sharply divided and turned out in such numbers that they overflowed the high school auditorium; a second meeting scheduled for those unable to get in to the first proved to be equally large. As in Vermont, discussions at town meetings are not dominated by the educated and affluent. Strong beliefs and a determination to have one's say are not by any means monopolized by a single socioeconomic group.

With all its limitations, assembly democracy has much to be said for it.

BUT BIGGER IS BETTER, SOMETIMES

As we saw in Chapter 2, the Greeks did not escape the dilemma. As they were aware, the Achilles heel of the small state is its military weakness in the face of a large state. Ingenious and valiant though the Athenians were in preserving their independence, they could not prevent defeat by the superior forces of Philip of Macedon in 322 B.C.E. or the centuries of foreign domination that followed. Once the centralized national state began to emerge, the remaining city-states were doomed. The last great city-state republic, Venice, fell without resistance to Napoleon Bonaparte's forces in 1797 and thereafter never regained independence.

In recent centuries, notably the twentieth, the limited capacities of self-governing units small enough for assembly democracy have shown up again and again, not only in military matters but in dealing with economic affairs, traffic, transportation, communications, the movement of people and goods, health, family planning, agriculture, food, crime, education, civil, political, human rights, and a host of other matters of concern.

Short of a world cataclysm that would drastically and permanently reduce the world's population and destroy its advanced technology, it is impossible to foresee a world in which all large political units will have vanished, to be replaced *entirely* by completely independent political units with populations so small (say fewer than fifty thousand persons at most) that its citizens could govern themselves, and would choose to govern themselves, exclusively by a system of assembly democracy. To make matters worse, a world of small and completely independent units would surely be unstable, for it would take only a few such units to coalesce, engage in military aggression, pick off one small unit after another, and thus create a system too large for assembly government. To democratize this new and larger unit, democratic reformers (or revolutionaries) would have to reinvent representative democracy.

THE DARK SIDE: BARGAINING AMONG ELITES

For all its advantages, representative government has a dark side. Most citizens in democratic countries are aware of it; for the most part they accept it as a part of the price of representation.

The dark side is this: under a representative government, citizens often delegate enormous discretionary authority over decisions of extraordinary importance. They delegate authority not only to their elected representatives but, by an even more indirect and circuitous route, they delegate authority to administrators, bureaucrats, civil servants, judges, and at a still further remove to international organizations. Attached to the institutions of polyarchal democracy that help citizens to exercise influence over the conduct and decisions of their government is a nondemocratic process, *bargaining among political and bureaucratic elites*.

In principle, elite bargaining takes place within limits set through democratic institutions and processes. But these limits are often broad, popular participation and control are not always robust, and the political and bureaucratic elites possess great discretion. Despite the limits on popular control, the political elites in democratic countries are not despots, out of control. Far from it. Periodic elections compel them to keep a ready eye on popular opinion. In addition, as they arrive at decisions the political and bureaucratic elites mutually influence and check one another. Elite bargaining has its own system of mutual checks and balances. To the extent that elected representatives participate in the bargaining process, they are a channel through which popular desires, goals, and values enter into governmental decisions. Political and bureaucratic elites in democratic countries are powerful, far more powerful than ordinary citizens can be; but they are not despots.

CAN INTERNATIONAL ORGANIZATIONS BE DEMOCRATIC?

So far we have been concerned with the possibilities of democracy in units of a smaller scale than a country or nation-state. But what about units of a larger scale, or at least a very different scale: international organizations?

During the late twentieth century democratic countries increasingly felt the consequences of internationalization—economic, cultural, social, political, bureaucratic, military. What does the future hold for democracy? Even if the governments of independent countries yield much of their power to international governments of one kind or another, won't the democratic process simply move up to the international level? If so, as emerging international governments are democratized, democratic values won't be impaired and may even be enhanced.

One might draw on history for an analogy. As we saw in Chapter 2, the original locus for the idea and practice of democracy was the city-state. But city-states could not withstand the increasing power of national states. Either the city-states ceased to exist as recognizable entities or, like Athens and Venice, they became local governments subordinate to the government of the country. In the twenty-first century, then, won't national governments simply become more like local governments that are subordinate to democratic international governments?

After all, one might say, the subordination of smaller local governments to a national government was not the end of democracy. On the contrary, the democratization of national governments not only vastly extended the domain of democracy but allowed an important place for democratic processes in the subordinate units—towns, cities, cantons, states, provinces, regions, and the like. So, in this view, the challenge is not to halt internationalization in its tracks, which is impossible. The challenge is to democratize international organizations.

Appealing as this vision is to anyone who places a high value on democracy, to my regret I am compelled to conclude that it is excessively optimistic. Even in countries where democratic institutions and practices have long existed and are well established, it is extremely difficult for citizens to exercise effective control over many key decisions on foreign affairs. It is far more difficult for them to do so in international organizations.

The European Union offers telling evidence. There, such nominally democratic structures as popular elections and a parliament are formally in place. Yet virtually all observers agree that a gigantic "democratic deficit" remains. Crucial decisions mainly come about through bargaining among political and bureaucratic elites. Limits are set not by democratic processes but mainly by what negotiators can get others to agree to and by considering the likely consequences for national and international markets. Bargaining, hierarchy, and markets determine the outcomes. Except to ratify the results, democratic processes hardly play a role.

If democratic institutions are largely ineffective in governing the European Union, the prospects for democratizing other international systems seem even more remote. To achieve a level of popular control that is anywhere near the level already existing within democratic countries, international organizations would have to solve several problems about as well as they are now dealt with in democratic countries. Political leaders would have to create political institutions that would provide citizens with opportunities for political participation, influence, and control roughly equivalent in effectiveness to those already existing in democratic countries. To take advantage of these opportunities, citizens would need to be about as concerned and informed about the policy decisions of international organizations as they now are about government decisions in their own countries. In order for citizens to be informed, political and communication elites would need to engage in public debate and discussion of the alternatives in ways that would engage the attention and emotions of the public. To insure public debate, it would be necessary to create an international equivalent to national political competition by parties and individuals seeking office. Elected representatives, or functional equivalents to them (whatever they might be), would need to exercise control over important international bureaucracies about as well as legislatures and executives now do in democratic countries.

How the representatives of a hypothetical international citizen body would be distributed among the people of different countries poses an additional problem. Given huge differences in the magnitude of the populations of different countries, no system of representation could give equal weight to the vote of each citizen and yet prevent small countries from being steadily outvoted by large countries; thus all solutions acceptable to the smaller democracies will deny political equality among the members of the larger demos. As with the United States and other federal systems, acceptable solutions may be cobbled together as one has been for the European Union. But whatever compromise is reached, it could easily be a source of internal strain, particularly in the absence of a strong common identity.

Strain is all the more likely because, as I have said, just as in national democracies most decisions are bound to be seen as harming the interests of some persons, so, too, in international organizations. The heaviest burden of some decisions might be borne by particular groups, regions, or countries. To survive these strains, a political culture supportive of the specific institutions would help—

might indeed be necessary. But developing a political culture takes time, perhaps many generations. In addition, if policy decisions are to be widely acceptable and enforceable among the losers, probably some common identity, equivalent to that in existing democratic countries, would have to develop.

It seems to me highly unlikely that all these crucial requirements for the democratization of international organizations will be met. But if the requirements are not met, by what process will international decisions be made? They will be made mainly, I think, by bargaining among political and bureaucratic elites—chief executives, ministers, diplomats, members of governmental and nongovernmental bureaucracies, business leaders, and the like. Although democratic processes may occasionally set the outside limits within which the elites strike their bargains, to call the political practices of international systems "democratic" would be to rob the term of all meaning.

A ROBUST PLURALISTIC SOCIETY WITHIN DEMOCRATIC COUNTRIES

Although democracy is unlikely to move up to the international level, it's important for us to keep in mind that every democratic country needs smaller units. In a modern country, these are of staggering variety. Even the smallest democratic countries require municipal governments. Larger countries may have others: districts, counties, states, provinces, regions, and others. No matter how small a country may be on a world scale, it will require a rich array of independent associations and organizations—that is, a pluralistic civil society.

How best to govern the smaller associations of state and society—trade unions, economic enterprises, specialized interest groups, educational organizations, and the rest—admits of no single answer. Democratic government may not be justified in all associations;

marked differences in competence may impose legitimate limits on the extent to which democratic criteria should be met. And even where democracy is justified no single form is necessarily the best.

Yet no undemocratic aspect of any government should go unchallenged, whether of the state and its units or independent associations in a pluralist civil society. Democratic principles suggest some questions we might ask about the government of any association.

- In arriving at decisions, does the government of the association insure equal consideration to the good and interest of every person bound by those decisions?
- Are any of the members of the association so definitely better qualified than others to govern that they should be entrusted with complete and final authority over the government of the association? If not, then in governing the association, must we not regard the members of the association as political equals?
- If the members are political equals, then should the government of the association not meet democratic criteria? If it should, then to what extent does the association provide its members with opportunities for effective participation, equality in voting, gaining enlightened understanding and exercising final control over the agenda?

In almost all, perhaps all, organizations everywhere there is some room for some democracy; and in almost all democratic countries there is considerable room for more democracy.

CHAPTER 10

Varieties II

CONSTITUTIONS

Just as democracy comes in different sizes, so, too, democratic constitutions come in a variety of styles and forms. But, you might well ask, do differences in the constitutions of democratic countries really matter? The answer, it seems, is no, yes, and maybe.

To explain why, I'll begin by drawing mainly on the constitutional experience of the older democracies, countries where the basic democratic institutions have existed continuously since about 1950—twenty-two in all (Australia, Austria, Belgium, Canada, Costa Rica, Denmark, Finland, France, Germany, Iceland, Ireland, Israel, Italy, Japan, Luxembourg, the Netherlands, New Zealand, Norway, Sweden, Switzerland, the United Kingdom, and the United States).[1]

The variations among them are sufficient to provide a fair idea of the range of possibilities. The constitutional arrangements of newly democratized countries, however, are no less important. Indeed, they may be even more because they can be crucial to the success of democratization.

In describing *constitutions* and *constitutional arrangements* I wish to use these terms broadly so as to include important practices that may not be specified in the constitution, such as electoral and party systems. My reason for doing so will become clear in the next chapter.

What then are the important variations in democratic constitutions, and how much do they matter?

CONSTITUTIONAL VARIATIONS

Written or unwritten? An unwritten constitution may seem to be a contradiction in terms, yet in a few countries certain well-established institutions and practices are understood as comprising the constitutional system, even though they are not prescribed in a single document adopted as the country's constitution. Among the older democracies (and assuredly among the newer ones), an unwritten constitution is a result of highly unusual historical circumstances, as it was in the three exceptional cases of Great Britain, Israel,[2] and New Zealand. The adoption of written constitutions has, however, become the standard practice.

Bill of Rights? Does the constitution include an explicit bill of rights? Again, although an explicit constitutional bill of rights is not universal among the older democracies, it is now standard practice. For historical reasons and because of the absence of a written constitution, the notable exception has been Britain (where, however, there is significant support for the idea).

Social and economic rights? Although the American constitution and those that survive from the nineteenth century in the older democratic countries generally have little to say explicitly about social and economic rights,[3] those adopted since World War II typically do include them. Sometimes, however, the social and economic rights prescribed (occasionally at great length) are little more than symbolic.

Federal or unitary? In a federal system the governments of certain smaller territorial units—states, provinces, regions—are guaranteed permanence and a significant range of authority; in unitary systems their existence and authority depend on decisions by the national government. Among the twenty-two older democratic countries, only six are strictly federal (Australia, Austria, Canada, Germany,

Switzerland, and the United States). In all six countries, federalism is the result of special historical circumstances.[4]

Unicameral or bicameral legislature? Although bicameralism predominates, Israel has never had a second chamber, and since 1950 the four Scandinavian countries, Finland, and New Zealand have abolished their upper houses.

Judicial review? Can a supreme court declare unconstitutional laws properly enacted by the national legislature? This practice, known as judicial review, has been a standard feature in democratic countries with federal systems, where it is seen as necessary if the national constitution is to prevail over laws enacted by the states, provinces, or cantons. But the more relevant issue is whether a court can declare a law enacted by the *national* parliament unconstitutional. Switzerland, in fact, limits the power of judicial review *only* to cantonal legislation. As we have just seen, however, most democratic countries are not federal, and among the unitary systems only about half have some form of judicial review. Moreover, even among countries where judicial review does exist, the extent to which courts attempt to exercise this power varies from the extreme case, the United States, where the Supreme Court sometimes wields extraordinary power, to countries where the judiciary is highly deferential to the decisions of the parliament. Canada provides an interesting variant. A federal system, Canada has a supreme court endowed with the authority to declare both provincial and federal laws unconstitutional. The provincial legislatures and the federal parliament can override the court's decision, however, by voting a second time to pass the act in question.

Tenure of judges for life or limited term? In the United States members of the federal (that is, national) judiciary are, by constitutional provision, given life tenure. The advantage of life tenure is to insure judges greater independence from political pressures. But if they also have the power of judicial review, their judgments may reflect the influence of an older ideology no longer supported by popular and legislative majorities. Consequently, they may employ judicial review to impede reforms, as they sometimes have in the United States, famously during the great reform period from 1933 to 1937 under the leadership of President Franklin D. Roosevelt. With American experience in view, some democratic countries that have explicitly provided for judicial review in constitutions written after World War II have rejected life tenure and instead have chosen to provide for limited, though lengthy, terms, as in Germany, Italy, and Japan.

Referenda? Are national referenda possible, or in the case of constitutional amendments, perhaps obligatory? Switzerland provides the limiting case: there, referenda on national issues are permissible, obligatory for constitutional amendments, and frequent. At the other extreme, the U.S. Constitution makes no provision for referenda (and no national referenda have ever been held), although they are common in many states. In contrast to the United States, however, in more than half the older democracies a referendum has been held at least once.

Presidential or parliamentary? In a presidential system the chief executive is elected independently of the legislature and is constitutionally vested with important powers. In a parliamentary or cabinet system the chief executive is chosen and may be removed by the parliament. The classic example of presidential government is the United States; the classic example of parliamentary government is Great Britain.

Presidential government was invented by the delegates to the American Constitutional Convention in 1787. Most of the delegates admired the British (unwritten) constitution for its "separation of powers" into a judiciary independent of both the legislature and the executive; a legislature (Parliament) independent of the executive;

and an executive (the monarchy) independent of the legislature. Although the delegates sought to emulate the virtues of the British constitution, a monarchy was clearly out of the question; so they were stumped by the problem of the executive. Left with no relevant historical models, they wrestled over the question for almost two months before producing their solution.

Although the convention was an extraordinary assembly of constitutional talent, the passage of time has endowed the delegates with far greater foresight than the historical records reveal to us or that human fallibilities would seem to allow. As with many inventions, the originators of the American presidential system (or, better, presidential-congressional system) could not possibly foresee how their creation would evolve over the next two centuries. Nor could they foresee that parliamentary government was just about to develop as an alternative and more widely adopted solution.

Although by now parliamentary government is all but unthinkable among Americans, had their Constitutional Convention been held some thirty years later it is altogether possible that the delegates would have proposed a parliamentary system. For what they (and, for that matter, observers in Britain as well) did not understand was that the British constitutional system was itself undergoing rapid change. In short, it was evolving into a parliamentary system in which executive authority would effectively rest with the prime minister and cabinet, not with the monarch. And though nominally chosen by the monarch, the prime minister would in actuality be chosen by the majority in Parliament (in due time, the House of Commons) and would remain in office only with the support of a parliamentary majority. The prime minister in turn would chose the other members of the cabinet. This system was pretty much in place by about 1810.

As it turned out, in most of the older, stable democratic countries of today, where democratic institutions evolved during the nineteenth and early twentieth centuries and endured, variants of parliamentary government, not presidential government, came to be the accepted constitutional arrangement.

Electoral system? How precisely are seats in the national legislature allocated in proportion to the preferences of the voters in elections? For example, will a party whose candidates get, say, 30 percent of the votes in an election gain close to 30 percent of the seats? Or might they win only 15 percent or so? Although the electoral system need not be specified in the "constitution" in a strict sense, as I suggested earlier it is useful to consider it a part of the constitutional system because of the way electoral systems interact with other parts of the constitution. More about this subject in the next chapter.

Although the list of alternatives could be extended even further, it is surely enough to show that constitutional arrangements among the older democracies vary widely. Moreover, the variations I have mentioned are rather general; if we were to move to a more concrete level of observation we would discover further important differences.

So, you might now conclude, the constitutions of democratic countries differ in important ways. But do variations make some constitutions *better*, or perhaps *more democratic?* Is there perhaps one best type of democratic constitution?

These questions raise yet another: How are we to appraise the relative desirability of different constitutions? Evidently we need some criteria.

HOW CONSTITUTIONS MAKE A DIFFERENCE

Constitutions might matter to a country's democracy in many ways.

Stability. A constitution might help to provide *stability* for the basic democratic political institutions described in Chapter 8. It could not only lay down a democratic framework of government but also insure all the necessary rights and guarantees that the basic political institutions require.

Fundamental rights. A constitution might protect majority and minority rights. Even though this criterion is implicitly included in the first, because of variations among democratic constitutions it is useful to give special attention to the basic rights and duties that provide guarantees for both majorities and minorities.

Neutrality. A constitution could maintain neutrality among the country's citizens. Having insured fundamental rights and duties, the constitutional arrangements could also insure that the process of making laws is designed neither to favor nor to penalize the views or the legitimate interests of any citizen or group of citizens.

Accountability. The constitution could be designed to enable citizens to hold political leaders accountable for their decisions, actions, and conduct within a "reasonable" interval of time.

Fair representation. What constitutes "fair representation" in a democracy is the subject of endless controversy, in part because it bears on the next two criteria.

Informed consensus. A constitution might help citizens and leaders to develop an informed consensus on laws and policies. It could do so by creating opportunities and incentives for political leaders to engage in negotiations, accommodation, and coalition building that would facilitate the conciliation of diverse interests. More about this in the chapters to come.

Effective government. By effectiveness I mean that a government acts to deal with what citizens understand to be the major issues and problems they confront and for which they believe government action is appropriate. Effective government is particularly important in times of great emergency brought on by war, the threat of war, acute international tension, severe economic hardship, and similar crises. But it is also relevant in more ordinary times, when major issues head the agendas of citizens and leaders. To be sure, in the short run a nondemocratic government might sometimes meet this criterion better than a democratic government; though whether it would do so in the long run seems more doubtful. In any case, we are concerned with governments functioning within democratic limits. Within those limits, it seems reasonable to want a constitutional system that has procedures to discourage protracted deadlock, delay, or evasion in confronting major issues and encourage taking action to deal with them.

Competent decisions. Desirable as effective government may be, we would hardly admire a constitution that facilitates decisive and resolute action yet makes it hard for a government to draw on the best knowledge available for solving the urgent problems on the country's agenda. Decisive action is no substitute for wise policy.

Transparency and comprehensibility. By this pair of criteria I mean that the operation of the government is sufficiently open to public view and simple enough in its essentials that citizens can readily understand how and what it is doing. Thus it must not be so complexly constructed that citizens cannot understand what is going on and, because they do not understand their government, cannot readily hold their leaders accountable, particularly at elections.

Resiliency. A constitutional system need not be so rigidly constructed or so immutably fixed in writing and tradition that it cannot be adapted to novel situations.

Legitimacy. Meeting the previous ten criteria would surely go a long way toward providing a constitution with sufficient legitimacy and allegiance among citizens and political elites to insure its survival. Yet in a specific country certain constitutional arrangements could be more compatible than could others with widespread traditional norms of legitimacy. For example, paradoxical though it may seem to many republicans, maintaining a monarch as head of state and yet adapting the monarchy to the requirements of polyarchy has conferred additional legitimacy on democratic constitutions in the Scandinavian countries, the Netherlands, Belgium, Japan, Spain, and Britain. In most democratic countries, by contrast, an attempt to blend a monarch as head of state would clash with widespread republican beliefs. Thus Alexander Hamilton's proposal at the Constitutional Convention in 1787 for an executive with life tenure—an "elective monarchy"—was rejected almost without debate. As another delegate, Elbridge Gerry remarked, "There were not 1/1000 part of our fellow citizens who are not agst. every approach towards monarchy."[5]

HOW MUCH OF A DIFFERENCE DO THE DIFFERENCES MAKE?

Do constitutional differences like these really matter?

To answer this question we need to add two more bodies of evidence to that of the twenty-two older democratic countries. One collection of experiences can be drawn from the "newer" democracies, countries in which the basic democratic institutions were established and maintained during the second half of the twentieth century. Another consists of the tragic but illuminating history of countries in which the democratic institutions were established at some point in the twentieth century but broke down and yielded, at least for a time, to an authoritarian regime.

Although these three immense sources of evidence are by no means fully reported or analyzed, I believe that they produce some important conclusions.

To begin with, each of the constitutional alternatives listed earlier has existed in at least one stable democracy. Consequently, it is perfectly reasonable, indeed logically necessary, to conclude that many different constitutional arrangements are compatible with the basic political institutions of polyarchal democracy that were described in Chapter 8. The political institutions of polyarchal democracy can, it appears, take many specific forms.

Why is this so? Certain underlying conditions highly favorable to the stability of the basic democratic institutions (discussed in Chapter 12) have prevailed in all these older and highly stable democracies. Given these favorable conditions, constitutional variations like those I have described have no great effect on the *stability* of the basic democratic institutions. Judged solely by that criterion, the variations I've described don't appear to matter. Within broad limits, then, democratic countries have a wide choice of constitutions.

In contrast, where the underlying conditions are highly unfavorable, it is improbable that democracy could be preserved by *any* constitutional design.

With only slight exaggeration we might summarize the first two points like this:

If the underlying conditions are highly favorable, stability is likely with almost any constitution the country is likely to adopt. If the underlying conditions are highly unfavorable, *no* constitution will save democracy.

There is, however, a third and more intriguing possibility: in a country where the conditions are neither highly favorable nor highly unfavorable but mixed, so that democracy is chancy but by no means impossible, the choice of constitutional design might matter. In brief: if the underlying conditions are mixed in a country, and some are favorable but others are unfavorable, a *well-designed constitution might help democratic institutions to survive,* whereas a *badly designed constitution might contribute to the breakdown of democratic institutions.*

Finally, crucial as it is, stability isn't the only relevant criterion. If we were to judge constitutional arrangements by other criteria, they might have important consequences even in countries where conditions are highly favorable to democratic stability. And they do. They shape the concrete political institutions of democratic countries: executives, legislatures, courts, party systems, local governments, and so on. The shape of these institutions might in turn have important consequences for the fairness of the representation in the legislature, or the effectiveness of the government, and as a result they might even affect the legitimacy of the government. In countries where the underlying conditions are mixed and the prospects for democratic stability are somewhat uncertain, these variations might prove to be exceptionally important.

Indeed, this does appear to be the case, for reasons we explore in the next chapter.

Varieties III

PARTIES AND ELECTORAL SYSTEMS

Probably no political institutions shape the political landscape of a democratic country more than its electoral system and its political parties. And none display a greater variety.

Indeed, the variations are so great that a citizen familiar only with his or her own country's electoral arrangements and party system may well find the political landscape of another democratic country incomprehensible, or, if understandable, unappealing. To a citizen of a country where only two major political parties contest elections, a country with a multiplicity of parties may look like political chaos. To a citizen in a multiparty country, having only two political parties to choose from may look like a political straitjacket. If either were to examine the other country's party system, they might find the differences even more confusing.

How can we account for these variations? Are some electoral or party systems more democratic than others or better in other respects?

Let's begin with the main variations in electoral systems.

ELECTORAL SYSTEMS

Electoral systems vary without end.[1] One reason they vary so much is that no electoral system can satisfy all the criteria by which you might reasonably wish to judge it. There are, as usual, trade-offs. If we choose one system we achieve some values at the expense of others.

Why so? To provide a tolerably brief answer, let me reduce the baffling array of possibilities to just two.

PR. Among the older democracies the most common electoral system is one deliberately designed to produce a close correspondence between the proportion of the total votes cast for a party in elections and the proportion of seats the party gains in the legislature. For example, a party with 53 percent of the votes will win 53 percent of the seats. An arrangement like this is usually known as a system of *proportional representation,* or PR.

FPTP. If PR systems are designed to meet one test of fairness, you might suppose that all democratic countries would have adopted them. Yet some have not. They have chosen instead to maintain electoral arrangements that may greatly increase the proportion of seats won by the party with the largest number of votes. For example, a party with, say, 53 percent of the votes may win 60 percent of the seats. In the variant of this system employed in Great Britain and the United States, a single candidate is chosen from each district and the candidate with the most votes wins. Because of the analogy with a horse race, this is sometimes called a *first-past-the-post* system (in short, FPTP).

Words About Words

In the United States, such an arrangement is often referred to as a *plurality system* because the candidate with a plurality (not necessarily a majority) of votes is the winner. Political scientists often refer to it as a system of "single member districts with plurality elections," a more literal but excessively cumbersome title. *First-past-the-post* is standard usage in Britain, and I'll adopt it here.

PR versus FPTP. As I pointed out earlier, debate continues over the question of what kind of electoral system best satisfies the requirement that elections should be both free and *fair*. But critics of FPTP contend that it generally fails the test of fair representation and sometimes fails it badly. For example, in the British parliamentary elections of 1997 the Labor Party gained 64 percent of the seats in Parliament—the largest majority in modern parliamentary history; yet it did so by winning only 44 percent of the votes cast. The Conservative Party, with 31 percent of the votes, won just 25 percent of the seats, and the unfortunate Liberal Democrats, who were supported by 17 percent of the voters, ended up with only 7 percent of the seats! (The candidates of other parties won a total of 7 percent of the votes and 4 percent of the seats.)

How do differences like these between the percentage of votes cast for a party and the percentage of the seats it wins come about? Imagine a tiny democratic system with only a thousand members, who are divided among ten equal districts from each of which the voters elect just one representative to the legislative body. Suppose that in our little democracy 510 voters (or 51 percent) vote for the Blue Party and 490 (or 49 percent) vote for the Purple Party. Now let us imagine (unlikely though it may be) that the support for each is perfectly uniform throughout our minidemocracy: each of the ten districts happens to contain 51 Blue voters and 49 Purple voters. How would the election turn out? The Blue Party wins in every district and thus gains 100 percent of the seats and a "majority" in parliament of ten to zero (table 2, example 1)! You could expand the size of the system to include a whole country and greatly increase the number of districts. The result would remain the same.

We can be reasonably certain that no democratic country would retain FPTP under these conditions. What prevents this bizarre— and completely undemocratic—outcome is that party support is *not*

TABLE 2.

Hypothetical illustration of the First-Past-the-Post electoral system
There are ten districts, each with one hundred voters, divided between the two parties (Blue and Purple) as shown.

EXAMPLE 1. Support for the parties is uniform

District	Votes for		Seats won by	
	Blue (number)	Purple (number)	Blue	Purple
1	51	49	1	0
2	51	49	1	0
3	51	49	1	0
4	51	49	1	0
5	51	49	1	0
6	51	49	1	0
7	51	49	1	0
8	51	49	1	0
9	51	49	1	0
10	51	49	1	0
Total	510	490	10	0

EXAMPLE 2. Support for the parties is not uniform

District	Votes for		Seats won by	
	Blue (number)	Purple (number)	Blue	Purple
1	55	45	1	0
2	60	40	1	0
3	40	60	0	1
4	45	55	0	1
5	52	48	1	0
6	51	49	1	0
7	53	47	1	0
8	45	55	0	1
9	46	54	0	1
10	55	45	1	0
Total	502	498	6	4

spread evenly across a country: in some districts the Blues may have 65 percent of the voters, whereas in others they have only 40 percent, say, and the Purples have the remaining 60 percent. The districts, that is, vary around the national average. For a hypothetical illustration, see table 2, example 2.

It is obvious, then, that in order for FPTP to result in acceptably fair representation, party support must *not* be distributed evenly across a country. Conversely, the more evenly voting support is distributed, the greater the divergence between votes and seats will be. Thus if regional differences decline in a country, as appears to have been the case in Britain in 1997, the distortion caused by FPTP grows.

If that is so, then why don't democratic countries with FPTP systems switch to PR? For one thing, we can't ignore the heavy weight of history and tradition in countries like Britain and the United States, where this system has prevailed from the beginnings of representative government. The United States provides a prime example. The American system of FPTP can result in depriving a substantial minority of African Americans of fair representation in state legislatures and the national House of Representatives. To make sure that African-American voters can gain at least some representatives in their state legislature or Congress, legislatures and judges have sometimes deliberately drawn district boundaries so as to form an area with an African-American majority. The shape of the resulting district occasionally bears no relation to geography, economy, or history. Under a PR system, if African Americans chose to vote for African-American candidates, they would be represented in proportion to their numbers: in a state where, say, 20 percent of the voters were black, they could be sure of filling about 20 percent of the seats with African Americans, if that were their choice.

But if this is so, why hasn't PR been adopted as a solution? Mainly because hostility to PR is so widespread in the United States that neither legislatures nor judges give it serious consideration as a possible alternative to racial gerrymandering.

Words About Words

Gerrymandering, or carving out electoral districts to obtain strictly political ends, is an old practice in the United States. It takes its name from Elbridge Gerry, whom we encountered earlier as a delegate to the American Constitutional Convention. Elected governor of Massachusetts, in 1812 Gerry brought about a redrawing of district boundaries for representatives to the state legislature that helped Democrats to maintain a majority. When someone noticed that one district bore the shape of a salamander, a critic remarked that it looked more like a "Gerrymander." The term *gerrymander,* including the verb form *to gerrymander,* subsequently entered into the American vocabulary.

Historical prejudices in favor of FPTP are buttressed, however, by more reasonable arguments. In the view of its supporters, the tendency of FPTP systems to amplify the legislative majority of the winning party has two desirable consequences.

Two-party versus multiparty systems. FPTP is often defended precisely because it does handicap third parties, and by doing so it helps to produce a two-party system. The usual outcome of PR, in contrast, is a multiparty system. Particularly in the English-speaking democracies, two-party systems are much admired and multiparty systems are correspondingly disliked and denigrated. Which is better?

An enormous debate whirls around the relative virtues of two-party and multiparty systems. Generally speaking, the advantages of each mirror their disadvantages. For example, one advantage of a two-party system is that it places a smaller burden on voters by simplifying their options to two. But from the point of view of an advocate of PR, this drastic reduction of the alternatives available seriously impairs voters' freedom of choice. Elections may be perfectly free, they would say, but because they deny representation to minorities they certainly aren't fair.

Effective government. Advocates of two-party systems also support FPTP because it has a further consequence. By amplifying the legislative majority of the winning party, FPTP makes it harder for the minority party to form a coalition able to prevent the majority party from carrying out its program—or, as the leaders of the majority would claim, their "popular mandate." With an amplified majority of party members in the legislature, party leaders will usually have enough votes to spare even if some of their party members defect to the opposition. Thus, it is argued, FPTP helps governments to meet the criterion of effectiveness. By contrast, in some countries PR has helped to produce so many competing and conflicting parties and alliances in the parliament that majority coalitions are extremely difficult to form and highly unstable. As a result, the effectiveness of the government is greatly reduced. Italy is often cited as an example.

What the advocates of FPTP often ignore, however, is that in some countries with PR systems extensive reform programs have been enacted by stable parliamentary majorities consisting often of a coalition of two or three parties. Indeed, several democracies with PR systems, such as the Netherlands and the Scandinavian countries, are veritable models of pragmatic reform combined with stability.

SOME BASIC OPTIONS FOR
DEMOCRATIC CONSTITUTIONS

We can now see why the task of designing a new constitution or redesigning an existing one should not be taken lightly. The task is as difficult and complex as designing a crewed rocket ship for probing outer space. Just as no sensible person would hand over the task of designing a rocket ship to amateurs, so, too, framing a constitution requires a country's best talents. Yet unlike rocket ships, if important constitutional innovations are to endure they will also require the assent and consent of the governed.

The main constitutional options and the various ways of combining them present a formidable array of alternatives. By now I hardly need to repeat my previous warning that every general alternative permits an almost limitless variety of more specific choices.

However, with this caution firmly in mind, let me offer some general guidelines for thinking about constitutional alternatives.

A good place to start is with five possible combinations of electoral systems and chief executives.

The continental European option: parliamentary government with PR elections. Parliamentary government is the overwhelming choice of the older democracies, and among democracies it generally predominates over presidential government.[2] The favored combination among the older democracies, as we have seen, is a parliamentary system in which members are elected by some system of PR. Because this combination is predominant in Europe, where the newer democracies have also followed the standard European path, I'll call this combination the continental European option.

The British (or Westminster) option: parliamentary government with FPTP elections. Because of its origins and its prevalence in English-speaking democracies other than the United States, I'll call this the British option. (It is sometimes also called the Westminster model, after the British seat of government.) Only four of the older democracies have maintained this solution over a lengthy period; not surprisingly, they are the United Kingdom, Canada, Australia, and New Zealand (which, however, abandoned it in 1993).[3]

The U.S. option: presidential government with FPTP elections. Because the United States stands alone among the older democracies in employing this combination, we may call it the U.S. option. A half-dozen newer democracies have also chosen this arrangement.

The Latin American option: presidential government with PR elections. In their strong preference for presidential government, Latin American countries have followed the same constitutional path as the United States. But in their choice of electoral systems, during the late twentieth century they generally followed European practice. As a result, in the fifteen Latin American countries where democratic institutions were more or less in place in the early 1990s, the basic constitutional pattern was a combination of presidential government and PR.[4] So we might call this combination the Latin American option.

It is striking that—with one exception, Costa Rica—none of the older democracies has opted for this combination. Although the older democracies are strongly predisposed to PR, as we have seen they have overwhelmingly rejected presidential government. Costa Rica stands out as the exception. Because Costa Rica, unlike every other country in Latin America, has been steadily democratic since about 1950, I count it among the older democracies. Unlike the others, however, it combines presidentialism with PR.

The mixed option: other combinations. Alongside these more or less "pure" types, several older democracies have created constitutional arrangements that depart in important respects from pure types. They have done so in an effort to minimize the undesirable consequences of the pure types while retaining their advantages. France, Germany, and Switzerland provide important illustrations of constitutional ingenuity.

The constitution of the French Fifth Republic provides for both an elected president with considerable power and a prime minister dependent on the parliament. France has also modified the FPTP electoral system. In a constituency where no candidate for the national assembly receives a majority of votes, a second runoff election is held. In the runoff, any candidate who won more than 12.5 percent of the registered voters in the first election can compete. Small parties thus have a shot at winning a seat here and there in the first round; but in the second round they and their supporters may decide to throw in their lot with one of the two top candidates.

In Germany, half the members of the Bundestag are chosen in FPTP elections and the other half by PR. Versions of the German solution have also been adopted in Italy and New Zealand.

In order to adapt their political system to their diverse population, the Swiss have created a plural executive consisting of seven councillors elected by the parliament for four years. The Swiss plural executive remains unique among the older democracies.[5]

THINKING ABOUT DEMOCRATIC CONSTITUTIONS: SOME GUIDELINES

Drawing on the experiences of the older democracies touched on in the last two chapters, I would offer the following conclusions:

- Most of the basic problems of a country cannot be solved by constitutional design. No constitution will preserve democracy in a country where the underlying conditions are highly unfavorable. A country where the underlying conditions are highly favorable can preserve its basic democratic institutions under a great variety of constitutional arrangements. Carefully crafted constitutional design may be helpful, however, in preserving the basic democratic institutions in countries where the underlying conditions are mixed, both favorable and unfavorable. (More about this in the next chapter.)

- Essential as it is, maintaining fundamental democratic stability is not the only relevant criterion for a good constitution. Fairness in representation, transparency, comprehensibility, responsiveness, and effective government are, among others, also important. Specific constitutional arrangements can and probably will have consequences for values like these.

- All constitutional arrangements have some disadvantages; none satisfy all reasonable criteria. From a democratic point of view, there is no perfect constitution. Moreover, the results of introducing or changing a constitution are bound to be somewhat uncertain. Consequently, constitutional design or reform requires judgments about acceptable trade-offs among goals and the risks and uncertainties of change.

- Over two centuries Americans seem to have developed a political culture, skills, and practices that enable their presidential-congressional system with FPTP, federalism, and strong judicial review to function satisfactorily. But the American system is exceedingly complicated and would probably not work nearly as well in any other country. In any case, it has not been widely copied. Probably it should not be.

- Some scholars contend that the Latin American combination of presidential government with PR has contributed to the breakdowns of democracy that have been so frequent among the republics of Central and South America.[6] Although it is difficult to sort out the effects of constitutional form from the adverse conditions that were the underlying causes of political polarization and crisis, democratic countries would probably be wise to avoid the Latin American option.

Moved by his optimism about the French and American revolutions, Thomas Jefferson once asserted that a revolution about every generation would be a good thing. That romantic idea was shot down during the twentieth century by the numerous revolutions that failed tragically or pathetically or, worse, produced despotic regimes. Yet it might not be a bad idea if a democratic country, about once every twenty years or so, assembled a group of constitutional scholars, political leaders, and informed citizens to evaluate its constitution in the light not only of its own experience but also of the rapidly expanding body of knowledge gained from the experiences of other democratic countries.

PART IV *Conditions Favorable and Unfavorable*

CHAPTER 12

What Underlying Conditions Favor Democracy?

The twentieth century was a time of frequent democratic failure. On more than seventy occasions democracy collapsed and gave way to an authoritarian regime.[1] Yet it was also a time of extraordinary democratic success. Before it ended, the twentieth century had turned into an age of democratic triumph. The global range and influence of democratic ideas, institutions, and practices had made that century far and away the most flourishing period for democracy in human history.

So we face two questions—or, rather, the same question put two ways. How can we account for the establishment of democratic institutions in so many countries in so many parts of the world? And how can we explain its failure? Although a full answer would be impossible, two interrelated sets of factors are undoubtedly of crucial importance.

FAILURE OF THE ALTERNATIVES

First, in the course of the century the main alternatives pretty much lost out in the competition with democracy. Even by the end of the century's first quarter the nondemocratic forms of government that from time immemorial had dominated beliefs and practices throughout most of the world—monarchy, hereditary aristocracy, and open oligarchy—had fatally declined in legitimacy and ideological strength. Although they were replaced by more widely popular antidemocratic alternatives in the form of fascism, Nazism, Leninism, and other authoritarian creeds and governments, these flourished only briefly. Fascism and Nazism were mortally wounded by the defeat of the Axis powers in World War II. Later in the century, military dictatorships, notably in Latin America, fell under the weight of their failures economic, diplomatic, and even military (Argentina). As the last decade of the century approached, the remaining and most important totalitarian rival to democracy, Leninism as embodied in Soviet communism, abruptly collapsed, irreparably weakened by internal decay and external pressures.

So was democracy now secure throughout the globe? As the American president Woodrow Wilson optimistically (and, as it turned out, wrongly) proclaimed in 1919 after the end of World War I, had the world at last "been made safe for democracy"?

Unfortunately, no. A final victory for democracy had not been achieved, nor was it close. The most populous country on earth and a major world power, China, had not yet been democratized. During the four thousand years of an illustrious civilization, the Chinese people had never once experienced democracy; and the prospects that China would soon become democratic were highly dubious. Nondemocratic regimes persisted in many other parts of the world as well, in Africa, Southeast Asia, the Middle East, and some of the remnants of the dissolved USSR. In most of these countries the conditions for democracy were not highly favorable; consequently, it was unclear whether and how they would make the transition to democracy. Finally, in more than a few countries that had made the transition and introduced the basic political institutions of polyarchal democracy, the underlying conditions were not favorable enough to guarantee that democracy would survive indefinitely.

Underlying conditions? I have suggested yet again that certain underlying or background conditions in a country are favorable to the stability of democracy and where these conditions are weakly

FIGURE 8. *What conditions favor democratic institutions?*

Essential conditions for democracy:
1. Control of military and police by elected officials
2. Democratic beliefs and political culture
3. No strong foreign control hostile to democracy
   Favorable conditions for democracy:
4. A modern market economy and society
5. Weak subcultural pluralism

present or entirely absent democracy is unlikely to exist, or if it does, its existence is likely to be precarious.

So it is now time to ask: What are these conditions?

To answer, we can draw on a large body of relevant experience provided by the twentieth century: countries that have undergone a transition to democracy, consolidated their democratic institutions, and retained them over many decades; countries where the transition has been followed by collapse; and countries that have never made the transition. These instances of democratic transition, consolidation, and breakdown indicate that five conditions (and there are probably more) significantly affect the chances for democracy in a country (fig. 8).

FOREIGN INTERVENTION

Democratic institutions are less likely to develop in a country subject to intervention by another country hostile to democratic government in that country.

This condition is sometimes sufficient to explain why democratic institutions failed to develop or persist in a country where other conditions were considerably more favorable. For example, were it not for the intervention of the Soviet Union after World War II, Czechoslovakia would probably be counted today among the older democracies. Soviet intervention also prevented Poland and Hungary from developing democratic institutions.

More surprisingly, until the last decades of the twentieth century the United States had compiled a dismal record of intervention in Latin America, where it had sometimes undermined a popularly elected government by intervening against it to protect American businesses or (in the official view) American national security. Although these Latin American countries where democracy was nipped in the bud were not necessarily fully democratic, had they been free from American intervention—or, better yet, strongly supported in their initial steps toward democratization—democratic institutions might well have evolved in time. A particularly egregious example was the clandestine intervention of U.S. intelligence agencies in Guatamala in 1954 to overthrow the elected government of a populist and left-leaning president, Jacopo Arbenz.

With the collapse of the Soviet Union, the countries of Central Europe and the Baltic moved speedily to install democratic institutions. In addition, the United States, and the international community generally, began to oppose dictatorships in Latin America and elsewhere and to support the development of democratic institutions throughout much of the world. Never in human history had international forces—political, economic, and cultural—been so supportive of democratic ideas and institutions. During the last decades of the twentieth century, then, an epochal shift occurred in the world's political climate that greatly improved the prospects for democratic development.

CONTROL OVER MILITARY AND POLICE

Unless the military and police forces are under the full control of democratically elected officials, democratic political institutions are unlikely to develop or endure.

In contrast to the external threat of foreign intervention, perhaps the most dangerous internal threat to democracy comes from leaders who have access to the major means of physical coercion: the military and the police. If democratically elected officials are to achieve and maintain effective control over military and police forces, members of the police and military, especially among the officers, must defer to them. And their deference to the control of elected leaders must become too deeply ingrained to cast off. Why civilian control has developed in some countries and not in others is too complex to describe here. But for our purposes the important point is that without it, the prospects for democracy are dim.

Consider the unhappy history of Central America. Of the forty-seven governments in Guatemala, El Salvador, Honduras, and Nicaragua between 1948 and 1982, more than two-thirds gained power by means other than free and fair elections—most frequently by a military coup.[2]

In contrast, Costa Rica has been a beacon of democracy in the region since 1950. Why were Costa Ricans able to develop and maintain democratic institutions when all their neighbors could not? A part of the answer is to be found in the existence of the other favorable conditions. But even these would not have sustained a democratic government in the face of a military coup, as so often occurred in the rest of Latin America. In 1950, however, Costa Rica dramatically eliminated that threat: in a unique and audacious decision, the democratic president abolished the military!

No other country has followed Costa Rica's example, nor are many likely to. Yet nothing could illustrate more vividly how crucial it is for elected officials to establish and maintain control over the military and police if democratic institutions are to be established and preserved.

CULTURAL CONFLICTS WEAK OR ABSENT

Democratic political institutions are more likely to develop and endure in a country that is culturally fairly homogeneous and less likely in a country with sharply differentiated and conflicting subcultures.

Distinctive cultures are often formed around differences in language, religion, race, ethnic identity, region, and sometimes ideology. Members share a common identity and emotional ties; they sharply distinguish "us" from "them." They turn toward other members of their group for personal relationships: friends, companions, marriage partners, neighbors, guests. They often engage in ceremonies and rituals that, among other things, define their group boundaries. In all these ways and others, a culture may become virtually a "way of life" for its members, a country within a country, a nation within a nation. In this case society is, so to speak, vertically stratified.

Cultural conflicts can erupt into the political arena, and typically they do: over religion, language, and dress codes in schools, for example; or equality of access to education; or discriminatory practices by one group against another; or whether the government should support religion or religious institutions, and if so, which ones and in what ways; or practices by one group that another finds deeply offensive and wishes to prohibit, such as abortion, cow slaughter, or "indecent" dress; or how and whether territorial and political boundaries should be adapted to fit group desires and demands. And so on. And on.

Issues like these pose a special problem for democracy. Adherents of a particular culture often view their political demands as matters of principle, deep religious or quasi-religious conviction, cultural preservation, or group survival. As a consequence, they consider their demands too crucial to allow for compromise. They are nonnegotiable. Yet under a peaceful democratic process, settling political conflicts generally requires negotiation, conciliation, compromise.

It should come as no surprise to discover, then, that the older and politically stable democratic countries have for the most part managed to avoid severe cultural conflicts. Even if significant cultural differences exist among citizens, they have generally allowed more negotiable differences (on economic issues, for example) to dominate political life most of the time.

Are there no exceptions to this seemingly happy state of affairs? A few. Cultural diversity has been particularly significant in the United States, Switzerland, Belgium, the Netherlands, and Canada. But if diversity threatens to generate intractable cultural conflicts, how have democratic institutions been maintained in these countries?

Their experiences, though very different, show that in a country where all the other conditions are favorable to democracy, the potentially adverse political consequences of cultural diversity can sometimes be made more manageable.

Assimilation. This was the American solution. From the 1840s to 1920, the dominant culture, which during two centuries of colonial rule and independence had been solidly established by white settlers who mainly came from Great Britain, confronted waves of non-British immigrants from Ireland, Scandinavia, Germany, Poland, Italy, and elsewhere—immigrants who could often be distinguished by differences in language (except for the Irish), religion, food, dress, customs, manners, neighborhood, and other characteristics. By 1910 almost one in five white persons residing in the United States had been born elsewhere; in addition, the parents of more than one in four of the native-born whites had been born abroad. Yet within a generation or two after immigrants reached the United States, their descendants were already assimilated into the dominant culture, so fully indeed that although many Americans today retain (or develop) a certain attachment to their ancestral country or culture, their dominant political loyalty and identity is American.

In spite of the impressive success of assimilation in reducing the cultural conflicts that massive immigration might otherwise have produced in the United States, the American experience reveals some crucial shortcomings in that solution.

To begin with, the challenge of assimilation was greatly eased because a great many of the adult immigrants who came to the United States to achieve the better life it promised were fairly eager to assimilate, to "become real Americans." Their descendants were even more so. Thus assimilation was mainly voluntary or enforced by social mechanisms (such as shame) that minimized the need for coercion by the state.[3]

If a massive population of immigrants was, on the whole, successfully assimilated, when American society confronted deeper racial or cultural differences the limits of that approach were soon revealed. In the encounters between the white population and the native peoples who had long occupied the New World, assimilation gave way to coercion, forced resettlement, and isolation from the main society. Nor could American society assimilate the large body of African-American slaves and their descendants, who, ironically, had like the Indians been living in America well before most other immigrants arrived. Coercively enforced caste barriers based on race effectively barred assimilation. A somewhat similar failure also occurred in the late nineteenth century when immigrants arrived from Asia to work as laborers on railroads and farms.

There was one further great divide that assimilation could not bridge. During the early nineteenth century a distinctive subculture, economy, and society based on slavery developed in the southern states. Americans living in the southern states and their compatriots in the northern and western states were divided by two fundamentally incompatible ways of life. The ultimate outcome was an "irrepressible conflict" that could not be resolved, despite great effort, by peaceful negotiation and compromise.[4] The resulting civil war lasted for four years and took a huge toll in human lives. Nor did the conflict end even after the defeat of the South and the abolition of slavery. A distinctive southern subculture and social structure then emerged in which the subjection of African-American citizens was enforced by the threat and actuality of violence and terror.

So much for the past failures of assimilation. By the end of the twentieth century it was unclear whether the historic American practice of assimilation could cope successfully with the steadily increasing Hispanic minority and other self-conscious minorities as well. Will the United States develop into a multicultural society where assimilation no longer insures that cultural conflicts are managed peacefully under democratic procedures? Or will it become one in which cultural differences produces a higher level of mutual understanding, toleration, and accommodation?[5]

Deciding by consensus. Distinctive and potentially conflicting subcultures have existed in Switzerland, Belgium, and the Netherlands. What can we learn from the experiences of these three democratic countries?

Each created political arrangements that required unanimity or broad consensus for decisions made by the cabinet and the parliament. The principle of majority rule yielded (in varying degrees) to a principle of unanimity. Thus any government decision that would significantly affect the interests of one or more of the subcultures would be made only with the explicit agreement of the representatives of that group in the cabinet and parliament. This solution was facilitated by PR, which insured that representatives from each of the groups would be fairly represented in parliament. They were also represented in the cabinet. And under the consensual practices adopted in these countries, the cabinet members from each subculture could exercise a veto over any policy with which they disagreed. (Arrangements like these, which political scientists refer to as "consociational democracy," vary greatly in details among the three countries. For more, see Appendix B.)

Clearly, consensual systems like these cannot be created or will not work successfully except under very special conditions. These include a talent for conciliation; high tolerance for compromise; trustworthy leaders who can negotiate solutions to conflicts that gain the assent of their followers; a consensus on basic goals and values that is broad enough to make agreements attainable; a national identity that discourages demands for outright separation; and a commitment to democratic procedures that excludes violent or revolutionary means.

These conditions are uncommon. Where they are absent, consensual arrangements are unlikely. And even if they are somehow put in place, as the tragic example of Lebanon indicates, they may collapse under the pressure of acute cultural conflict. Once described by political scientists as a highly successful "consociational democracy," Lebanon plunged into a prolonged civil war in 1958, when internal stress proved too great for its consensual system to manage.

Electoral systems. Cultural differences often get out of hand because they are fueled by politicians competing for support. Authoritarian regimes sometimes manage to use their massive coercive power to overwhelm and suppress cultural conflicts, which then erupt as coercion declines with steps toward democratization. Tempted by the easy pickings provided by cultural identities, politicians may deliberately fashion appeals to members of their cultural group and thereby fan latent animosities into hatreds that culminate in "cultural cleansing."

To avoid this outcome, political scientists have suggested that electoral systems could be designed to change the incentives of politicians so as to make conciliation more profitable than conflict. Under the arrangements they propose, no candidates could be elected with the support of only a single cultural group; they would need to gain votes from several major groups. The problem, of course, is to persuade political leaders early in the process of democratization to adopt arrangements of this kind. Once a more divisive electoral system is in place, the spiral into cultural conflict may be all but irreversible.

Separation. When cultural cleavages are too deep to be overcome by any of the previous solutions, the only remaining solution may be for cultural groups to separate themselves into different political units within which they possess enough autonomy to maintain their identity and achieve their main cultural goals. In some situations the solution might be a federal system in which the units—states, provinces, cantons—are sufficiently autonomous to accommodate the different groups. A critical element in the remarkable harmonious multicultural society created by the Swiss is their federal system. Most of the cantons are fairly homogeneous culturally; for example, one canton may be Francophone and Catholic and another German-speaking and Protestant. And the powers of the cantons are adequate for cultural needs.

Like the other democratic political solutions to the problem of multiculturalism, the Swiss solution also requires unusual conditions—in this case, at least two. First, citizens in different subcultures must be already separated along territorial lines, so that the solution imposes no severe hardships. And second, though divided for some purposes into autonomous units, the citizens must have a national identity and common goals and values sufficiently strong to sustain the federal union. Although both conditions hold for Switzerland, neither is at all common.

Where the first condition exists but not the second, cultural differences are likely to produce demands for full independence. If one democratic country becomes two by peacefully separating, the solution seems impeccable when judged purely by democratic standards. For example, after almost a century of near independence in a union with Sweden, in 1905 Norway peacefully gained full independence.

But if the first condition exists only imperfectly because the groups are intermingled, then independence may impose severe hardships on the minority (or minorities) to be included in the new country. These may in turn justify their own claims either for independence or for remaining, somehow, within the mother country. This problem has complicated the issue of independence from Canada for the province of Quebec. Although many French-speaking citizens of Quebec wish to gain full independence, the province also includes a sizable number of non-Francophones—English-speakers, aboriginal groups, and immigrants—who wish to remain Canadian citizens. Although a complicated territorial solution is theoretically possible that would allow most of those who preferred to remain in Canada to do so, whether it will prove to be political possible is unclear.[6]

The disheartening fact is, then, that all the solutions to the potential problems of multiculturalism in a democratic country that I have described, and there may be others, depend for their success on special conditions that are likely to be rare. Because most of the older democratic countries have been only moderately heterogeneous, they have largely been spared from severe cultural conflicts. Yet changes began to set in toward the end of the twentieth century that will almost certainly end this fortunate state of affairs during the twenty-first century.

DEMOCRATIC BELIEFS AND CULTURE

Sooner or later virtually all countries encounter fairly deep crises—political, ideological, economic, military, international. Consequently, if a democratic political system is to endure it must be able to survive the challenges and turmoil that crises like these present. Achieving stable democracy isn't just fair-weather sailing; it also means sailing sometimes in foul and dangerous weather.

During a severe and prolonged crisis the chances increase that democracy will be overturned by authoritarian leaders who promise to end the crisis with vigorous dictatorial methods. Their methods, naturally, require that basic democratic institutions and procedures be set aside.

During the twentieth century the collapse of democracy was a frequent event, as the seventy instances of democratic breakdown mentioned at the beginning of this chapter attest. Yet some democracies did weather their gales and hurricanes, not just once but many times. Several, as we saw, even overcame the dangers arising from sharp cultural differences. And some emerged with the democratic ship of state even more seaworthy than before. The survivors of these stormy periods are precisely the countries we can now call the older democracies.

Why did democratic institutions weather crises in some countries but not in others? To the favorable conditions I have already described, we need to add one more. The prospects for stable democracy in a country are improved if its citizens and leaders strongly support democratic ideas, values, and practices. The most reliable support comes when these beliefs and predispositions are embedded in the country's culture and are transmitted, in large part, from one generation to the next. In other words, the country possesses a democratic political culture.

A democratic political culture would help to form citizens who believe that: democracy and political equality are desirable goals; control over military and police should be fully in the hands of elected leaders; the basic democratic institutions described in Chapter 8 should be maintained; and political differences and disagreements among citizens should be tolerated and protected.

I don't mean to suggest that every person in a democratic country must be formed into perfect democratic citizens. Fortunately not, or surely no democracy would ever exist! But unless a substantial majority of citizens prefer democracy and its political institutions to any nondemocratic alternative and support political leaders who uphold democratic practices, democracy is unlikely to survive through its inevitable crises. Indeed, even a large minority of militant and violent antidemocrats would probably be sufficient to destroy a country's capacity for maintaining its democratic institutions.

How do people in a country come to believe in democratic ideas and practices? How do democratic ideas and practices become an intrinsic part of the country's culture? Any attempt to answer these questions would require us to delve deeply into historical developments, some general, some specific to a particular country, a task well beyond the limits of this book. Let me say only this: Lucky is the country whose history has led to these happy results!

But of course history is not always so generous. Instead, it endows many countries with a political culture that, at best, supports democratic institutions and ideas only weakly and, at worst, strongly favors authoritarian rule.

ECONOMIC GROWTH WITH A MARKET ECONOMY

Historically, the development of democratic beliefs and a democratic culture has been closely associated with what might loosely be called a market economy. More specifically, a highly favorable condition for democratic institutions is a market economy in which economic enterprises are mainly owned privately, and not by the state, that is, a capitalist rather than a socialist or statist economy. Yet the close association between democracy and market-capitalism conceals a paradox: a market-capitalist economy inevitably generates inequalities in the political resources to which different citizens have access. Thus a market-capitalist economy seriously impairs political equality: citizens who are economically unequal are unlikely to be politically equal. In a country with a market-capitalist economy, it appears, full political equality is impossible to achieve. Consequently, there is a permanent tension between democracy and a market-capitalist economy. Is there a feasible alternative to market-capitalism that would be less injurious to political equality? I return to this question, and more generally to the relation between democracy and market-capitalism, in the next two chapters.

Meanwhile, however, we cannot escape the conclusion that a market-capitalist economy, the society it produces, and the economic growth it typically engenders are all highly favorable conditions for developing and maintaining democratic political institutions.

A SUMMARY

Probably other conditions would also be helpful—the rule of law, prolonged peace, and no doubt others. But the five conditions I have just described are, I believe, among the most crucial.

We can sum up the argument of this chapter in three general propositions: First, a country that enjoys all five of these conditions is almost certain to develop and maintain democratic institutions. Second, a country that lacks all five conditions is extremely unlikely to develop democratic institutions, or, if it somehow does, to maintain them. What about a country where the conditions are mixed—where some are favorable but some are unfavorable? I'll postpone the answer, and the third general proposition, until we have considered the strange case of India.

INDIA: AN IMPROBABLE DEMOCRACY

You might already have begun to wonder about India. Doesn't it lack all the favorable conditions? If so, doesn't it stand in contradiction to my entire argument? Well, not quite.

That India could long sustain democratic institutions seems, on the face of it, highly improbable. With a population approaching one billion at the end of the twentieth century, Indians are divided among themselves along more lines than other country in the world. These include language, caste, class, religion, and region—and infinite subdivisions within each.[7] Consider:

India has no national language. The Indian constitution officially recognizes fifteen languages. But even that understates the magnitude of the language problem: at least a million Indians speak one of thirty-five distinct languages. What is more, Indians speak about twenty-two thousand distinct dialects.

Although 80 percent of the people are Hindus (the rest are mainly Muslim, though one state, Kerala, contains many Christians), the unifying effects of Hinduism are severely compromised by the caste system that Hinduism has prescribed for Indians since about 1500 B.C.E. Like language, even the caste system is infinitely divisive. To begin with, a huge number of people are excluded from the four prescribed hereditary castes: these are the "outcastes," the "untouchables" with whom contact is defiling. In addition, however, each caste is further divided into innumerable hereditary subcastes within whose social, residential, and often occupational boundaries its members are rigidly confined.

India is one of the poorest countries in the world. Pick your number: From 1981 to 1995 about half the population lived on the equivalent of less than one U.S. dollar a day. By this measure, only four countries were poorer. In 1993–1994, more than a third of India's population—more than three hundred million people—officially lived in poverty, mainly in small villages and engaged in agriculture. In 1996 among seventy-eight developing countries India was ranked forty-seventh on a Human Poverty Index, next to Rwanda in forty-eighth place. In addition, about half of all Indians over age fifteen, and more than 60 percent of females over age six, are illiterate.

Although India gained independence in 1947 and adopted a democratic constitution in 1950, given the conditions I have just described no one should be surprised that India's political practices have displayed some egregious shortcomings from a democratic point of view. It has suffered from recurring violations of basic rights.[8] India is viewed by businesspeople as among the ten most corrupt countries in the world.[9] Worse, in 1975 India's democratic institutions were overturned and replaced by dictatorship when the prime minister, Indira Gandhi, staged a coup d'état, declared a state of emergency, suspended civil rights, and imprisoned thousands of leading opponents.

Yet most of the time most Indians support democratic institutions. In an action that would not have been taken by a people unqualified for democracy, two years after Indira Gandhi's seizure of power, she was voted out of office in a reasonably fair election. Not just the political elites but the Indian people as a whole, it appeared, were more attached to democratic institutions and practices than she had assumed; and they would not permit her to govern by authoritarian methods.

Although Indian political life is highly turbulent and often violent, somehow the basic democratic institutions, blemishes and all, continue to operate. This observation seems to confound all reasonable expectations. How can we account for it? Any answer to the Indian conundrum must be tentative. Yet surprising as it may seem, certain aspects of India help to explain why it manages to maintain its democratic institutions.

To begin with, several of the favorable conditions I've described do exist in India. Growing out of its past as a British colony, the Indian military developed and has maintained a code of obedience to elected civilian leaders. Thus India has been free of the major threat to democratic government in most developing countries. In contrast to Latin America, for example, Indian military traditions provide little support for a military coup or a military dictatorship. The police, though widely corrupt, are not an independent political force capable of a coup.

In addition, the founders of modern India who led it to independence and helped to shape its constitution and political institutions all adhered to democratic beliefs. The political movements they led strongly advocated democratic ideas and institutions. Democracy, one might say, is the national ideology of India. There is no other. Weak as India's sense of nationhood may be, it is so intimately bound up with democratic ideas and beliefs that few Indians advocate a nondemocratic alternative.

Furthermore, although India is culturally diverse, it is the only country in the world where Hindu beliefs and practices are so widely shared. After all, eight out of ten Indians are Hindus. Even though the caste system is divisive and Hindu nationalists are a standing danger to the Muslim minority, Hinduism does provide something of a common identity for a majority of Indians.

Yet even if these conditions provide support for democratic institutions, India's widespread poverty combined with its acute multicultural divisions would appear to be fertile grounds for the rampant growth of antidemocratic movements powerful enough to overthrow democracy and install an authoritarian dictatorship. Why has this not happened? A closer view reveals several surprises.

First, every Indian is a member of a cultural minority so tiny that its members cannot possibly govern India alone. The sheer number of cultural fragments into which India is divided means that each is small, not only far short of a majority but far too small to rule over that vast and varied subcontinent. No Indian minority could rule without employing overwhelming coercion by military and police forces. But the military and police, as we have noted, are not available for that purpose.

Second, with few exceptions, members of a cultural minority do not live together in a single area but tend instead to be spread over different regions of India. As a consequence, most minorities cannot hope to form a separate country outside India's boundaries. Whether they like it or not, most Indians are destined to remain citizens of India. Because disunion is impossible, the only alternative is union, within India.[10]

Finally, for most Indians there is simply no realistic alternative to democracy. None of India's minorities, by itself, can overturn democratic institutions and establish an authoritarian regime, count on the military and police support it would need to sustain an authoritarian government, hope to form a separate country, or propose an appealing ideological and institutional alternative to democracy. Experience indicates that any sizable coalition of different minorities will be too divided to sustain a takeover, much less an authoritarian government. Democracy, it seems, is the only feasible option for most Indians.

The full story of democracy in India is more complex, as the full story of any country is bound to be. But in the end, India confirms the third proposition I promised earlier. In a country that lacks one or several but not all of the five conditions that favor democracy, democracy is chancy, perhaps improbable, but not necessarily impossible.

WHY DEMOCRACY HAS SPREAD THROUGHOUT THE WORLD

I began this chapter by noting how often in the course of the twentieth century democracy had collapsed and yet how widely it had spread by the end of that century. We can now explain that triumph: the favorable conditions I have described became much more widely dispersed among the countries of the world.

- The danger of intervention by an outside power hostile to democratization declined as colonial empires dissolved, peoples gained their independence, the major totalitarian regimes collapsed, and the international community largely supported democratization.

- The lure of military dictatorship declined as it became apparent, not just to civilians but to military leaders themselves, that military rulers were usually not able to meet the challenges of a modern society. Indeed, they often proved to be grossly incompetent. Thus in many countries one of the oldest and most dangerous threats to democracy was at last eliminated or greatly reduced.

- Many countries where democratization took place were sufficiently homogeneous to be able to avoid serious cultural conflicts. Often these were smaller countries, not large agglomerations of diverse cultures. In some countries that were more culturally divided, consensual arrangements were worked out. In at least one country, India, no minority culture was substantial enough to govern. In contrast, where cultural conflicts were acute, as they were in parts of Africa and ex-Yugoslavia, democratization was pretty much a disaster.

- With the visible failures of totalitarian systems, military dictatorships, and many other authoritarian regimes, antidemocratic beliefs and ideologies lost their previous appeal throughout much of the world. Never before in human history had so many people supported democratic ideas and institutions.

- The institutions of market-capitalism were spread to one country after another. Market-capitalism not only resulted in higher economic growth and well-being but also fundamentally altered a country's society by creating a large and influential middle class sympathetic to democratic ideas and institutions.

So for these reasons, and perhaps others, the twentieth century turned out to be the Century of Democratic Triumph. Yet we should view that triumph with caution. For one thing, in many "democratic" countries the basic political institutions were weak or defective. In figure 1 (p. 8), I counted sixty-five countries as democratic. But we might reasonably divide them them into three groups: most democratic, 35; fairly democratic, 7; and marginally democratic, 23 (see Appendix C for sources).[11] Thus the "triumph of democracy" was considerably less complete than it was sometimes portrayed.

In addition, it is reasonable to wonder whether democratic successes will be sustained in the twenty-first century. The answer depends on how well democratic countries meet their challenges. One of these, as I've already suggested, arises directly from the contradictory consequences of market-capitalism: in some respects it is favorable to democracy, yet in others it is unfavorable. We'll see why in the next two chapters.

CHAPTER 13

Why Market-Capitalism Favors Democracy

Democracy and market-capitalism are like two persons bound in a tempestuous marriage that is riven by conflict and yet endures because neither partner wishes to separate from the other. To shift the simile to the botanical world, the two exist in a kind of antagonistic symbiosis.

Although the relation is extraordinarily complicated, from the profuse and constantly growing array of experiences with political and economic systems we can, I believe, draw five important conclusions. I offer two in this chapter, the other three in the next.

1. *Polyarchal democracy has endured only in countries with a predominantly market-capitalist economy; and it has never endured in a country with a predominantly nonmarket economy.*

Although I have limited this conclusion to polyarchal democracy, it also applies pretty well to the popular governments that developed in the city-states of Greece, Rome, and medieval Italy and to the evolution of representative institutions and the growth of citizen participation in northern Europe. But I'm going to bypass that history, some of which we encountered in Chapter 2, in order to focus exclusively on the institutions of modern representative democracy—that is, polyarchal democracy.

Here the record is amazingly unambiguous. Polyarchal democracy has existed *only* in countries with predominantly market-capitalist economies and *never* (or at most briefly) in countries with predominantly nonmarket economies. Why is this so?

2. *This strict relation exists because certain basic features of market-capitalism make it favorable for democratic institutions. Conversely, some basic features of a predominantly nonmarket economy make it harmful to democratic prospects.*

In a market-capitalist economy, the economic entities are either individuals or enterprises (firms, farms, and whatnot) that are privately owned by individuals and groups, and not, for the most part, by the state. The main goal of these entities is economic gain in the form of wages, profits, interest, and rent. Those who manage the enterprises have no need to strive for broad, lofty, and ambiguous goals such as the general welfare or the public good. They can be guided solely by self-interested incentives. And because markets supply owners, managers, workers, and others with much of the crucial information they need, they can make their decisions without central direction. (This doesn't mean they can do without laws and regulations, which I'll come back to in the next chapter.)

Contrary to what our intuition might tell us, markets serve to coordinate and control the decisions of the economic entities. Historical experience shows pretty conclusively that a system in which countless economic decisions are made by innumerable independent but competing actors, each acting from rather narrow self-regarding interests and guided by the information supplied by markets, produces goods and services much more efficiently than any known alternative. What is more, it does so with a regularity and orderliness that is truly astonishing.

As a result, in the long run market-capitalism has typically led to economic growth; and economic growth is favorable to democracy. To begin with, by cutting acute poverty and improving living standards, economic growth helps to reduce social and political conflicts. Furthermore, when economic conflicts do arise, growth provides more resources that are available for a mutually satisfactory settlement in which each side gains something. (In the absence of growth, economic conflicts, to use the language of game theory, become "zero-sum": what I gain you lose, what you gain I lose. So cooperation is useless.) Growth also provides individuals, groups, and governments with surplus resources to support education and thus to foster a literate and educated citizenry.

Market-capitalism is also favorable to democracy because of its social and political consequences. It creates a large middling stratum of property owners who typically seek education, autonomy, personal freedom, property rights, the rule of law, and participation in government. The middle classes, as Aristotle was the first to point out, are the natural allies of democratic ideas and institutions. Last, and perhaps most important, by decentralizing many economic decisions to relatively independent individuals and firms, a market-capitalist economy avoids the need for a powerful, even authoritarian central government.

A nonmarket economy can exist where resources are scarce and economic decisions few and obvious. But in a more complex society, to avoid economic chaos and to provide at least a moderate standard of living, a substitute for the coordination and control provided by markets is necessary. The only feasible substitute is the government of the state. So whatever the formal legal ownership of enterprises might be in a nonmarket economy, their decisions are, in effect, made and controlled by the government. Without the coordination of the market, it necessarily becomes the government's task to allocate all scarce resources: capital, labor, machinery, land, buildings, consumer goods, dwellings, and the rest. To do so, the government needs a detailed and comprehensive central plan and thus government officials charged with making the plan, carrying it out, and seeing to its enforcement. These are prodigious tasks, requiring staggering quantities of reliable information. To gain compliance with their directives, government officials must discover and apply appropriate incentives. These may run from rewards, both legal (such as salaries and bonuses) and illegal (for example, bribery), to coercion and punishment (such as execution for "economic crimes"). Except under rare and transitory conditions, which I'll come to in a moment, no government has proved up to the task.

It is not the inefficiencies of a centrally planned economy, however, that are most injurious to democratic prospects. It is the economy's social and political consequences. A centrally planned economy puts the resources of the entire economy at the disposal of government leaders. To foresee the likely consequences of that fantastic political windfall, we might recall the aphorism that "power corrupts and absolute power corrupts absolutely." A centrally planned economy issues an outright invitation to government leaders, written in bold letters: *You are free to use all these economic resources to consolidate and maintain your power!*

Political leaders would have to have superhuman powers of self-denial to resist this temptation. Alas, the melancholy record of history is clear: rulers with access to the enormous resources provided by a centrally planned economy have all confirmed the wisdom of the aphorism. To be sure, leaders may use their despotism for good ends or bad. History records some of both—though overall, I think, despots have achieved considerably more ill than good. In any case, centrally planned economies have always been closely associated with authoritarian regimes.

SOME QUALIFICATIONS

Although the two conclusions are valid, they need several qualifications.

For one thing, economic growth is not unique to democratic

countries, nor is economic stagnation unique to nondemocratic nations. Indeed, there appears to be no correlation between economic growth and a country's type of government or regime.[1]

Moreover, although democracy has existed only in countries with a market-capitalist economy, market-capitalism has existed in nondemocratic countries. In several of these—Taiwan and South Korea in particular—the factors I mentioned earlier that tend to accompany economic growth and a market economy in turn helped to bring about democratization. In these two countries authoritarian leaders, whose policies helped to stimulate the development of a successful market economy, export industries, economic growth, and a large, educated middle class, also unwittingly planted the seeds of their own destruction. Thus although market-capitalism and economic growth are favorable to democracy, in the long run they may be far less favorable, indeed downright unfavorable for nondemocratic regimes. Consequently, the dénouement of a momentous historical drama to be played out during the twenty-first century will reveal whether China's nondemocratic regime can withstand the democratizing forces generated by market-capitalism.

A market-capitalist economy need not exist, however, only in its familiar twentieth-century urban-industrial or postindustrial form. It may also be—or at least has been—agricultural. As we saw in Chapter 2, during the nineteenth century the basic democratic institutions, with the exception of female suffrage, developed in several countries—the United States, Canada, New Zealand, and Australia—that were predominantly agricultural. In 1790, the first year of the American republic under its new (and still continuing) constitution, out of a total population of just under four million persons, only 5 percent lived in places with more than twenty-five hundred inhabitants; the remaining 95 percent lived in rural areas, mainly on farms. By 1820, when the political institutions of (white male) polyarchal democracy were already solidly established, in a population of fewer than ten million people, more than nine out of ten still lived in rural areas. On the eve of the Civil War in 1860, when the country had more than thirty million inhabitants, eight of ten Americans lived in rural areas. The America that Alexis de Tocqueville described in *Democracy in America* was agrarian, not industrial. The economic enterprises of that agrarian society were, of course, principally farms, owned and managed by individual farmers and their families. Much of what they produced was used for their own consumption.

The important point, however, is that the economy was highly decentralized (more, indeed, than it was to become with industrialization); it gave political leaders little access to its resources; and it created a large middle class of free farmers. Thus it was highly favorable for democratic development. Indeed, in Thomas Jefferson's vision of the Republic, the necessary foundation for democracy was an agrarian society consisting of independent farmers.

Are these preindustrial origins of several of the oldest democracies irrelevant to countries in the postindustrial era? No. That body of experience reinforces a crucial point: whatever its dominant activity, a decentralized economy that helps to create a nation of independent citizens is highly favorable for the development and maintenance of democratic institutions.

A moment ago I mentioned "rare and transitory conditions" under which governments have efficiently managed central planning. What is more, the governments were democratic. These were the wartime governments of Britain and the United States during World War I and even more emphatically during World War II. But in these cases, the planning and allocation of resources had a clearly defined goal, which was to insure that military needs were met along with a basic supply of goods and services for civilians. The war aims were widely supported. Though some black markets developed, they were not so extensive as to diminish the effectiveness of the centralized system for allocating resources and controlling prices. Finally, the system was dismantled after peace arrived. As a result, political leaders were deprived of the opportunities they would have enjoyed for exploiting their dominant economic role for political purposes.

If we put these wartime systems to one side, centrally directed economies have existed only in countries where the leaders were fundamentally antidemocratic. Thus we cannot easily untangle the undemocratic consequences of the economic order from the undemocratic consequences of leaders' beliefs. Lenin and Stalin were so hostile to democracy that with or without a centrally directed economy, they would have prevented democratic institutions from developing. The centrally directed economy simply made their task easier by providing them with greater resources for inflicting their will on others.

Strictly speaking, then, the historical experiment that combines democratic institutions with a centrally directed peacetime economy has never been tried. I for one hope that it never will. The likely consequences are, I believe, fully foreseeable. And they bode ill for democracy.

Yet even if market-capitalism is far more favorable to democratic institutions than any nonmarket economy that has so far existed, it also has some profoundly unfavorable consequences. We examine these in the next chapter.

CHAPTER 14

Why Market-Capitalism Harms Democracy

If we approach market capitalism from a democratic point of view we discover, when we look closely, that it has two faces. Like the emblem of the Greek god Janus, they face in opposite directions. One, a friendly face, points toward democracy. The other, a hostile face, points the other way.

3. *Democracy and market-capitalism are locked in a persistent conflict in which each modifies and limits the other.*

By 1840, a market economy with self-regulating markets in labor, land, and money had been fully installed in Britain. Market-capitalism had triumphed over its enemies on all fronts: not only in economic theory and practice but in politics, law, ideas, philosophy, and ideology as well. Its opponents, so it appeared, were completely routed. Yet in a country where people have a voice, as they had in England even in those predemocratic times, such a complete victory could not endure.[1] As it always does, market-capitalism brought gains for some; but as it always does, it also brought harm to others.

Though suffrage was highly restricted, the other political institutions of representative government were largely in place. And in due time—in 1867 and again in 1884—suffrage was expanded; after 1884 most males could vote. Thus the political system provided opportunities for the effective expression of opposition to unregulated market-capitalism. Turning for help to political and governmental leaders, those who felt themselves injured by unregulated markets sought protection. Opponents of laissez-faire economics found effective expression of their grievances through political leaders, movements, parties, programs, ideas, philosophies, ideologies, books, journals, and, most important, votes and elections. The newly formed Labour Party focused on the plight of the working classes.

Although some opponents proposed only to regulate market-capitalism, others wished to abolish it outright. And some compromised: let's regulate it now, they said, and eliminate it later. Those who proposed to abolish capitalism never achieved their goals. Those who demanded government intervention and regulation often did.

As in Britain, so, too, in Western Europe and the other English-speaking countries. In any country where governments could be influenced by popular movements of discontent, laissez-faire could not be sustained. Market-capitalism without government intervention and regulation was impossible in a democratic country for at least two reasons.

First, the basic institutions of market-capitalism themselves require extensive government intervention and regulation. Competitive markets, ownership of economic entities, enforcing contracts, preventing monopolies, protecting property rights—these and many other aspects of market capitalism depend wholly on laws, policies, orders, and other actions carried out by governments. A market economy is not, and cannot be, completely self-regulating.

Second, without government intervention and regulation a market economy inevitably inflicts serious harm on some persons; and those who are harmed or expect to be harmed will demand government intervention. Economic actors motivated by self-interest have little incentive for taking the good of others into account; on the contrary, they have powerful incentives for ignoring the good of others if by doing so they themselves stand to gain. Conscience is easily quieted by that seductive justification for inflicting harm on others: "If I don't do it, others will. If I don't allow my factory to discharge its wastes into the river and its smoke into the air, others will. If I don't sell my products even if they may be unsafe, others will. If I don't . . . others will." In a more or less competitive economy, it is virtually certain that, in fact, others will.

When harm results from decisions determined by unregulated competition and markets, questions are bound to arise. Can the harm be eliminated or reduced? If so, can this be achieved without excessive cost to the benefits? When the harm accrues to some persons and the benefits to others, as is usually the case, how are we to judge what is desirable? What is the best solution? Or if not the best, at least an acceptable solution? How should these decisions be made, and by whom? How and by what means are the decisions to be enforced?

It is obvious that these are not just economic questions. They are also moral and political questions. In a democratic country citizens searching for answers will inevitably gravitate toward politics and government. The most easily accessible candidate for intervening in a market economy in order to alter an otherwise harmful outcome, and the most effective, is . . . the government of the state.

Whether discontented citizens succeed in getting the government to intervene depends, of course, on many things, including the relative political strengths of the antagonists. However, the historical record is clear: in all democratic countries,* the harm produced by, or expected from, unregulated markets has induced governments to intervene in order to alter an outcome that would otherwise cause damage to some citizens.

In a country famous for its commitment to market-capitalism,

---

*And in many nondemocratic countries as well. But our concern here is with the relation between democracy and market-capitalism.

the United States, national, state, and local governments intervene in the economy in ways too numerous to list. Here are just a few examples:

- unemployment insurance;
- old age annuities;
- fiscal policy to avoid inflation and economic recession;
- safety: food, drugs, airlines, railroads, highways, streets;
- public health, control of infectious diseases, compulsory vaccination of school children;
- health insurance;
- education;
- the sale of stocks, bonds, and other securities;
- zoning: business, residential, and so on;
- setting building standards;
- insuring market-competition, preventing monopolies, and other restraints on trade;
- imposing and reducing tariffs and quotas on imports;
- licensing physicians, dentists, lawyers, accountants, and other professional persons;
- establishing and maintaining state and national parks, recreation areas, and wilderness areas;
- regulating business firms to prevent or repair environmental damage; and belatedly,
- regulating the sale of tobacco products in order to reduce the frequency of addiction, cancer, and other malign effects.

And so on. And on, and on.

To sum up: In no democratic country does a market-capitalist economy exist (nor in all likelihood can it exist for long) without extensive government regulation and intervention to alter its harmful effects.

Yet if the existence in a country of democratic political institutions significantly affects the operation of market-capitalism, the existence of market-capitalism in a country greatly affects the operation of democratic political institutions. The causal arrow, so to speak, goes both ways: from politics to economics and from economics to politics.

4. *Because market capitalism inevitably creates inequalities, it limits the democratic potential of polyarchal democracy by generating inequalities in the distribution of political resources.*

Words About Words

Political resources include everything to which a person or a group has access that they can use to influence, directly or indirectly, the conduct of other persons. Varying with time and place, an enormous number of aspects of human society can be converted into political resources: physical force, weapons, money, wealth, goods and services, productive resources, income, status, honor, respect, affection, charisma, prestige, information, knowledge, education, communication, communications media, organizations, position, legal standing, control over doctrine and beliefs, votes, and many others. At one theoretical limit, a political resource might be distributed equally, as with votes in democratic countries. At the other theoretical limit, it might be concentrated in the hands of one person or group. And the possible distributions between equality and total concentration are infinite.

Most of the resources I just listed are everywhere distributed in highly unequal fashion. Although market-capitalism is not the only cause, it is important in causing an unequal distribution of many key resources: wealth, income, status, prestige, information, organization, education, knowledge . . . .

Because of inequalities in political resources, some citizens gain significantly more influence than others over the government's policies, decisions, and actions. These violations, alas, are not trivial. Consequently, citizens are not political equals—far from it—and thus the moral foundation of democracy, political equality among citizens, is seriously violated.

5. *Market-capitalism greatly favors the development of democracy up to the level of polyarchal democracy. But because of its adverse consequences for political equality, it is unfavorable to the development of democracy beyond the level of polyarchy.*

For the reasons advanced earlier, market-capitalism is a powerful solvent of authoritarian regimes. When it transforms a society from landlords and peasants to employers, employees, and workers; from uneducated rural masses barely capable of surviving, and often not even that, to a country of literate, moderately secure, urbanized inhabitants; from the monopolization of almost all resources by a small elite, oligarchy, or ruling class to a much wider dispersion of resources; from a system in which the many can do little to prevent the domination of government by a few to a system in which the many can effectively combine their resources (not least their votes) and thereby influence the government to act in their favor—when it helps to bring about these changes, as it often has and will continue to do in many countries with developing economies, it serves as a vehicle for a revolutionary transformation of society and politics.

When authoritarian governments in less modernized countries undertake to develop a dynamic market economy, then, they are likely to sew the seeds of their own ultimate destruction.

But once society and politics are transformed by market-capitalism and democratic institutions are in place, the outlook fundamentally changes. Now the inequalities in resources that market-capitalism churns out produce serious political inequalities among citizens.

Whether and how the marriage of polyarchal democracy to market-capitalism can be made more favorable to the further democratization of polyarchy is a profoundly difficult question for which there are no easy answers, and certainly no brief ones. The relation between a country's democratic political system and its nondemocratic economic system has presented a formidable and persistent challenge to democratic goals and practices throughout the twentieth century. That challenge will surely continue in the twenty-first century.

CHAPTER 15

The Unfinished Journey

What lies ahead? As we saw, the twentieth century, which at times appeared to many contemporaries likely to turn into a dark and tragic period for democracy, proved instead to be its era of un-paralleled triumph. Although we might find comfort in believing that the twenty-first century will be as kind to democracy as the twentieth, the historical record tells us that democracy has been rare to human experience. Is it destined once again to be replaced by nondemocratic systems, perhaps appearing in some twenty-first century version of Guardianship by political and bureaucratic elites? Or might it instead continue its global expansion? Or, in yet another transformation, might what is called "democracy" become both broader in reach and shallower in depth—extending to more and more countries as its democratic qualities grow ever more feeble?

The future is, I think, too uncertain to provide firm answers. Having completed our exploration of the questions set out in Chapter 3, we have now run off our charts. The known world mapped from experience must give way to a future where the maps are, at best, unreliable—sketches made by cartographers without reliable reports on a distant land. Nonetheless, we can predict with considerable confidence, I believe, that certain problems democratic countries now face will remain, and may even grow more daunting.

In this final chapter I shall provide a brief sketch of several challenges. I'll focus mainly on the older democracies partly to make my task more manageable but also because I believe that sooner or later—probably sooner than later—countries recently democratized or still in transition will confront problems like those that lie ahead for the older democracies.

Given what has gone before, none of the problems I'll mention should come as a great surprise. I have little doubt that there will be others. Regrettably, I cannot hope to offer solutions here, for that task that would take another book—or, rather, many books. We can be reasonably certain, however, of one thing: the nature and quality of democracy will greatly depend on how well democratic citizens and leaders meet the challenges I am about to describe.

CHALLENGE 1: THE ECONOMIC ORDER

Market-capitalism is unlikely to be displaced in democratic countries. Consequently, the antagonistic cohabitation described in Chapters 13 and 14 is sure to persist in one form or another.

No demonstrably superior alternative to a predominantly market economy is anywhere in sight. In a seismic change in perspectives, by the end of the twentieth century few citizens in democratic countries had much confidence in the possibility of discovering and introducing a non-market system that would be more favorable to democracy and political equality and yet efficient enough in producing goods and services to be equally acceptable. During the two preceding centuries, socialists, planners, technocrats, and many others had nurtured visions in which markets would be widely and permanently replaced by, so they thought, more orderly, better planned, and more just processes for making economic decisions about the production, pricing, and distribution of goods and services. These visions have nearly faded into oblivion. Whatever the defects of a predominantly market economy may be, it appears to be the only option for democratic countries in the new century.

Whether a predominantly market economy requires that economic enterprises be owned and controlled in their prevailing capitalist forms is, by contrast, much less certain. The internal "governments" of capitalist firms are typically undemocratic; sometimes, indeed, they are virtually managerial despotisms. Moreover, the ownership of firms and the profits and other gains resulting from ownership are distributed in highly unequal fashion. Unequal ownership and control of major economic enterprises in turn contribute massively to the inequality in political resources mentioned in Chapter 14 and thus to extensive violations of political equality among democratic citizens.

In spite of these drawbacks, by the end of the twentieth century the historic alternatives to capitalist ownership and control had lost most of their support. Labor, socialist, and social-democratic parties had long abandoned nationalization of industry as a goal. Governments led by such parties, or at least including them as eager partners, were rapidly privatizing existing state-owned enterprises. The only major experience with a socialist market-economy, in which "socially owned" enterprises operating in a market context were internally governed by representatives of the workers (at least in principle), died when Yugoslavia and its hegemonic communist government disintegrated. To be sure, in the older democratic countries some employee-owned firms not only exist but actually flourish. Yet trade union movements, labor parties, and workers in general do not seriously advocate an economic order consisting predominantly of firms owned and controlled by their employees and workers.

So: the tension between democratic goals and a market-capitalist economy will almost certainly continue indefinitely. Are there better ways of preserving the advantages of market-capitalism while reducing its costs to political equality? The answers provided by citizens and leaders in democratic countries will largely determine the nature and quality of democracy in the new century.

CHALLENGE 2: INTERNATIONALIZATION

We've already seen why internationalization is likely to expand the domain of decisions made by political and bureaucratic elites at the expense of democratic controls. As I suggested in Chapter 9, from a democratic perspective the challenge posed by internationalization is to make sure that the costs to democracy are fully taken into account when decisions are shifted to international levels, and to strengthen the means for holding political and bureaucratic elites accountable for their decisions. Whether and how these may be accomplished is, alas, far from clear.

CHALLENGE 3: CULTURAL DIVERSITY

As we saw in Chapter 12, a moderate level of cultural homogeneity was favorable to the development and stability of democracy in many of the older democratic countries. During the last decades of the twentieth century, however, two developments in these countries contributed to an increase in cultural diversity. Both seemed likely to continue into the twenty-first century.

First, some citizens who had habitually incurred discrimination joined others like themselves in movements of cultural identity that sought to protect their rights and interests. These movements included people of color, women, gays and lesbians, linguistic minorities, ethnic groups living in their historic regions, such as the Scots and Welsh in Great Britain and French-speakers in Quebec, and others.

Second, cultural diversity in the older democratic countries was magnified by an increased number of immigrants, who were usually marked by ethnic, linguistic, religious, and cultural differences that made them distinguishable from the dominant population. For many reasons, immigration, both legal and illegal, is likely to contribute indefinitely to a significant increase in cultural diversity within the older democracies. For example, economic differences between the rich democratic countries and poorer countries encourage people in the poorer countries in the hope that they can escape their poverty by moving to the richer countries. Others simply want to improve the quality of their lives by emigrating to a rich country with greater opportunities. The number seeking to move to the older democracies was further increased during the last years of the twentieth century by a flood of terror-stricken refugees desperately trying to escape from the violence, repression, genocidal terror, "ethnic cleansing," starvation, and other horrors they faced in their home countries.

Pressures from inside added to these pressures from outside. Employers hoped to hire immigrants at wage levels and under working conditions that no longer attracted their fellow citizens. Recent immigrants wanted their relatives abroad to reunite with them. Citizens moved by considerations of humanity and simple justice were unwilling to force refugees to remain forever in refugee camps or face the misery, terror, and possibly outright murder confronting them at home.

Faced with pressures from outside and within, democratic countries discovered that their boundaries were more porous than they had assumed. Illegal entry by land or sea was impossible to prevent, it appeared, without heavy expenditures for policing borders in ways that, aside from the expense, many citizens found distasteful or intolerably inhumane.

It seems unlikely to me that cultural diversity and the challenge it poses will decrease during the new century. If anything, diversity seems likely to increase.

If, in the past, democratic countries have not always dealt with cultural diversity in ways consistent with democratic practices and values, can they, and will they, do better in the future? The various arrangements described in Chapter 12 and in Appendix B offer possible solutions that extend from assimilation at one extreme to independence at the other. There may be others. In any case, here again the nature and quality of democracy will greatly depend on the arrangements that democratic countries develop for dealing with the cultural diversity of their people.

CHALLENGE 4: CIVIC EDUCATION

Although I have not said much in the previous pages about civic education, you may recall that one basic criterion for a democratic process is enlightened understanding: within reasonable limits as to time, each member (citizen) must have equal and effective opportunities for learning about relevant alternative policies and their likely consequences.

In practice, how *do* citizens tend to acquire their civic education? The older democratic countries have created many routes to political understanding. To begin with, most citizens receive a level of formal education sufficient to insure literacy. Their political understanding is augmented further by the widespread availability of relevant information that they can acquire at low cost through the media. Political competition among office seekers organized in political parties adds to the supply, as parties and candidates eagerly offer voters information (sometimes laced with misinformation) about their records and intentions. Thanks to political parties and interest organizations, the amount of information that citizens *need* in order to be adequately informed, actively engaged in politics, and politically effective is actually reduced to more easily attainable levels. A political party usually has a history known in a general way to voters, a present direction that is ordinarily an extension of its past, and a rather predictable future. Consequently, voters have less need to understand every important public issue. Instead, they can simply vote for candidates from the party of their choice with some confidence that, if elected, their representatives will generally pursue policies that accord broadly with their interests.

Many citizens also belong to associations organized to protect and promote their specific concerns—interest groups, lobbying organizations, pressure groups. The resources, political skills, and expert knowledge available to organized interest groups provide citizens with a special kind of representation in political life that is often highly effective.

Because of party competition, the influence of interest organizations, and competitive elections, political leaders generally assume that they will be held accountable for carrying out, or at least trying to carry out, their party programs and campaign promises. What is more, despite widely held beliefs to the contrary, in the older democratic countries they usually have in fact done so.[1]

Last, important governmental decisions are typically made incrementally, not by great leaps into the unknown. Because they are made a step at a time, incremental changes tend to avoid crippling disasters. Citizens, experts, and leaders learn from mistakes, see what corrections are needed, modify the policy, and so on. If necessary the process is repeated again and again. Although each step might look disappointingly small, over time gradual steps can produce profound, one might say revolutionary, changes. Yet these gradual changes occur peacefully and gain such broad public support that they tend to endure.

Although to some observers such muddling through in incremental fashion seems hopelessly irrational, on inspection it appears to be a fairly rational way of making important changes in a world of high uncertainty.[2] The most disastrous decisions in the twentieth century turned out to be those made by authoritarian leaders freed from democratic restraints. While democracies muddled through, despotic leaders trapped within their own narrow visions of the world blindly pursued policies of self-destruction.

With all its imperfections, then, this standard solution for achieving an adequate level of civic competence has much to be said for it.[3]

Yet I fear that it will not continue to be satisfactory in the future. Three interrelated developments seem to me likely to render the standard solution seriously deficient.

Changes in scale. Because of increased internationalization, actions that significantly affect the lives of citizens are made over larger and larger areas that include more and more people within their boundaries.

Complexity. Although the average level of formal education has risen in all democratic countries, and probably will continue to rise, the difficulty of understanding public affairs has also increased and may have outstripped the gains from higher levels of education. Over the course of the previous half-century or so the number of different matters relevant to politics, government, and the state have increased in every democratic country. Indeed, no person can be expert in them all—in more than a few, in fact. Finally, judgments about policies are not only fraught with uncertainty but usually required difficult judgments about trade-offs.

Communications. During the twentieth century the social and technical framework of human communication in advanced countries underwent extraordinary changes: telephone, radio, television, fax, interactive TV, the Internet, opinion surveys almost instantaneous with events, focus groups, and so on. Because of the relatively low costs of communication and information, the sheer amount of information available on political matters, at all levels of complexity, has increased enormously.[4] Yet this increased availability of information may not lead to greater competence or heightened understanding: scale, complexity, and the greater quantity of information imposes ever stronger demands on citizens' capacities.

As a result, one of the imperative needs of democratic countries is to improve citizens' capacities to engage intelligently in political life. I don't mean to suggest that the institutions for civic education developed in the nineteenth and twentieth centuries should be abandoned. But I do believe that in the years to come these older institutions will need to be enhanced by new means for civic education, political participation, information, and deliberation that draw creatively on the array of techniques and technologies available in the twenty-first century. We have barely begun to think seriously about these possibilities, much less to test them out in small-scale experiments.

Will democratic countries, whether old, new, or in transition, rise to these challenges and to others they will surely confront? If they fail to do so, the gap between democratic ideals and democratic realities, already large, will grow even greater and an era of democratic triumph will be followed by an era of democratic deterioration and decline.

Throughout the twentieth century, democratic countries never lacked for critics who confidently announced that democracy was in crisis, in grave peril, even doomed. Well, probably it was, at times, in grave peril. But it was not, after all, doomed. Pessimists, it turned out, were all too ready to give up on democracy. Confounding their dire predictions, experience revealed that once democratic institutions were firmly established in a country, they would prove to be remarkably sturdy and resilient. Democracies revealed an unexpected capacity for coping with the problems they confronted— inelegantly and imperfectly, true, but satisfactorily.

If the older democracies confront and overcome their challenges in the twenty-first century, they just might transform themselves, at long last, into truly advanced democracies. The success of the advanced democracies would then provide a beacon for all, throughout the world, who believe in democracy.

CHAPTER 16

Continuing the Journey?

The Arab spring that erupted in 2010 forced dictators from power in Tunisia, Egypt, Libya, and Yemen in quick succession. Waves of protest spread across the Middle East, prompting widespread comparisons to the collapse of communism that had snowballed through Eastern Europe and dismembered the Soviet Union two decades earlier. It was the biggest burst of democratic enthusiasm since the historic transition that had replaced South Africa's Apartheid regime with a democratically elected government in 1994. Democracy seemed once again to be on the march.

By 2014, the picture was more sobering, underscoring Dahl's caution that democratic progress is seldom linear. The prospects still looked good in Tunisia and somewhat more shakily in Yemen. But Libya was a failed state, Iraq seemed to be becoming one, and Syria's protests had evolved into a civil war and then a humanitarian catastrophe. Egypt's military had ousted its elected government and anointed a general as president in dubiously democratic elections. No other authoritarian regime in the region showed signs of democratizing any time soon. Rather than the Europe of 1989, commentators were reaching instead for comparisons with 1830 and 1848, when democratic revolutions across the European continent had also been stillborn.

Dahl also reminded us that, for all democracy's setbacks, the longer-term picture has been one of democratic advance. In 1998 he identified 65 democracies out of a total of 192 countries in the world, a ratio he found encouraging. He noted that there are various ways to measure democracy, and some regimes are difficult to classify (see Appendix D). Nonetheless, the overall picture continues to be encouraging despite the recent democratic failures. By most measures the number of democracies today outstrips the non-democracies, even if billions of the world's people continue to live under authoritarian rule.

This raises the question: Can we expect more countries to democratize? It is difficult to answer, and distinguished political scientists have been dramatically wrong about it in the past. In 1984, when the number of democracies in the world numbered in the low thirties, Samuel Huntington voiced the conventional wisdom by saying that it was unlikely that there would be many more.[1] That prediction turned out to be wrong by orders of magnitude. Can we do better?

Today, scholars generally distinguish the prospects for transitions to democracy from the likelihood that democracies, once established, will survive. We refer to the latter as democratic consolidation. We have much more confidence in what we can say about the second subject than the first. This is partly because the conditions that make for a successful transition often depend on obviously unpredictable contingencies. It seems highly unlikely that South Africa would have enjoyed a successful transition to democracy between 1990 and 1994 had it not been for the remarkable leadership skills of African National Congress leader Nelson Mandela and South Africa's president F. W. De Klerk, not to mention propitious external factors such as the disappearance of communism as a serious force in Sub-Saharan Africa by the late 1980s.[2] This made democracy less terrifying to white South African elites, many of whom began to realize that the end of Apartheid need not mean its replacement by something resembling Cuba.

Moreover, the South African transition would likely have collapsed midstream had either Mandela or De Klerk been assassinated during the transition negotiations, as Yitzhak Rabin was by a disgruntled right-wing extremist when he came close to concluding a promising settlement between Israelis and Palestinians in November 1995.[3] If King Juan Carlos of Spain, who succeeded Francisco Franco as head of state in 1975, had not turned out to be a closet reformer, it seems unlikely that Spanish democracy would so easily have been restored. Juan Carlos's actions would surely have surprised Franco, who had named him as the future head of state six years earlier. Other examples could be given. The general point is that it seems implausible that we will ever be able to predict democratic transitions, given their vital dependence on contingencies of this sort.

However, we understand more about what makes democracies survive. For a long time political scientists, following Alexis de Tocqueville, maintained that political culture was an important factor in democracy's viability. This is difficult to establish empirically, however. Dahl's view was not that culture per se is important but rather that a pluralist culture depends on crosscutting cleavages of interest within the population. On this, he agreed with James Madison's argument in *Federalist* Number 10 that a single "majority faction" is bad for democracy because it means that the minority has no reason to accept the result.[4] But if there are many intersecting cleavages, then those who lose in one election have reason to think they might prevail later—perhaps as part of a different coalition. Unlike the economist Kenneth Arrow, for whom the instability of majority rule was a problem in pluralist societies, Dahl's Madisonian insight was that it is actually an advantage.[5] It keeps majorities fluid in ways that stop politics from becoming winner-take-all contests in which losers might as well reach for their guns.

Madison was right that enduring factions would not emerge within a perfectly homogenous population whose members had the same interests, beliefs, and values, but it is worth pausing to note that, even in that limiting case, majority rule would render prevailing arrangements potentially unstable. Game theorists have long been aware that any allocation of a divisible good—say a dollar—can be upended by majority rule so long as there is open-ended iteration. If Anna and Beth agree to split the dollar equally, giving Cleo nothing, she can respond in a future round by proposing a different split—perhaps sixty/forty—to Anna or Beth, either one of whom can then find a majority partner to upend the new status quo. And so on, ad infinitum. Even if all three agreed on an equal division, any two might form a majority coalition to change this—dividing the dollar among themselves at the expense of the third. Notice that this logic assumes nothing about motivation. People might upset the status quo to get more for themselves, but they could also do it to advance a particular conception of justice or fairness.

The divide-a-dollar result is general and carries the implication that any possible distribution of a divisible good is potentially unstable under majority rule. But it is a desirable kind of instability in that it gives everyone a reason to remain in the system, create coalitions in support of the outcomes they favor, and try to stop others from pulling their coalitions apart. In this sense, the perpetual instability of majority rule actually reinforces democracy in pluralist societies.

The danger derives from the presence of indivisible goods, like ethnicity, race, or religion, in the politicized mix. If they become dominant sources of political mobilization, overwhelming the divisible goods, then politics is more likely to be experienced as—and to become—winner-take-all. In the former Yugoslavia, for instance, relatively high levels of ethnic intermarriage and concomitant social integration did not prevent destructive ethnic conflict from erupting once the country was split into states in which citizenship was defined by reference to the majority national group in each former republic. Indeed, the highest levels of violence occurred in what had previously been the most integrated areas, as people found that they were either noncitizens or second-class citizens in lands they had inhabited all their lives.

Israel's Jewish public identity has had comparable consequences for Palestinians and Israeli Arabs, who are for all practical purposes second-class citizens. Their low rates of political participation reflect alienation from what, for them, must be the oxymoronic identity of a "Jewish democracy." The lesson of the seventeenth-century wars of religion is that it is best to take indivisible goods off the political table. If the church is disestablished, there are less likely to be religious battles over the commanding heights of the state.

A good deal of attention has also been paid to the role played by institutions in maintaining democracy. It is often assumed, for example, that constitutional arrangements and, especially, independent courts are important. Dahl was always skeptical of these claims, and his skepticism has turned out to be well founded. It is difficult to show that constitutional arrangements, including the existence of independent judiciaries, have much—if anything—to do with democracy's viability. This is not to say that institutions are irrelevant. It seems, for instance, that all else equal presidential systems of the sort that are common in Latin America are somewhat less stable than the parliamentary systems that prevail in Western Europe. But the differences are not great, and can be mitigated by such factors as a strong presence of the president's party in the legislature.[6] Many presidential systems—including the American one—have been stable for long periods of time.

The bulk of the story for democratic survival seems to be economic. Specifically, if per capita income (PCI) reaches and remains above about $13,000 (measured in 2014 dollars), an existing democracy will likely survive indefinitely. But as PCI falls below that threshold, democracy becomes vulnerable, and the further it falls, the more vulnerable democracy becomes. PCI seems to matter much more than inequality. Democracy survives in some of the most unequal countries in the world as measured by the Gini coefficient, a standard measure of inequality. These include much-celebrated new democracies such as Brazil and South Africa. It is unclear whether democracy could endure in less socially and economically diversified unequal countries like Saudi Arabia, for reasons I take up below. But the general finding seems to be robust: PCI matters more for democratic consolidation than do inequality, institutions, culture, or other variables that have been studied.

Why democracy survives in comparatively rich countries is an interesting question, to which answers are mainly speculative. Some suggest that in wealthy countries, both the rich and the poor have reasons to maintain democracy—if it exists—over support for a coup. Seymour Martin Lipset said more than half a century ago, "If there is enough wealth in the country so that it does not make too much difference whether redistribution takes place, it is easier to accept the idea that it does not matter too much which side is in power. But if loss of office means serious losses for major groups, they will seek to retain office by any means available."[7] And if there is wealth to redistribute, the poor are less likely to reach the point at which Karl Marx and Friedrich Engels predicted that they would become revolutionary—when they have "nothing to lose but their chains."[8]

There might be something to arguments of this sort, but they rest on large assumptions about just how "the rich" and "the poor" translate their economic preferences into effective political action.

As the divide-a-dollar story reminds us, majoritarian electoral politics creates the possibility of cross-class coalitions. These can occur in poor countries as well as rich ones. This means that, if we are to understand the links between the economy and democratic consolidation, more must be said about the incentives facing those who are in a position to destroy the democratic order should they choose to do so.

Democracy depends minimally, but vitally, on the willingness of office-holders to give up power when they lose an election. This, in turn, means that there must be reasonably appealing alternatives to holding political office. Poor countries tend to be marked by winner-take-all (and, hence, loser-lose-all) politics, whereas richer democracies offer other opportunities to formerly employed political elites. When George Herbert Walker Bush lost the presidency in 1992, he could go onto corporate boards, create foundations, and get wealthier than he could ever have done had he remained in office. Sending the tanks down Pennsylvania Avenue is scarcely worth contemplating in such circumstances. The practice of giving up power—known among political scientists as alternation—was by then so deeply entrenched in American politics that it would have been hard to imagine a losing candidate even considering a coup—even when, as with Al Gore and the Democrats in 2000, the losers believed that the election had been stolen.

The best predictor of alternation is alternation. Adam Przeworski has pointed out that it is hard for alternation to get going, but once it starts it becomes established fairly quickly.[9] This raises the question: How did alternation become established in the United States in the first place? It is difficult to read the historical literature on the early American republic without concluding that the prospects for alternation in America's critical first few elections depended substantially on the low appeal that politics held for George Washington, John Adams, Thomas Jefferson, Aaron Burr, and James Madison, especially in light of the more lucrative and appealing ways in which they could spend their time. Even at that early stage, the American polity and economy offered elites opportunities that dampened the costs of losing office.[10] It probably did not hurt that Washington, D.C., remained a dismal city surrounded by malaria-infested swamps for many decades after the government moved there from Philadelphia in 1800.

This reasoning suggests a mechanism for why democracy often struggles to survive in single-commodity export economies (the "oil curse"), where access to the levers of political power is often vital to the continuing well-being of elites. In such settings, even if PCI reaches levels that are expected to make democracy sustainable, it might nonetheless be vulnerable to a coup by those who fear losing power or who find themselves in a position to grab it. In this line of thinking, the diversification of the economy matters more than inequality, and perhaps even as much as PCI. What counts is the extent to which everyone's eggs are in the same basket. If they are, then the incentive to fight over access to the basket is high. Politics all too easily becomes a zero-sum battle for monopoly control of the commanding heights of the economy.

Like Madison before him, Dahl was right that diversification of factional interests serves democracy best when interests multiply and intersect with one another. As with the disappointed competitors whose team has just lost the World Series, losers in democratic competition need to be able to tell themselves—and believe—that there's always next year. This requires that most people believe there is going to be another season. If the economy is in shambles or in the corrupt control of a few, then it seems unlikely that people will give up political power when they hold it or resist the temptation to grab it when they can.

The moral of the story is that the prospects for democratic consolidation will grow for any country if it builds and sustains a diversified economy that disperses opportunities among different sectors of the population and renders people less dependent on access to political power for their survival and success. The recent calls, at the UN Conference on Sustainable Development held in Rio de Janeiro in 2012 and elsewhere, for broad-based inclusive economic growth that ranges over multiple economic sectors are therefore on the right track. Apart from the considerable economic benefits that they promise, inclusive growth strategies increase the odds that when democracy gets a foothold, it will survive.

CHAPTER 17

Democracy and Inequality

I noted in the last chapter that highly unequal countries can survive as democracies. They can hold elections that are widely seen as free and fair. These elections might offer genuine possibilities for alternation. The media might be free enough of censorship and other forms of government interference for people to have genuinely independent sources of information. Robust civic and political freedoms might ensure meaningful liberty to criticize government policies and try to get them changed. These are all important features of democracy, as anyone who has lived in a country where they are missing, or seriously threatened, will attest.

Dahl agreed, but he also argued that beyond a certain point, inequality undermines the quality of democracy. If small minorities get disproportionate control over the political process as a result of their wealth, then his requirement that everyone should have an equal ability to influence the political agenda becomes compromised. Dahl's worries about the political effects of inequality grew in the years after he published *On Democracy*, when his main concern about the older democracies had been whether they would "perfect and deepen" their democracy. Deepening, for Dahl, had meant extending democratic governance to other spheres of collective life, notably the economy.

But in the early part of the new century Dahl began to worry that inequality might compromise basic democratic institutions.

By the time he published his last book, *On Political Equality*, in 2006, Dahl was openly wondering whether inequality might soon become so extreme as to "push some countries—including the United States—below the threshold at which we regard them as 'democratic.'" When he wrote that, economic inequality had been increasing in the United States for three decades. The Gini coefficient had grown from under 0.4 in the early 1970s to almost 0.5, making the United States the most unequal of the advanced capitalist democracies.

We know now that in 2006 the world was living in a bubble. It burst two years later, producing the sharpest recession since the Great Depression. Millions lost jobs and millions more were unable to find them. Real estate values plummeted and wages stagnated. Major companies like Lehman Brothers, Chrysler, and General Motors went bankrupt. Massive investment banks like Merrill Lynch were forced into overnight mergers at the cost of tens of billions of dollars to avoid the same fate. Many of these events would have been unthinkable weeks—in some cases, days or even hours—before they happened. Untold billions vanished from the portfolios of America's wealthiest individuals. At the time it looked as if a major reordering of economic fortunes might be in the cards.

But, unlike the decades that followed the Great Depression, the United States did not see an enduring reduction in inequality after 2006. The great bulk of the wealth that had been lost at the top was restored within five years. This was partly due to the federal government's quick bailouts of major financial, insurance, and auto companies, and partly because financial markets soon recovered from the steep losses of the 2008 crash—also with substantial government help in the form of trillions of dollars of cheap money plowed into the economy by the Federal Reserve. And because lower and middle incomes continued to stagnate, the longer-term trend of growing inequality resumed. In January 2014, Oxfam reported that the wealthiest 1 percent of Americans had captured 95 percent of the postfinancial crisis growth while the bottom 90 percent had become poorer since 2009.[1] Study after study reveals that inequality now exceeds the levels of the Gilded Age in the late nineteenth century.[2] Dahl's concern has not been rendered moot by events.

One way in which economic inequality undermines democracy is when money is used to influence electoral politics. In its 1976 decision in *Buckley v. Valeo*, the Supreme Court ruled that Congress could regulate contributions to political campaigns. But the justices also equated money with speech protected by the First Amendment, a fateful decision that they deployed to justify prohibiting the regulation of political "expenditures." Dismissing concerns that expenditures promote corruption (on the grounds that there is no quid-pro-quo relationship if the funds are not given to a campaign), the justices held that any restraints on expenditures unacceptably limit free expression. They insisted that protecting that freedom is more important than "equalizing the relative ability of individuals and groups to influence the outcome of elections." Even when wealthy individuals finance their own campaigns, the First Amendment "simply cannot tolerate" any restriction on a candidate's freedom "to speak without legislative limit on behalf of his own candidacy."[3] *Buckley* opened the floodgates to unlimited spending in electoral politics, sanctified by the fig leaf that allows campaign commercials to be copied verbatim by groups and individuals engaged in "expenditures."

In 2010, the Court extended *Buckley* to corporations in *Citizens United v. Federal Election Commission.*[4] Shortly thereafter, the D.C. Court of Appeals extended the proscription to cover contributions to advocacy groups in *SpeechNow.org v. Federal Election Commis-*

sion.[5] This led to the birth and rapid growth of a new creature, the "independent expenditure only" political action committee, or Super PAC.[6] One of the few remaining limits to contributions fell four years later, when the Court struck down limits on aggregate contributions, which had stood at $117,200 per election cycle, with the implication that a single donor can now give some $3.5 million per election cycle divided among candidates, PACs, and parties.[7] Moreover, although *Citizens United* allows Congress to require the disclosure of corporate political expenditures, prior Court decisions and rulings by the Federal Election Commission have made this all but unenforceable.[8] The net effect, first seen in the 2012 elections, is that unlimited amounts can be spent, much of it anonymously, by corporations as well as individuals to shape election results.

Citizens United is a troubling threat to democracy, but the underlying problem is *Buckley*'s insistence that money is speech. The answer to this, as Justice Byron White said in his dissent at the time, is that money is not speech. Money is money. And it is a vital resource for competing in elections. The decision to regulate expenditures reflected "a considered judgment of Congress that elections are to be decided among candidates none of whom has overpowering advantage by reason of a huge campaign war chest."[9]

Buckley alleged that limiting how much money people can spend on political communication during a campaign "necessarily" restricts "the number of issues discussed" or "the depth of their exploration."[10] Far from being a necessary truth, this dubious claim ignores what happens when many millions of dollars are spent to support (or attack) a candidate or policy, saturating the relevant media markets and drowning out competing views. Saturation spending might actually reduce the number of issues discussed or the depth of their exploration. People have finite capacities to listen. Those with massive war chests can decide unilaterally whether they will be deployed to add issues to the agenda and promote in-depth discussion or, conversely, to drown out opposing views and engage in attack-ad character assassination.

The spillover effects of opening these floodgates in the United States should stand as a warning to others. Public financing of campaigns has fallen by the wayside as candidates, trapped in the arms-race logic of fundraising, find that they cannot bind themselves to the voluntary limits that come with accepting public funds. The billion-dollar threshold crossed by Barack Obama and Mitt Romney in the 2012 presidential election is a likely harbinger of the future, as are Senate campaigns in the tens of millions and the need for House members, facing reelection every two years, to run permanent fundraising machines.[11] Even if some version of compulsory public funding could pass constitutional muster in the post-*Buckley* era (surely a nonstarter), this would not address the limitless expenditures that Buckley authorizes and the more recent decisions amplify.

The reality is that it would require a constitutional amendment to undo the damage to American democracy wrought by the Supreme Court in this area over the past four decades. Though many politicians would benefit from such a change, there are huge collective action obstacles to their getting behind it. This is to say nothing of the monied interests that would throw their weight behind maintaining a new status quo that so substantially increases their political clout.

Second, inequality also affects who participates in politics. Nolan McCarty, Keith Poole, and Howard Rosenthal have shown, for the United States, that the concentration of income and wealth at the top and the growth of a low-paid class at the bottom skews the incentives for politicians in both parties away from the interests of the poor. The reason is that poor people vote in comparatively low numbers, whereas the rich participate both directly by voting and indirectly by giving money to campaigns and political causes. The net effect is that as inequality increases, the policies of both parties shift to the right. This happened during the Gilded Age; it declined steadily as inequality fell in the middle part of the twentieth century; and it has returned with the resurgence of inequality driven by increased immigration and lopsided income growth at the top since the 1960s.[12]

This problem could perhaps be mitigated to a degree by compulsory voting. Turnout is somewhat higher in countries like Australia that mandate voting, and it seems reasonable to think that this supplies political parties with incentives to attend to broader swaths of the electorate. Whether a systematic study of the ten or so countries that enforce compulsory voting would confirm this conjecture is an open question.[13] In any case it would not deal with the failures to regulate the role of private money in electoral politics, which, perhaps surprisingly, is extensive and lightly regulated in Australia. So long as politicians need money, those who are in a position to give or withhold it will be able to get, and keep, their attention.

A third major way in which money matters in democratic politics has to do with the complexity of the political system. This problem, too, is particularly acute in the United States. I noted in my preface that Dahl was skeptical that the separation of powers system designed by the American founders would do the work that they hoped it would. The system of multiple vetoes they created was intended to make change difficult, as it did. Making change difficult is one way to protect important constitutional guarantees that might otherwise fall victim to the whims of tyrannous majorities—though as I noted, Dahl was right that there is scant evidence of this being a significant problem in democracies. Making change difficult does not make it impossible, however. And in a world in which political action requires resources, those who have them are more likely to be able to achieve change—or shape its direction— than those who lack resources.

Consider a contrast between the minimum wage and legislation that affects the well-to-do. The minimum wage has steadily been eroded by inflation in recent decades, yet Democrats have found it difficult to enact minimum wage increases. They have never managed to override the blocking power of their Republican adversaries to get it indexed for inflation, which would solve the problem.[14] By contrast, the alternative minimum tax, which limits the deductions available to higher-income taxpayers, has been amended eleven times since 1986 to avoid bracket creep, and in 2013 it was indexed for inflation.[15] The threshold for paying estate taxes has also seen significant increases in recent years. It, too, was indexed for inflation in 2013.[16] In short, status-quo bias is not neutral; it works to the systematic advantage of those with the resources to keep the pressure up on politicians and pay the rents that they are in a position to extract for doing the benefactors' bidding.

Institutional complexity also works to the disproportionate benefit of the well resourced by fostering opacity. This allows those who understand the system to exploit, and sometimes even create, principal-agent problems in the bureaucracy and between bureaucrats and politicians. This was well illustrated during the 2009–2010 battle over the Dodd-Frank financial regulation bill passed by Congress in response to the financial crisis. Intense financial sector lobbying weakened the bill in various ways as it worked its way through Congress, but there was one area in which public sentiment was strong enough to force politicians to resist: the ban on proprietary trading. Investment banks had been free to trade on their own accounts since the 1999 repeal of the Glass-Steagall Act (itself the achievement of an effective multiyear lobbying campaign).[17] This was widely seen as having worsened the crisis, contributing to the perception that bankers had to be reined in.

Former Federal Reserve chairman Paul Volker championed a reintroduction of the ban on proprietary trading, which eventually prevailed despite stiff industry opposition. But once it became obvious that some version of the Volker rule would survive in the final bill, lobbyists pushed for strings of exceptions that would make it all but unenforceable.[18] They also lobbied for much of the detail to be deferred to the implementation stage and then deluged the rule writers with tens of thousands of comments and objections that made meaningful rule-writing all but impossible.[19] When the 867-page rule was finally adopted (more than two years late) in December 2013, it was still beset by more than eighteen hundred outstanding questions and what *Forbes* magazine described as hundreds of pages "full of loopholes for the well-paid lawyers from Sullivan & Cromwell, Cleary Gottlieb, Skadden Arps and the other $1,400 an hour attorneys to interpret favorably for Goldman Sachs and J.P. Morgan Chase."[20] Shortly after the bill passed, I asked a partner at a major investment bank whether they were now out of the proprietary trading business. His reply: "It will be at least five years before we will know whether we have managed to kill that part."

That is a sobering note to end on. It underscores the prescience of Dahl's worry about the corrupting effects of inequality on democratic politics. It also suggests that Dahl perhaps understated things when he said that judicial review provides no additional civic protections over and above those achieved by democracy. In this area the Court's decisions since *Buckley* have ushered in decades of cumulative corrosion of democratic politics by money that shows no signs of abating. It is no small irony that it is the United States Supreme Court that has fostered this result by repeatedly striking down as unconstitutional laws passed by the people's elected representatives. In this area at least, judicial review subverts democracy, reinforcing the disproportionate political power of the monied few.

On Electoral Systems

If you would like to learn more about electoral systems, a good place to start is *The International IDEA Handbook of Electoral System Design,* edited by Andrew Reynolds and Ben Reilly (Stockholm: International Institute for Democracy and Electoral Assistance, 1997).

It divides "the world of electoral systems" into three main families: Plurality-Majority systems, Proportional Representation (PR) systems, and Semi-PR systems. First-Past-the-Post (FPTP, which I compared with PR in Chapter 11) is just one of four types of Plurality-Majority systems. Others include the Alternative Vote (AV) system (also known as Preferential Voting) and the Two Round system used in France.

Although the Alternative Vote system is used only in Australia (and in modified form in the Pacific island state of Nauru), some political scientists strongly support it. Under this system, candidates may be chosen from single-member districts as in FPTP. But unlike as in FPTP, voters rank the candidates—one for their first choice, two for second, three for third, and so on. If no candidate wins a majority of votes, the candidate with the lowest total is eliminated and the second preferences of the voters are then counted. This continues until a candidate wins 50 percent of the votes. The French Two Round system is intended to achieve a similar result. Both avoid the potential defect in FPTP: if more than two candidates contest a seat, the seat might be won by a candidate whom a majority of voters would reject if they were given the choice. In effect, AV gives them that opportunity.

PR systems fall into three groups. Far and away the most common is the List system, under which voters choose candidates from lists provided by political parties; the number of candidates elected is strictly related to the proportion of votes cast for the candidate's party. Under the Mixed Member Proportional system used in Germany, Italy, and more recently New Zealand, some candidates, for example half, are chosen from a national PR list and the others from single-member districts. Thus, its advocates contend, the List system provides some of the proportionality of PR but, like FPTP, is more likely than a pure PR system to produce a parliamentary majority.

One PR system often advocated by political scientists but rarely used (the exception is Ireland, where it has been employed since 1921) is the Single Transferable Vote system (STV). As with the Alternative Vote described above, voters rank the candidates. But unlike AV, STV is employed in *multimember districts*. Following a method of counting votes too complex to describe here, STV insures that the seats in the multimember districts will be won by the most highly ranked candidates and produces an approximately proportional distribution of seats among the political parties. Although voters in Ireland seem satisfied with STV, its complexity has probably discouraged its use elsewhere.

The handbook describes nine systems and their consequences. In addition, it also provides sage "Advice for Electoral System Designers." Some of the precepts it offers (followed by short explanations) are:

- Keep it simple.
- Don't be afraid to innovate.

- Err on the side of inclusion.
- Build legitimacy and acceptance among all key actors.
- Try to maximize voter influence.
- But balance that against encouraging coherent political parties.

That a rather large number of alternative electoral systems exist suggests three observations. First, if a democratic country happens to have an electoral system that ill suits its needs, the country should replace it. Second, the electoral system of a country can probably be tailored to its particular features—historical, traditional, cultural, and so on. Third, before a country adopts a new electoral system (or decides to retain the existing one), the alternatives should be carefully explored with the aid of competent experts on electoral systems.

Political Accommodation in Culturally or Ethnically Divided Countries

Arrangements in democratic countries designed to secure a satisfactory degree of political accommodation among different subcultures fall roughly into two types, "consociational democracy" and electoral arrangements:

Consociational democracies result in the formation of *grand coalitions* of political leaders *after* elections under PR electoral systems that insure each subculture a share of seats in the legislature roughly proportional to the relative size of its vote. The leading authority on this subject is Arend Lijphart, who provides an overview in *Democracy in Plural Societies: A Comparative Exploration* (New Haven and London: Yale University Press, 1977, chap. 3, 53–103).

Systems of consociational democracy have existed in Switzerland, in Belgium, in the Netherlands from about 1917 to the 1970s, and in Austria from 1945 to 1966. The subcultural patterns and the political arrangements for gaining consensus are (were) different in each country. The *Swiss* differ among themselves in their native tongue (German, French, Italian, and Romanch), religion (Protestant, Catholic), and canton. The differences in language and religion to some extent cut across one another: some German-speakers are Protestant and some are Catholic, while some French-speakers are Catholic and some are Protestant. These crosscutting differences have mitigated conflicts over language and religion, which have been almost nonexistent in modern Switzerland. The smaller cantons, however, are typically fairly homogeneous with respect to both language and religion. This has come about both by history and by design. Although the Swiss consensual political arrangements are mainly prescribed by the constitution of the Swiss Confederacy, they are also strongly supported, it appears, by Swiss attitudes and political culture.

In *Belgium* separate parties first developed around three subcultures: Catholic, Liberal, and Socialist. In time, these parties split even further over a difference in language that was partly regional as well, since French was predominant in Wallonia and Flemish in Flanders. Demands for greater autonomy for the subcultures led to extensive federalization, with separate regional and linguistic public authorities and a special status for the bilingual capital, Brussels. It was also standard practice to maintain a strict parity between Flemings and Walloons in forming federal cabinets.

In *the Netherlands*, a long tradition of elite-accommodation, which first took root in the confederal Dutch Republic (1579–1795), facilitated the development of separate subcultures of Liberals, Calvinists, Catholics, and Socialists, which penetrated practically all relationships and activities, from politics to marriage, neighborhood, clubs, trade unions, newspapers, and others. The chief lines of division around which these subcultures developed were religion and class. In 1917 a national compromise resulted in the granting of full financial parity of religious schools and public schools, universal suffrage, and a system of strong proportional representation, which further strengthened the separate ideological families. Although these political practices did not normally result in all-party coalitions, they did provide for collegial decision-making, mutual recognition of minority interests, and autonomous group rights, and at the same time they also produced relatively effective government.

The Dutch system became the prototype of the consociational democracy model described in 1968 in Arend Lijphart's influential analysis, *The Politics of Accommodation: Pluralism and Democracy in the Netherlands* (Berkeley: University of California Press). By then, however, the subcultures were already becoming less distinctive, as the Socialists were increasingly integrated into the national system and the two religious subcultures underwent far-reaching secularization. But established collegial practices and a general respect for autonomous group claims have generally persisted.

Successful consociational democracies are rare, doubtless because the conditions that make them workable are rare. Criticisms of consociationalism as a solution in divided societies are that: (1) in many culturally divided countries, the favorable (perhaps even necessary) conditions for its success are too frail or entirely absent; (2) consociational arrangements greatly reduce the important role of *opposition* in democratic government; and (3) some critics worry that mutual vetoes and the need for consensus might lead to excessive deadlock. However, the experience of the Netherlands and some other one-time consociational systems casts doubt on the validity of the second criticism and clearly belies the third.

Some political scientists argue that a possible alternative would be to construct electoral arrangements that provide strong incentives for political leaders to build enduring *electoral* coalitions *before* and *during* parliamentary or presidential elections (see, for example, Donald L. Horowitz, *Ethnic Groups in Conflict* [Berkeley: University of California Press, 1985], and *A Democratic South Africa? Constitutional Engineering in a Divided Society* [Berkeley: University of California Press, 1991]). How this may best be achieved is, however, far from evident. Clearly FPTP is the least desirable system because it may allow one group to gain such an overwhelming majority of seats as to make negotiation, compromise, and coalition-formation unnecessary. Some observers find merit in the Alternative Vote system described in Appendix A. *Distribution requirements* might compel candidates for the presidential office to gain a minimum percentage of votes from more than one main subculture or ethnic group. (However, in Kenya, despite the requirement that "to be elected president a candidate had to receive at least 25% of the vote in at least five out of eight provinces . . . , in 1992 a divided opposition allowed Daniel Arap Moi to become President with only 35% of the vote" [*The International IDEA Handbook of Electoral System Design*, edited by Andrew Reynolds and Ben Reilly (Stockholm: International Institute for Democracy and Electoral Assistance, 1997), 1090].) Or major offices might be distributed among the main ethnic groups according to a fixed formula to which they have all agreed. However, none of these guarantee a permanent end to divisive cultural conflicts. Ingenious arrangements that brought stability for a time in Lebanon, Nigeria, and Sri Lanka all broke down under the strain of ethnic conflict into civil war or authoritarian rule.

One conclusion seems inescapable: there are no *general* solutions to the problems of culturally divided countries. Every solution will need to be custom tailored to the features of each country.

On Counting Democratic Countries

How many democratic countries are there? Where would a specific nation, such as your own, fit on a scale running, say, from "democracy" to "autocracy"?

Although few readers of this book, I imagine, will feel that they have much need for a precise, well-based, and up-to-date count of the number of democratic countries in the world, some might well wish to find an answer to the second question. Yet to find that answer may require an answer to the first.

And that is not easy. For it is one thing to say that a democratic country must possess all the institutions of polyarchy described in Chapter 8, but it is quite another to judge whether they do exist in a particular country. To conclude that a country is democratic, in the sense of possessing the political institutions of polyarchal democracy, requires at least two judgments: that the institutions *actually exist* in the country and that they exist at or above some *lower limit or threshold* below which we would want to say that the country is not democratic. A huge supply of information about the countries of the world provided by independent observers helps greatly in arriving at the first judgment. The second is trickier, and somewhat arbitrary. One solution is to assume that the threshold is roughly set by the level existing in the European and English-speaking countries—the older democracies. Implicitly or explicitly, this, I believe, is the standard solution. We judge a country to be "democratic" only if the major democratic political institutions exist there at a comparable level.

In recent years many scholars and research organizations have tried to reach reasonably well grounded judgments as to the countries that do or not satisfactorily meet democratic criteria. In doing so, they have often used similar but not identical criteria. Fortunately, the results tend to agree, even though drawing the exact boundary between "democracy" and "nondemocracy" is a bit arbitrary.

To illustrate, I'll mention three such efforts. A table in my work *Democracy and Its Critics* (New Haven and London: Yale University Press, 1989) shows the growth in the number of polyarchal democracies from 1850 to 1979, and I've drawn on that table for figure 1 (p.8). Another table from that work (table 17.3, p.241) classifies 168 countries, circa 1981–1985, into seven categories ranging from full polyarchies, where four of the major democratic political institutions exist, to extreme authoritarian regimes in which none exist. Both tables were based on work by Michael Coppedge and Wolfgang Reinicke, who used the best information available to judge the relative level in each country for each of four basic democratic institutions: free and fair elections, freedom of expression, alternative and independent sources of information, and associational autonomy. They explain their method in "Measuring Polyarchy," in *Studies in Comparative International Development* 25, 1 (Spring 1990): 51–72; it involves an enormous amount of careful research and has not been repeated. (Coppedge, however, briefly describes the scale and fruitfully employs the earlier rankings in "Modernization and Thresholds of Democracy: Evidence for a Common Path," in *Inequality, Democracy, and Economic Development,* edited by Manus I. Midlarsky [Cambridge: Cambridge University Press, 1997], 177–201.)

A different useful source that is readily available and current is the annual publication by the nonpartisan organization Freedom

House, *Freedom in the World: The Annual Survey of Political Rights and Civil Liberties, 1996–1997*. If you have access to the Internet you will find their list of countries at: http://www.freedomhouse.org/political/frtable1.htm. The Freedom House ratings rank countries on two scales, each of which runs from most free (1) to least free (7), one for Political Rights and the other for Civil Liberties. When I counted all the countries that ranked 1, or most free, on Political Rights, and 1, 2, or 3 on Civil Liberties, I found that 56 countries met both criteria and all, I think, fit well with other judgments about democratic institutions in these countries. However, neither India, Brazil, nor Russia reached these levels: Freedom House ranks India 2 on Political Rights and 4 on Civil Liberties, Russia 3 on Political Rights and 4 on Civil Liberties. If we were to include them, the total would amount to 58 countries.

Another source is an analysis in 1994 of 157 countries at the University of Colorado, which maintains Polity III.

The 157 countries are scored on a 10-point democracy scale (0 = low, 10 = high) and a 10-point autocracy scale (0 = low, 10 = high). Of these, 65 countries are assigned an Autocracy score of 0 and a democracy score of 8, 9, or 10. It is this total that is shown for 1990 in figure 1. Yet although we might reasonably choose to call all these countries "democratic," we could still judge them to be "democratic" in varying degrees, so to speak. Thus we could classify the thirty-five countries that score 10 on the democracy scale as the "most democratic," the seven scoring 9 as "fairly democratic," and the twenty-three scoring 8 as "marginally democratic."

Polity III, however, omits most of the microstates, tiny countries like San Marino (population 24,000) or small islands in the Caribbean and the Pacific, like Barbados (population 256,000) and Micronesia (population 123,000). Yet on the Freedom House scale San Marino, Barbados, and Micronesia are all ranked at the top in both Political Rights and Civil Liberties and thus deserve to be regarded as among the "most democratic" countries.

In sum: although a complete, reliable, and current count of all the democratic countries in the world appears to be unavailable, the two sources allow fairly good estimates. Perhaps of more importance for most readers of this book, the two sources will enable you to see how independent experts rank a particular country on measures directly relevant to democracy.

On Counting Democratic Countries II

Political scientists and sociologists have developed a number of ways to assess empirically whether a country is democratic.

One of the first and most influential systematic attempts to identify specific attributes of democratic regimes is due to Dahl (1971). He developed a measure of "polyarchy" based on what he considered to be the two main dimensions of democratization: opportunities to participate in elections and opportunities to compete for political power. With data for 1969, he used ten indicators of what he considered to be the seven institutional requirements for democracy.[1] With these data he produced a scale that placed countries on a continuum ranging from the least to the greatest opportunity for participation and contestation. This measure was later extended for 1985 by Coppedge and Reinicke (1990).

Although these measures of democracy cover a large number of countries, they are limited to one or two years.[2] Today, there are three different measures of democracy that cover most, if not all, countries for a relatively large number of years. These are the measures that are used by most political scientists, sociologists, and economists who study empirically the causes and consequences of democratic regimes. They are:

- The Polity IV measures of political regime characteristics and transitions, which cover 1800 to 2012 (found at: http:// www.systemicpeace.org/polity/polity4.htm).

- The Freedom House (FH) measure of political and civil liberties, which covers all countries of the world between 1973 and 2014 (found at http://www.freedomhouse.org/).
- The classification of democracies and dictatorships developed by Przeworski et al. (2000) in *Democracy and Development* (DD), covering all countries in the world between 1946 and 2008.

Although similar in that they cover a large number of countries for a relatively large number of years, these measures differ in at least three important ways:

- the conception of democracy that underlies each of them;
- the nature of the data used to assess political regimes; and
- the type of measurement they develop.

As illustrated by the selections in Chapter 1, conceptions of democracy differ in terms of whether they adopt a strictly procedural view as opposed to a more substantive one. In the first case, democracy depends exclusively on the presence of certain institutions, with no reference to the kinds of outcomes that are generated by their operation. Thus, the authors of DD state that "'democracy' is a regime in which those who govern are selected through contested elections" (2000:15). Since they are interested in studying the relationship between democracy and normatively desirable aspects of political, social, and economic life, they need to define democracy narrowly so that they can avoid the tautology that a broader definition might imply (2000:14).

In substantive conceptions of democracy, institutions are seen as necessary but not sufficient to characterize a political regime. Although it may be that no democracy exists that does not have contested elections, not all regimes that are based on contested elections may be called democratic. What matters is that, through these elections, something else happens: the public good is achieved, citizen preferences are represented, governments become account-able, citizen participation in political life is maximized, economic equality is enhanced, rationality is implemented, economic condi-tions improve, and so on. Those who use FH, therefore, believe that the measure of "freedom" it offers can be used to indicate "de-mocracy." Similarly, Polity IV conceives of democracy as the pres-ence of institutions that allow citizens to choose alternative poli-cies and leaders, in combination with "institutionalized constraints on the exercise of power by the executive" and "the guarantee of civil liberties to all citizens in their daily lives and in acts of politi-cal participation" (manual, p. 14). Finally, Bollen (1980:372) defined democracy as "the extent to which the political power of the elite is minimized and that of the nonelite is maximized." In a later for-mulation, he stated that "it is the relative power between élites and nonélites that determines the degree of political democracy. Where the nonélites have little control over the élites, political democracy is low. When the élites are accountable to the nonélites, political democracy is higher" (Bollen 1991:4).

A second difference between the measures of democracy has to do with the type of information that is used, or required, to assess a political regime. Most measures are based on data that require largely subjective judgments by the coder. Thus, FH re-quires answers to the following questions, with no clear attempt to define what the relevant terms or qualifiers mean: Are there *fair* electoral laws, *equal* campaigning opportunities, *fair* polling, and *honest* tabulation of ballots? Are voters able to endow their representatives with *real* power? Do minorities have *reasonable* self-determination, self-government, autonomy, or participation through informal consensus in the decision-making process? Are the people *free from domination* by the military, foreign powers, totalitarian parties, religious hierarchies, economic oligarchies, or any other *powerful* group? Are there *free* and *independent* media? Are there *free* trade unions and other professional organizations, and is there *effective* collective bargaining? Is there *personal autonomy*? Is there *equality of opportunity*? Similarly, the Polity IV democracy scale requires one to decide whether constraints on the chief executive in any given country are close to *parity*, face *substantial limitations*, or are located in one of two possible *intermediate* categories.

The Polity IV approach contrasts with the one adopted by the authors of DD, who classify democracy on the basis of four observational criteria. Thus, for them, in order to be a democracy a regime has to have an elected executive, an elected legislature, elections in which two or more political parties compete, and incumbents who have lost power at least once. These rules unambiguously classify the vast majority of regimes in all countries in every year since 1946. They do not, however, account for a small proportion of cases where history has not yet provided the necessary information to apply the rules. Rather than creating "intermediate" categories to accommodate these cases, they decide to keep them separate and allow each user to decide how or whether to use them in their analysis.

Finally, measures of democracy differ as to the level at which they make the observation. Most measures are either continuous or, although categorical, transformed into a continuous scale. This is true of both Polity IV and FH. The former offers separate indices of democracy and autocracy (each ranging from 0 to 10), which are often combined into a 21-point scale for democracy (with high values indicating higher levels of democracy). The latter provides separate indicators of civil and political liberties (ranging from 1 to 7), which are often combined into a single measure of the degree of democracy, ranging from 2 (highest levels of democracy) to 14 (lowest levels of democracy). In contrast, DD classifies political regimes simply into two categories: democracies and dictatorships.

Among the debates that have engaged those who study democracy empirically, this is probably the one that has generated the highest level of controversy. The most forceful proponents of a continuous measure of democracy have been Bollen and Jackman (1989) who assert "the inherently continuous nature of the concept of political democracy" and claim that "since democracy is conceptually continuous, it is best measured in continuous terms" (1989:612) and that "democracy is always a matter of degree" (1989:618).

A different argument states that measures that allow for gradation should be preferred over dichotomies because they will contain more information, and that even though dichotomous measures may contain less error than continuous measures, they are less sensitive to variations in the underlying concept of democracy (Elkins 2000).

This issue has probably been blown out of proportion. The matter is not whether one should adopt a continuous or a categorical measure of democracy that is observable across all political regimes. The issue is whether there is a natural zero-point that divides democracies and nondemocracies. Even those who develop and use categorical measures of democracy may agree, given some appropriate criteria to use as a yardstick, that democratic regimes can differ as to how democratic they are, and that some measure to assess their degree of democracy may make sense. Note, however, that this refers to democratic regimes, as opposed to nondemocratic regimes. It assumes that some regimes fail whatever minimum requirement there is for them to be called democratic.

The belief that democracy is an attribute that can and should be measured over the spectrum of cases leads to assertions that may be absurd, for example, the claim that the level of democracy in Albania in 1950 and 1955, under the communist regime of Enver Hoxa, was, according to the Bollen scale, about 24 out of 100. The level of democracy in North Korea in 1960 and 1965 was about 21 according to Bollen, and it went down to 11 in 1980. The average score for Cuba between 1960 and 1999 was –7 in the Polity scale (which, as we know, has a minimum of –10). The level of democracy in Chile between 1974 and 1980, according to Bollen, was a low, but positive, 5.56; it averaged –7 according to the Polity scale and 11.6 according to the combined Freedom House scale. Singapore was more democratic than Cuba, scoring –2 as opposed to –7. Zaire under Mobuto, although almost close to the bottom, was not *at* the bottom of the Polity scale: often it scored a –9, but sometimes things improved and it scored –8; and according to the FH scale, its score ranged from the least democratic 14 to the somewhat more democratic 11. According to FH, South Africa under apartheid had scores that were similar to Russia since 1993, the Dominican Republic in the 1990s, postcommunist Albania and Romania, and Sri Lanka in the 1990s. Thus, if one believes that democracy can be continuously measured over all regimes, one has to be prepared to argue that it makes sense to speak of positive levels of democracy in places like Albania under Hoxa, North Korea, and Chile under Pinochet; that it makes sense to speak of a change from one value to another along these scales; and, finally, that we can meaningfully interpret scores across countries.

As for the informational content of different measures, it is not true that a continuous scale will necessarily contain more information than a dichotomous classification of political regime. The informational content of a measure depends on the way in which it is conceptualized and observed, at least as much as it depends on the level of measurement. What kind of information is being conveyed when we say that the level of democracy in Singapore in 1965 was 76.94 according to the Bollen scale? Or that the Burmese junta scored a –6 in the Polity scale? Which measure conveys more information: the one that says that North Korea scored 21.04 in Bollen's democracy scale in 1965, or the one that says that North Korea was a dictatorship in 1965 because leaders were not selected on the basis of contested elections?

Measures are only as good as their components. Consider the FH scale. It is based on answers to 8 questions for the political liberty scale and 14 for the civil liberty scale. Given the nature of the questions and information required, as seen above, these answers often require highly subjective judgment on the part of coders. Coders assign "raw points" ranging from 0 to 4 for each of those questions, for a maximum of 32 political rights points and 56 civil liberties points. Countries are then distributed into one of the seven categories that make up the final political and civil liberties scales according to the number of raw points they received. For example, a country with 28 to 32 raw political rights points is placed in category 1 of the political rights scale; with 23 to 27 points, it is placed in category 2; and so on.

What needs to be true for the FH scale to convey meaningful information? For one, it is necessary that each of the 22 items that compose the checklist of political rights and civil liberties be sufficiently defined. Adjectives such as *equal, fair, honest, reasonable,* and so on that appear in the description of the checklist items must have been sufficiently defined so that one may separate the cases of *unequal, unfair, dishonest, and unreasonable* practices that take place across countries. Then, there must be rules that allow one to decide when a practice related to political or civil liberty deserves a 0, as opposed to a 1, 2, 3, or 4 in each of these items. Not only must these items make sense, but one must be able to distinguish the levels in which they materialize. Moreover, it must also be true that different constellations of attributes that add up to the same number be equivalent. Having "personal autonomy" with no "equality of opportunity" must be equivalent to the opposite. Finally, assuming that one knows what to do once one has the facts, one still has to get the facts about each of these items. What is needed is information about the policymaking activities of both executive and legislative bodies, political campaigning, political parties (both in government and in opposition), trade unions, professional organizations, the judiciary, the military, religious organizations, economic oligarchies, and so on.

If these conditions are met, indeed the FH scale will convey more information than a dichotomous measure based simply on whether or not contested elections took place. However, if these conditions are not met, then at each step of the process the numbers that are generated make less and less sense. One is left with a scale that is more refined than a dichotomy in the sense that it contains more categories and allows for more values, but certainly not because it conveys more information about the political regime in each country. It is possible that what they convey is information about the subjectivity of those involved in generating the scale.

So which measure should one use to study democracy? As with anything else, the best measure is a function of the question being asked and of its conceptual clarity. The measures of democracy, however, are all very highly correlated, thus making it irrelevant which measure one uses. Indeed, the correlation between Polity IV and FH is −0.90. Polity IV predicts correctly 87 percent of the cases classified as democracies by DD and 93 percent of those classified as dictatorships. FH predicts 87 percent and 93 percent, respectively. But continuous scales of democracy have a bimodal distribution, with a high concentration of cases at the low and high ends of the scales: 56 percent of the cases are classified in the three lowest and highest categories of FH's 13-point scale; 71 percent of the cases have scores that are −7 and lower or 7 and higher in the 21-point Polity IV scale. If one excludes the extremes of the democracy scales, the correlation among the different measures is considerably reduced. The correlation between Polity IV and FH becomes –0.67. Polity IV predicts 65 percent of the democracies in DD and 87 percent of dictatorships, whereas these numbers are 73 percent and 87 percent for FH. Thus it is the uncontroversial cases that drive the high correlation among different measures of democracy: No measure is likely to produce very different readings for, say, England, the United States, Sweden, North Korea, or Iraq. The problem arises with "difficult" cases, such as Mexico, Botswana, Malaysia, Peru, Guatemala, and scores of other countries that do not easily fit into the categories that make up existing measures. These countries are "difficult," however, not necessarily because they represent intermediate instances of democracy, thus calling for measures that allow for gradations; rather, they are difficult because the rules we have to sort the types of political regimes are not good enough to distinguish all the cases we encounter in the world. Perhaps rather than gradations of democracy, what we need is simply better rules for identifying democratic regimes.

None of this is necessarily an argument for the use of a dichotomous measure such as DD over scales such as FH, Polity, or Bollen. But given that once we get to these difficult cases—the cases that populate the middle of the distribution in these scales—no consensus seems to exist across measures; *the choice must be made on conceptual grounds and on the basis of the amount of error each measure may contain.* If one can make sense of what it means to be 4, or to move from 4 to 5 in the Polity scale, then one should probably use it. If one cannot make sense of what this means, and, for this reason, doubts the process that generated this number, then one might be better served by using a "cruder" measure, but one that has some theoretical and empirical meaning.

In what follows we use DD to characterize the distribution of democracies in the world across regions and over time since 1946. Table A.1 presents the frequency of democracies in each region of

TABLE A.1. *Distribution of democracies across regions, 1946–2008*

Region	Country-years	% democratic	% parliamentary	% mixed	% presidential
Sub-Saharan Africa	2153	14.17	24.26	39.34	36.39
South Asia	393	44.78	82.39	5.68	11.93
East Asia	308	17.53	5.56	55.56	38.89
South-East Asia	513	19.10	46.94	0.00	53.06
Pacific Islands/Oceania	342	65.79	85.33	0.00	14.67
Middle East/North Africa	741	18.22	100.00	0.00	0.00
Latin America	1197	59.06	0.00	0.28	99.72
Caribbean/Non-Iberic America	521	76.97	95.01	0.00	4.99
Eastern Europe/Ex-Soviet Union	945	32.59	38.96	61.04	0.00
Industrial Countries	1636	94.44	68.87	21.29	9.84
Oil Countries	322	0.00	0.00	0.00	0.00
All	9071	43.59	54.63	17.17	28.20

the world between 1946 and 2008. These figures refer to the countries that either existed in 1946 or became independent after that year. The second column in the table presents the number of country-years observed in each region.

The third column in table A.1 presents the percentage of country-years in each region that was spent under democracy. As we can see, the variation is large across regions. Only a small proportion of the time in sub-Saharan Africa, East Asia, and the Middle East/North Africa was spent under democracy. The opposite was true for the Caribbean and the industrial countries, where most of the time was spent under democracy. Latin America is unique in that it experienced democracy and dictatorship in equal proportions. No oil country has ever been a democracy.

The last three columns in table A.1 present the distribution of different types of democracy—parliamentary, mixed, and presidential—in each region. Recall that systems in which governments must enjoy the confidence of the legislature are parliamentary; systems in which they serve at the authority of the elected president are presidential; and systems in which governments respond both to legislative assemblies and elected presidents are mixed. As we can see, regional patterns are, again, very clear. Most democracies in the industrial countries are parliamentary. The same is true of the relatively few democracies that exist in South Asia, the Pacific Islands, the Middle East, and the Caribbean. Latin America, on the contrary, is overwhelmingly presidential, whereas the democracies that exist in sub-Saharan Africa tend to be equally split among the three types.

Figure A.1 presents the evolution of democratic regimes since 1946. As we can see, the postwar evolution of democracies can be approximated by a U-shaped curve. The proportion of democracies was relatively high at the end of the 1940s, when it started to decline,

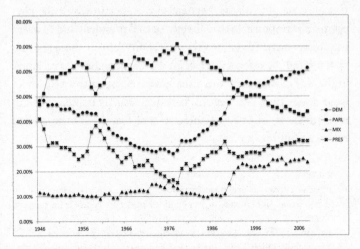

reaching a low of only 28 percent in 1977 to 1978. Since then the proportion of democracy in the world has been increasing, reaching almost 62 percent in 2008, the highest level since 1946. This pattern should not be immediately interpreted as evidence that democratization happens in waves, as argued by Huntington. As Przeworski et al. (2000) argue, the pattern we observe in figure A.1 is not so much the product of democracies becoming dictatorships and vice versa. Rather it is because many countries have entered the world, that is, have become independent, in the 1960s and 1970s, and they did so as dictatorships. The proportion of democracies and dictatorships in countries that existed prior to 1946, as they note, has remained mostly constant, and the variation that we observe is almost entirely due to regime changes in Latin America.

Figure A.1 also presents the proportion of democracies that are parliamentary, mixed, or presidential. The most striking feature in this picture is the recent increase in the proportion of democracies that have adopted a mixed system, that is, one in which the government is responsible to a directly elected president and to a legislative majority. We know very little about the way these regimes operate, and the category in fact masks a large amount of variation in the way governments are actually formed and dismissed. There is no doubt, however, that this is an increasingly popular form of government among new democracies, one that needs to be studied more carefully.

NOTES

1 These requirements are: freedom to form and join organizations, freedom of expression, right to vote, right of political leaders to compete for support, existence of alternative sources of information, free and fair elections, and institutions that make government policies depend on popular votes.

2 A similar limitation applies to the measure developed by Bollen (1980). Originally constructed for 1960 and 1965, it has been extended to 1955, 1970, 1975, and 1980, but not for other years.

REFERENCES

Bollen, Kenneth A. 1980. "Issues in the Comparative Measurement of Political Democracy." *American Sociological Review* 45(3): 370–390.

———. 1991. "Political Democracy: Conceptual and Measurement Traps," in Alex Inkeles, ed., *On Measuring Democracy: Its Consequences and Concomitants*. pp. 3–20. New Brunswick: Transaction Books.

Bollen, Kenneth A., and Robert W. Jackman. 1989. "Democracy, Stability, and Dichotomies." *American Sociological Review* 54(4): 612–621.

Cheibub, José Antonio, Jennifer Gandhi, and James Raymond Vreeland. 2010. "Democracy and Dictatorship Revisited." *Public Choice* 143(1):67–101.

Coppedge, Michael, and Wolfgang H. Reinicke. 1990. "Measuring Polyarchy." *Studies in Comparative International Development* 25(1): 51–72.

Dahl, Robert A. 1971. *Polyarchy: Participation and Opposition*. New Haven: Yale University Press.

Elkins, Zachary. 2000. "Gradations of Democracy: Empirical Tests of Alternative Conceptualizations." *American Journal of Political Science* 44(2): 293–301.

Marshall, Monty G., and Keith Jaggers. *Polity IV Project. Political Regime Characteristics and Transitions, 1800–1999. Dataset Users' Manual.* University of Maryland, College Park. Accessed at systemicpeace.org/inscr/p4manualv2012.pdf.

Przeworski. Adam, Mike Alvarez, José Antonio Cheibub, and Fernando Limongi. 2000. *Democracy and Development: Political Regimes and Economic Performance in the World, 1950–1990.* Cambridge: Cambridge University Press.

NOTES

CHAPTER 2: WHERE AND HOW DID DEMOCRACY DEVELOP?

1 For an extensive description of democracy in Athens, see Mogens Herman Hansen, *The Athenian Democracy in the Age of Demosthenes: Structure, Principles, and Ideology*, translated by J. A. Crook (Oxford: Blackwell, 1991).

2 James Madison, *The Federalist: A Commentary on the Constitutions of the United States* . . . (New York: Modern Library [1937?]), No. 10, 59.

3 Johannes Brøndsted, *The Vikings* (New York: Penguin, 1960), 241.

4 Benjamin R. Barber, *The Death of Communal Liberty: A History of Freedom in a Swiss Mountain Canton* (Princeton: Princeton University Press, 1974), 115.

5 Gwyn Jones, *A History of the Vikings*, 2d ed. (Oxford: Oxford University Press, 1985), 150, 152, 282–284.

6 Franklin D. Scott, *Sweden: The Nation's History* (Minneapolis: University of Minnesota Press, 1977), 111–112.

7 Dolf Sternberger and Bernhard Vogel, eds., *Die Wahl Der Parliamente*, vol. 1: *Europa* (Berlin: Walter de Gruyter, 1969), part 1, table A1, 632; part 2, 895, and table A2, 913.

CHAPTER 4: WHAT IS DEMOCRACY?

1 Thucydides, *Complete Writings: The Peloponnesian War*, unabridged Crawley translation with introduction by John H. Finley, Jr. (New York: Random House, 1951), 105.

2 American readers accustomed to applying the term *state* to the states that make up the federal system of the United *States* may sometimes find this usage confusing. But the term is widely used in international law, political science, philosophy, and in other countries, including several countries with federal systems, where the constituent parts may be called provinces (Canada), cantons (Switzerland), Lande (Germany), and so on.

CHAPTER 5: WHY DEMOCRACY?

1 These figures are from Robert Conquest, *The Great Terror, Stalin's Purge of the Thirties* (New York: Macmillan, 1968), 525ff., and a compilation in 1989 by eminent Russian historian Roy Medvedev (*New York Times*, February 4, 1989, 1).

2 An important exception was the United States, where de facto limits on the exercise of suffrage by black citizens were imposed in southern states until after the passage and enforcement of the Civil Rights Acts of 1964–1965.

3 To pursue the problem more deeply, see James S. Fishkin, *Tyranny and Legitimacy: A Critique of Political Theories* (Baltimore: Johns Hopkins University Press, 1979).

4 Thucydides, *The Peloponnesian War* (New York: Modern Library, 1951), 105.

5 The word *anarchy* is from the Greek word *anarchos* meaning rulerless, from *an* + *archos*, ruler. Anarchism refers to a political theory holding that a state is unnecessary and undesirable.

6 John Stuart Mill, *Considerations on Representative Government* [1861] (New York: Liberal Arts Press, 1958), 43, 55.

7 This important finding is substantiated by Bruce Russett, *Controlling the Sword: The Democratic Governance of National Security* (Cambridge: Harvard University Press, 1990), chap. 5, 119–145. In what follows I have drawn freely from Russett's discussion. The observation also appears to hold true for earlier democracies and republics. See Spencer Weart, *Never at War: Why Democracies Will Never Fight One Another* (New Haven and London: Yale University Press, 1998).

8 High levels of international trade seem to predispose countries toward peaceful relations regardless of whether they are democratic or undemocratic. John Oneal and Bruce Russett, "The Classical Liberals Were Right: Democracy, Interdependence, and Conflict, 1950–1985," *International Studies Quarterly* 41, 2 (June 1997): 267–294.

CHAPTER 6: WHY POLITICAL EQUALITY I?

1 For further on this matter, see Garry Wills, *Inventing America: Jefferson's Declaration of Independence* (Garden City, N.Y.: Doubleday, 1978), 167–228.

2 Alexis de Tocqueville, *Democracy in America,* vol. 1 (New York: Schocken Books, 1961), lxxi.

CHAPTER 7: WHY POLITICAL EQUALITY II?

1 The philosophical status of ethical statements and how they differ from statements in empirical sciences like physics, chemistry, and so on has been a matter of vast debate. I could not hope to do justice to the issues here. However, for an excellent discussion of the importance of moral argument in public decisions, see Amy Gutmann and Dennis Thompson, *Democracy and Disagreement* (Cambridge: Belknap Press of Harvard University Press, 1996).

2 For these remarks at the Constitutional Convention, see Max Farrand, ed.,

The Records of the Federal Convention of 1787, 4 vols. (New Haven: Yale University Press, 1966), 1:82, 284, 578.

3 John Stuart Mill, *Considerations on Representative Government* [1861] (New York: Liberal Arts Press, 1958), 44.

CHAPTER 8: WHAT POLITICAL INSTITUTIONS DOES LARGE-SCALE DEMOCRACY REQUIRE?

1 "The Hats assumed their name for being like the dashing fellows in the tricorne of the day. . . . The Caps were nicknamed because of the charge that they were like timid old ladies in nightcaps." Franklin D. Scott, *Sweden: The Nation's History* (Minneapolis: University of Minnesota Press, 1977), 243.

2 Alexis de Tocqueville, *Democracy in America*, vol. 1 (New York: Schocken Books, 1961), 51.

3 Tocqueville, *Democracy in America*, 50.

4 John Stuart Mill, *Considerations on Representative Government* [1861] (New York: Liberal Arts Press, 1958), 55.

CHAPTER 9: VARIETIES I

1 Lenin, *The Proletarian Revolution and the Renegade Kautsky* (November 1918), cited in Jens A. Christophersen, *The Meaning of "Democracy" as Used in European Ideologies from the French to the Russian Revolution* (Oslo: Universitetsvorlaget, 1966), 260.

2 As I mentioned in Chapter 2, Greeks did not view as "democratic" the rudimentary representative governments formed by some cities for common defense, which in any case were irrelevant to later developments of representative government.

3 Destutt de Tracy, *A Commentary and Review of Montesquieu's Spirit of Laws* (Philadelphia: William Duane, 1811), 19, cited in Adrienne Koch, *The Philosophy of Thomas Jefferson* (Chicago, 1964), 152, 157.

4 Cited in George H. Sabine, *A History of Political Theory*, 3d ed. (New York: Holt, Rinehart and Winston, 1961), 695.

5 The quotation and estimates of the numbers of Athenian citizens are from Mogens Herman Hansen, *The Athenian Democracy in the Age of Demosthenes: Structure, Principles, and Ideology*, translated by J. A. Crook (Oxford: Blackwell, 1991), 53–54. Estimates for the other cities are from John V. Fine, *The Ancient Greeks: A Critical History* (Cambridge: Belknap Press of Harvard University Press, 1983).

6 E. F. Schumacher, *Small Is Beautiful: A Study of Economics as If People Mattered* (London: Blond and Briggs, 1973).

7 Frank M. Bryan, "Direct Democracy and Civic Competence," *Good Society* 5, 1 (Fall 1995): 36–44.

CHAPTER 10: VARIETIES II

1 See Arend Lijphart, *Democracies: Patterns of Majoritarian and Consensus Government in Twenty-One Countries* (New Haven and London: Yale University Press, 1984), table 3.1, 38. I have added Costa Rica to his list.

2 Through a series of enactments by the parliament sitting as a constitutional body Israel has been converting its constitutional arrangements into a written constitution.

3 Some social and economic rights have been added to the U.S. Constitution directly, as with the Thirteenth Amendment abolishing slavery, or via congressional and judicial interpretation of the Fifth and Fourteenth Amendments.

4 Lijphart, *Democracies*, tables 10.1 and 10.2, 174, 178. Because of its regional decentralization, Belgium might reasonably be added to the list. As with other constitutional arrangements, the categories "federal" and "unitary" include significant variations.

5 According to Madison's notes, in a lengthy speech on June 18, 1787, Hamilton remarked, "As to the Executive, it seemed to be admitted that no good one could be established on republican principles. . . . The English model was the only good one on this subject. . . . Let one branch of the Legislature hold their places for life or at least during good behavior. Let the Executive also be for life." See Max Farrand, ed., *The Records of the Federal Convention of 1787*, vol. 1 (New Haven: Yale University Press, 1966), 289. Gerry's comment on June 26 is at 425.

CHAPTER 11: VARIETIES III

1 The variations are, as an excellent study puts it, "countless." The same study suggests that "essentially they can be split into nine main systems which fall into three broad families." Andrew Reynolds and Ben Reilly, eds., *The International IDEA Handbook of Electoral System Design*, 2d ed. (Stockholm: International Institute for Democracy and Electoral Assistance, 1997), 17. The "three broad families" are plurality-majority, semi-PR, and PR. For further details, see Appendix A.

2 Incidentally, whether a country is federal or unitary has no particular bearing on its choosing between a parliamentary and a presidential system. Of the federal systems among the older democracies, four are parliamentary (Australia, Austria, Canada, and Germany) while only the United States is presidential, and Switzerland is a unique hybrid. We can thus discount fed-

eralism as a factor that determines the choice between presidentialism and parliamentarism.

3 In referendums held in 1992 and 1993 New Zealanders rejected FPTP. In the binding 1993 referendum a majority adopted a system that combines proportionality with the election of some members of parliament from districts and others from party lists.

4 For details, see Dieter Nohlen, "Sistemas electorales y gobernabilidad," in Dieter Nohlen, ed., *Elecciónes y sistemas de partidos en America Latina* (San José, Costa Rica: Instituto Interamericano de Derechos Humanos, 1993), 391–424. See also Dieter Nohlen, ed., *Enciclopedia electoral latinoamericana y del Caribe* (San José, Costa Rica: Instituto Interamericano de Derechos Humanos, 1993). Without exception, all twelve of the newly independent island countries of the Caribbean that had been British colonies adopted the British (Westminster) constitutional model.

5 And newer ones as well. For some years Uruguay had a plural executive, which, however, it abandoned.

6 See Juan J. Linz and Arturo Valenzuela, eds., *The Failure of Presidential Democracy* (Baltimore: Johns Hopkins University Press, 1994).

CHAPTER 12: WHAT UNDERLYING CONDITIONS FAVOR DEMOCRACY?

1 I derived this estimate by combining lists (eliminating overlaps) from two studies that used somewhat different criteria: Frank Bealey, "Stability and Crisis: Fears About Threats to Democracy," *European Journal of Political Research* 15 (1987): 687–715, and Alfred Stepan and Cindy Skach, "Presidentialism and Parliamentarism in Comparative Perspective," in Juan J. Linz and Arturo Valenzuela, eds., *The Failure of Presidential Government* (Baltimore: Johns Hopkins University Press, 1994), 119–136.

2 Mark Rosenberg, "Political Obstacles to Democracy in Central America," in James M. Malloy and Mitchell Seligson, eds., *Authoritarians and Democrats: Regime Transition in Latin America* (Pittsburgh: University of Pittsburgh Press, 1987), 193–250.

3 Though coercion was not, as is sometimes thought, nonexistent. Children in schools were uniformly compelled to speak English. Most rapidly lost competence in their ancestral language. And outside the home and neighborhood English was almost exclusively employed—and woe to the person who could not comprehend or respond in English, however poorly.

4 Many volumes have been written on the causes of the American Civil War. My brief statement does not, of course, do justice to the complex events and causes leading to that conflict.

5 For an excellent comparative analysis, see Michael Walzer, *On Toleration* (New Haven and London: Yale University Press, 1997). In an epilogue he offers "Reflections on American Multiculturalism" (93–112).

6 Scott J. Reid describes a two-round voting process that would allow most, though not all, persons in Quebec to remain in Canada or in an independent Quebec. He concedes that his "proposal and others like it may or may not be practical" ("The Borders of an Independent Quebec: A Thought Experiment," *Good Society 7* [Winter 1997]: 11–15).

7 The data that follow are mainly from the *Economist*, August 2, 1997, 52, 90; United Nations Development Programme, *Human Development Report* (New York: Oxford University Press, 1997), 51; "India's Five Decades of Progress and Pain," *New York Times*, August 14, 1997; and Shashi Tharoor, "India's Odd, Enduring Patchwork," *New York Times*, August 8, 1997.

8 After her electoral defeat in 1977 Indira Gandhi was voted in again as prime minister in 1980. In 1984 she ordered Indian troops to attack the holiest Muslim shrine in India, which was being occupied by members of the Sikh religious sect. Shortly after, she was assassinated by two of her Sikh bodyguards. Hindus then went on a rampage and killed thousands of Sikhs. In 1987, her son Rajiv Gandhi, who had become prime minister, suppressed an independence movement by a regional minority, the Tamils. In 1991 he was assassinated by a Tamil.

9 *Economist*, August 2, 1997, 52.

10 This is not true if members of a distinct cultural minority live together in a region on India's borders. There are several such minorities, most prominently the Kashmiris, whose attempts to gain independence have been frustrated by the Indian government's employing military force against them.

11 The criteria for the three categories are described in Appendix C.

CHAPTER 13: WHY MARKET-CAPITALISM FAVORS DEMOCRACY

1 For impressive evidence on this point, see Bruce Russett, "A Neo-Kantian Perspective: Democracy, Interdependence, and International Organizations in Building Security Communities," in Emanuel Adler and Michael Barnett, eds., *Security Communities in Comparative and Historical Perspective* (Cambridge: Cambridge University Press, 1998); and Adam Przeworski and Fernando Limongi, "Political Regimes and Economic Growth," *Journal of Economic Perspectives* 7, 3 (Summer 1993): 51–70.

CHAPTER 14: WHY MARKET-CAPITALISM HARMS DEMOCRACY

1 The classic account is Karl Polanyi, *The Great Transformation* (New York: Farrar and Rinehart, 1944). Polanyi was an exile from Austria and Hungary who moved to England and later taught in the United States.

CHAPTER 15: THE UNFINISHED JOURNEY

1 This is essentially the finding of several careful studies. Compare the study of thirteen democratic countries by Hans-Dieter Klingemann, Richard I. Hofferbert, and Ian Budge et al., *Parties, Policies and Democracy* (Boulder: Westview, 1994). A study of thirty-eight governments in twelve democratic countries also found considerable congruence between the views of citizens and those of policy makers, though the congruence was higher in countries with PR electoral systems than in countries with FPTP systems; John D. Huber and G. Bingham Powell, Jr., "Congruence Between Citizens and Policy Makers in Two Visions of Liberal Democracy," *World Politics* 46, 3 (April 1994): 29ff.

2 Charles E. Lindblom showed the rationality of "muddling through" by incremental methods in a seminal article, "The Science of Muddling Through," *Public Administration Review* 19 (1959): 78–88. See also Lindblom, "Still Muddling, Not Yet Through," in his *Democracy and Market System* (Oslo: Norwegian University Press, 1988), 237–262. Lindblom also used the term *disjointed incrementalism,* on which he wrote extensively. See his *The Intelligence of Democracy: Decision Making Through Mutual Adjustment* (New York: Free Press, 1965).

3 For example, Benjamin I. Page reaches a favorable verdict about American voters in *Choices and Echoes in Presidential Elections: Rational Man and Electoral Democracy* (Chicago: University of Chicago Press, 1978). Michael X. Delli Carpini and Scott Keeler conclude, however, that "one of the central—and most disturbing—findings of our research is the sizable gaps in knowledge found between socioeconomically disadvantaged groups and their more advantaged counterparts" (*What Americans Know About Politics and Why It Matters* [New Haven and London: Yale University Press, 1989], 287).

A more severe criticism, with recommendations for the introduction of new institutions to help overcome deficiencies in understanding, is James Fishkin, *The Voice of the People: Public Opinion and Democracy* (New Haven and London: Yale University Press, 1995).

4 In 1930 a three-minute telephone call from New York to London had cost three hundred dollars (in 1996 dollars); in 1996 it cost about one dollar (*Economist,* October 18, 1997, 79).

CHAPTER 16: CONTINUING THE JOURNEY?

1 Samuel P. Huntington, "Will More Countries Become Democratic?" *Political Science Quarterly* 99, 2 (Summer 1984): 193–218.

2 James H. Read and Ian Shapiro, "Transforming Power Relationships: Leadership, Risk, and Hope," *American Political Science Review* 108, 1 (February 2014): 40–53.

3 Courtney Jung, Ellen Lust, and Ian Shapiro, "Problems and Prospects for Democratic Settlements: South Africa as a Model for the Middle East and Northern Ireland?" in *The Real World of Democratic Theory*, ed. Ian Shapiro (Princeton: Princeton University Press, 2011), 80–142.

4 James Madison, "The Federalist No. 10," in *The Federalist Papers*, ed. Ian Shapiro (New Haven: Yale University Press, 2009), 47–53.

5 Kenneth Arrow, *Social Choice and Individual Values* (New York: John Wiley and Sons, 1951).

6 José Antonio Cheibub and Fernando Limongi, "Democratic Institutions and Regime Survival: Parliamentarism and Presidentialism Reconsidered," *Annual Review of Political Science* 5, 1 (2002): 151–179.

7 Seymour Martin Lipset, *Political Man: The Social Bases of Politics* (Garden City, N.J.: Doubleday, 1960), 62.

8 Karl Marx and Friedrich Engels, *Manifesto of the Communist Party*, ed. Jeffrey Isaac (New Haven: Yale University Press, 2012), 102.

9 Adam Przeworski, "Acquiring the Habit of Changing Governments through Elections" (mimeo, New York University, 2014).

10 See, e.g., Stanley Elkins and Eric McKitrick, *The Age of Federalism: The Early American Republic, 1788–1800* (New York: Oxford University Press, 1993), and Susan Dunn, *Jefferson's Second Revolution: The Election Crisis of 1800 and the Triumph of Republicanism* (New York: Houghton Mifflin, 2004).

CHAPTER 17: DEMOCRACY AND INEQUALITY

1 "Working for the Few: Political Capture and Economic Inequality," Oxfam Briefing Paper #178, January 20, 2014, http://www.oxfam.org/en/policy/working-for-the-few-economic-inequality.

2 Nolan McCarty, Keith Poole, and Howard Rosenthal, *Political Bubbles: Financial Crises and the Failure of American Democracy* (Princeton: Princeton University Press, 2013).

3 *Buckley v. Valeo* 424 U.S. 1 (1976), 39, 48, 59.

4 *Citizens United v. Federal Election Commission* 558 U.S. 310 (2010).

5 *SpeechNow.org v. Federal Election Commission* 599 F.3d 686, 689 (D.C. Cir. 2010).

6 As of July 2013, Super PACs had reported total receipts of $828,224,595 and to-
tal independent expenditures of $609,417,654 in the 2012 cycle. Open Secrets.
Center for Responsive Politics. http://www.opensecrets.org/pacs/superpacs
.php. See also "Koch-Backed Political Network, Designed to Shield Donors,
Raised $400 million in 2012," *Washington Post*, January 6, 2014.

7 *McCutcheon v. Federal Election Commission* 572 U.S. __ (2014).

8 Stephen Engelberg and Kim Barker, "Flood of Secret Campaign Cash: It's Not
All *Citizens United*," ProPublica, August 23, 2012, http://www.propublica.org/
article/flood-of-secret-campaign-cash-its-not-all-citizens-united.

9 *Buckley v. Valeo*, 259, 265, 266.

10 *Buckley v. Valeo*, 19.

11 Paul Hirschkorn, "The $1 Billion Presidential Campaign," CBS News, Oc-
tober 21, 2012, http://www.cbsnews.com/news/the-1-billion-presidential
-campaign/ [01–15–2015].

12 Nolan McCarty, Keith Poole, and Howard Rosenthal, *Polarized America: The
Dance of Ideology and Unequal Riches* (Princeton: Princeton University Press,
2006), 7–9, 71–138.

13 Most countries with compulsory voting laws do not enforce them, with the
result that their effects are modest. Somewhat surprisingly, their main impact
is to increase turnout of the elderly. See Ellen Quintelier, Marc Hooghe, and
Sofie Marien, "The Effect of Compulsory Voting on Turnout Stratification
Patterns: A Cross-National Analysis," *International Political Science Review*
32, 4 (2011): 396–416.

14 A federal minimum wage (FMW) was first set in 1938 at $0.25 an hour, or
$4.00 in 2012 dollars. By that benchmark the highest was $10.51 in 1968. The
FMW is congenitally eroded by inflation until Congress can be induced to
raise it (as it last did in 2009). In 2012 the FMW stood at $7.25, the real level
reached in 1960. See "Minimum Wage History," Oregon State University,
http://oregonstate.edu/instruct/anth484/minwage.html; Lawrence Mishel,
"Declining Value of the Federal Minimum Wage as a Major Factor Driving
Inequality," Report for the Economic Policy Institute, February 21, 2013, http://
www.epi.org/publication/declining-federal-minimum-wage-inequality/; and
McCarty, Poole, and Rosenthal, *Polarized America*, 166–169.

15 Internal Revenue Code section 55(d), as amended by section 104(b)(1) of the
American Taxpayer Relief Act of 2012 (January 2, 2013).

16 Matthew Dalton, "Permanent Estate Tax Ends Decade of Uncertainty," *Tax
Notes Today*, January 3, 2013, http://www.taxanalysts.com/www/website.nsf/
Web/RequestInformation?OpenDocument&trial=FTN&dn=2013–106
&title=Permanent%20Estate%20Tax%20Ends%20Decade%20of%20
Uncertainty.

17 The hundreds of millions of dollars spent by financial lobbies while the bill was moving through Congress and regulations were being written swamped anything that could be put together on the other side. See Gary Rivlin, "How Wall Street Defanged Dodd-Frank," The Investigative Fund, April 30, 2013, http://www.theinvestigativefund.org/investigations/politicsandgovernment/1778/how_wall_street_defanged_dodd-frank/.

18 Alan S. Blinder, *After the Music Stopped: The Financial Crisis, the Response, and the Work Ahead* (New York: Penguin, 2013), 290–319.

19 Blinder, *After the Music Stopped*, 315–316.

20 Robert Lenzner, "The 867 Page Volcker Rule Is Unfathomable and a Plague on Markets," Forbes online, December 10, 2013, http://www.forbes.com/sites/robertlenzner/2013/12/10/the-credit-markets-are-broken-due-to-the-disastrous-867-page-volcker-rule/.

FOR FURTHER READING

The number of books and articles that deal directly or indirectly with the subject of democracy is enormous. They date from the fourth century B.C.E. with works by Aristotle and Plato to no fewer than hundreds of works, I'd guess, published in the past year. So the following brief list is obviously incomplete, and the selections may be fairly arbitrary. But should you wish to pursue a topic further than my brief treatment allows or would like to explore democracy from other perspective than mine, these works should help. I've already cited some of them in the Notes.

THE ORIGINS AND DEVELOPMENT OF DEMOCRACY

Adcock, F. E. *Roman Political Ideas and Practice*. Ann Arbor: University of Michigan Press, 1959.

Agard, Walter R. *What Democracy Meant to the Greeks*. Madison: University of Wisconsin Press, 1965.

Hansen, Mogens Herman. *The Athenian Democracy in the Age of Demosthenes: Structure, Principles, and Ideology*. Translated by J. A. Crook. Oxford: Blackwell, 1991.

Huntington, Samuel P. *The Third Wave: Democratization in the Late Twentieth Century*. Norman: University of Oklahoma Press, 1991.

Jones, A. H. M. *Athenian Democracy*. Oxford: Blackwell, 1957.

Ober, Josiah. *Democracy and Knowledge: Innovation and Learning in Classical Athens*. Princeton: Princeton University Press, 2008.

Schwartzberg, Melissa. *Counting the Many: The Origins and Limits of Supermajority Rule*. New York: Cambridge University Press, 2013.

Taylor, Lily R. *Roman Voting Assemblies from the Hannibalic War to the Dictatorship of Caesar*. Ann Arbor: University of Michigan Press, 1966.

Vanhanen, Tatu. *The Process of Democratization: A Comparative Study of 147 States, 1980–88*. New York: Crane Russak, 1990.

DEMOCRATIC GOALS, IDEALS, AND ADVANTAGES

Barber, Benjamin R. *Strong Democracy: Participatory Politics for a New Age*. Berkeley: University of California Press, 1984.

Bobbio, Norberto. *The Future of Democracy: A Defence of the Rules of the Game*. Translated by Roger Griffin. Edited and introduced by Richard Bellamy. Cambridge: Polity Press, 1987. [Originally published as *Il futuro della democrazia*. Turin: Giulio Editore, 1984.]

Christophersen, Jens A. *The Meaning of "Democracy" as Used in European Ide-*
ologies from the French to the Russian Revolution. Oslo: Universitetsforlaget,
1968.

Fishkin, James. *Democracy and Deliberation: New Directions for Democratic*
Reform. New Haven and London: Yale University Press, 1991.

Gutmann, Amy. *Liberal Equality.* Cambridge: Cambridge University Press,
1980.

Held, David. *Models of Democracy,* 2d ed. Stanford: Stanford University Press,
1996.

Mansbridge, Jane J. *Beyond Adversarial Democracy.* New York: Basic Books,
1980.

Mill, John Stuart. *Considerations on Representative Government.* [1861] New
York: Liberal Arts Press, 1958.

Pateman, Carole. *Participation and Democratic Theory.* Cambridge: Cambridge
University Press, 1970

Przeworski, Adam. *Democracy and the Limits of Self-Government.* New York:
Cambridge University Press, 2010.

Rehfeld, Andrew. *The Concept of Constituency: Political Representation, Demo-*
cratic Legitimacy, and Institutional Design. New York: Cambridge University
Press, 2005.

Rousseau, Jean-Jacques. *Du Contrat social, ou Principes de droit politique.* [1762]
Paris: Editions Garnier Frères, 1962.

———. *On the Social Contract, with Geneva Manuscript and Political Economy.*
Edited by Roger D. Masters and translated by Judith R. Masters. New York:
St. Martin's Press, 1978.

Sartori, Giovanni. *The Theory of Democracy Revisited.* Chatham, N.J.: Chatham
House, 1987.

Sen, Amartya. "Freedoms and Needs." *New Republic,* January 10 and 17, 1994,
31–38.

Shapiro, Ian. *Democracy's Place.* Ithaca: Cornell University Press, 1996.

———. *Democratic Justice.* New Haven: Yale University Press, 1999.

Urbinati, Nadia. *Representative Democracy: Principles and Genealogy.* Chicago:
University of Chicago Press, 2006.

ACTUAL DEMOCRACY: INSTITUTIONS AND PRACTICES

Coppedge, Michael. *Democratization and Research Methods.* New York: Cambridge University Press, 2012.

Diamond, Larry, et al., eds. *Consolidating the Third Wave Democracies.* Baltimore: Johns Hopkins University Press, 1997.

Katznelson, Ira. *Fear Itself: The New Deal and the Origins of Our Time*. New York: W. W. Norton, 2013.

Klingemann, Hans-Dieter, Richard I. Hofferbert, and Ian Budge, et al. *Parties, Policies, and Democracy*. Boulder: Westview Press, 1994.

Lijphart, Arend. *Democracies: Patterns of Majoritarian and Consensus Government in Twenty-one Countries*. New Haven and London: Yale University Press, 1984.

———. *Democracy in Plural Societies: A Comparative Exploration*. New Haven and London: Yale University Press, 1977.

Lijphart, Arend, ed. *Parliamentary versus Presidential Government*. Oxford: Oxford University Press, 1992.

Linz, Juan J., and Arturo Valenzuela, eds. *The Failure of Presidential Democracy*. Baltimore: Johns Hopkins University Press, 1994.

Mayhew, David R. *Divided We Govern: Party Control, Lawmaking, and Investigations, 1946–2002*, 2d ed. New Haven: Yale University Press, 2005.

———. *Partisan Balance: Why Political Parties Don't Kill the U.S. Constitutional System*. Princeton: Princeton University Press, 2011.

Powell, G. Bingham, Jr. *Elections as Instruments of Democracy: Majoritarian and Proportional Representation*. New Haven: Yale University Press, 2000.

Rae, Douglas W. *The Political Consequences of Electoral Laws*. New Haven: Yale University Press, 1967.

Runciman, David. *The Confidence Trap: A History of Democracy in Crisis from World War I to the Present*. Princeton: Princeton University Press, 2013.

Sartori, Giovanni. *Comparative Constitutional Engineering: An Inquiry into Structures, Incentives, and Outcomes*. London: Macmillan, 1994.

Shapiro, Ian. *The Real World of Democratic Theory*. Princeton: Princeton University Press, 2012.

Shugart, Matthew Soberg, and John M. Carey. *Presidents and Assemblies: Constitutional Design and Electoral Dynamics*. New York: Cambridge University Press, 1992.

Stepan, Alfred, Juan J. Linz, and Yogendra Yadav. *Crafting State-Nations: India and Other Multinational Democracies*. Baltimore: Johns Hopkins University Press, 2011.

Stokes, Susan C., Thad Dunning, Marcelo Nazareno, and Valeria Brusco. *Brokers, Voters, and Clientelism: The Puzzle of Distributive Politics*. New York: Cambridge University Press, 2013.

Ware, Alan. *Citizens, Parties, and the State: A Reappraisal*. Princeton: Princeton University Press, 1988.

Archibugi, Daniele, and David Held, eds. *Cosmopolitan Democracy: An Agenda for a New World Order.* Cambridge: Polity Press, 1995.

Coleman, Isobel, and Terra Lawson-Remer, eds. *Pathways to Freedom: Political and Economic Lessons from Democratic Transitions.* New York: Council on Foreign Relations Press, 2013.

Diamond, Larry. *Developing Democracy: Toward Consolidation.* Baltimore: Johns Hopkins University Press, 1999.

Gutmann, Amy, and Dennis Thompson. *Democracy and Disagreement.* Cambridge: Belknap Press of Harvard University Press, 1996.

Hayek, Friedrich A. von. *The Road to Serfdom.* Chicago: University of Chicago Press, 1976.

Held, David, ed. *Prospects for Democracy, North, South, East, West.* Stanford: Stanford University Press, 1993.

Inglehart, Ronald. *Culture Shift in Advanced Industrial Society.* Princeton: Princeton University Press, 1990.

———. *Modernization and Postmodernization: Cultural, Economic, and Political Change in Forty-three Societies.* Princeton: Princeton University Press, 1997.

Lindblom, Charles E. *Democracy and Market System.* Oslo: Norwegian Universities Press, 1988.

———. *The Intelligence of Democracy: Decision Making Through Mutual Adjustment.* New York: Free Press, 1965.

———. *Politics and Markets: The World's Political Economic Systems.* New York: Basic Books, 1977.

Linz, Juan J., and Alfred Stepan. *Problems of Democratic Transition and Consolidation: Southern Europe, South America, and Post-Communist Europe.* Baltimore: Johns Hopkins University Press, 1996.

Polanyi, Karl. *The Great Transformation.* New York: Farrar and Rinehart, 1944.

Przeworski, Adam. *Democracy and the Market: Political and Economic Reforms in Eastern Europe and Latin America.* Cambridge: Cambridge University Press, 1991.

Przeworski, Adam, Michael Alvarez, José Cheibub, and Fernando Limongi. *Democracy and Development: Political Institutions and Well-Being in the World, 1950–1990.* New York: Cambridge University Press, 2000.

Putnam, Robert D. *Making Democracy Work: Civic Traditions in Modern Italy.* Princeton: Princeton University Press, 1993.

Sen, Amartya. *Inequality Reexamined.* New York: Russell Sage Foundation, and Cambridge: Harvard University Press, 1992.

Walzer, Michael. *On Toleration.* New Haven and London: Yale University Press, 1997.

CHALLENGES AND PROSPECTS

Budge, Ian. *The New Challenge of Direct Democracy*. Cambridge: Polity Press, 1996.

Burnheim, John. *Is Democracy Possible? The Alternative to Electoral Politics*. Berkeley: University of California Press, 1985.

Fishkin, James S. *The Voice of the People: Public Opinion and Democracy*. New Haven: Yale University Press, 1997.

Gutmann, Amy. *Democratic Education*. Princeton: Princeton University Press, 1987.

Hirst, Paul. *Associative Democracy: New Forms of Social and Economic Governance*. Cambridge: Polity Press, 1994.

King, Desmond, and Rogers M. Smith. *Still a House Divided: Race and Politics in Obama's America*. Princeton: Princeton University Press, 2011.

Levinson, Sanford. *Our Undemocratic Constitution: Where the Constitution Goes Wrong (And How We Can Correct It)*. New York: Oxford University Press, 2008.

Schweickart, David. *Capitalism or Worker Control? An Ethical and Economic Appraisal*. New York: Praeger, 1980.

Shapiro, Ian. *The State of Democratic Theory*. Princeton: Princeton University Press, 2003.

Skocpol, Theda. *Diminished Democracy: From Membership to Management in American Civic Life*. Norman: University of Oklahoma Press, 2004.

Stokes, Susan C. *Mandates and Democracy: Neoliberalism by Surprise in Latin America*. New York: Cambridge University Press, 2001.

ACKNOWLEDGMENTS

As I recall, it was to my wife, Ann Sale Dahl, that I first mentioned that I might like to write yet another book bearing on democratic theory and practice. The book I had in mind this time, I said, would be less academic than most I'd written. I wouldn't write the book primarily for other scholars and academics, or even specifically for Americans. I would like it to be helpful to any person, anywhere, who might be seriously interested in learning more about a vast subject that can easily become so complicated that the only people willing to pursue it in depth are political theorists, philosophers, and other scholars. To find just the right style, I confessed, would be a daunting challenge. Ann's enthusiastic response encouraged me to proceed. She was also the first reader of a nearly complete draft, and her deft editorial suggestions significantly improved my presentation.

Two very busy fellow scholars, James Fishkin and Michael Walzer, generously provided detailed comments on my finished draft—well, not quite finished, as it turned out. Their criticisms and suggestions were so relevant and helpful that I adopted almost all of them, regretfully ignoring only a few that seemed to me would require a longer book than the one I had in mind. I am also indebted to Hans Daalder, Arend Lijphart, and Hans Blokland for their helpful comments on the Netherlands.

I am grateful to Charles Hill, David Mayhew, Ian Shapiro, and Norma Thompson for responding to my appeal for the names of works that would be useful to readers who might wish to pursue the subject further. Their proposals have enriched the list entitled "For Further Reading."

Considerably before I had completed the manuscript, I mentioned it to John Covell, Senior Editor at Yale University Press, who immediately expressed his very strong interest in it. After I presented him with a copy of the manuscript, the queries and proposals he offered helped me to improve it in numerous ways.

I am happy that with this book I have continued a long relationship with Yale University Press. It is particularly gratifying to me that Yale University Press is publishing it, because in writing the book I have drawn unhesitatingly on earlier works of mine that the Press has published over many years. I am also delighted that Director John Ryden, Associate Director Tina Weiner, and Managing Editor Meryl Lanning not only expressed their enthusiasm for publishing the book but also strongly endorsed my proposal that it should be rapidly translated and published abroad in order to make it available to readers elsewhere in the world.

Finally, the editing of Laura Jones Dooley, Assistant Managing Editor, was both rapid and superb. Though her contribution is invisible to the reader, the author knows that the book is better for it. He hopes that she does, too.

INDEX

advantages of democracy, 45–61; fostering human development, 55–56; guaranteeing fundamental rights, 48–50; insuring freedoms, 50–52; peace, 57–58; prevention of tyranny, 46–48; prosperity, 58–59; protecting personal interests, 52–53; providing opportunities for exercising moral responsibility, 55; providing opportunities for self-determination, 53–54; providing political equality, 56–57

Africa, 192–193

African Americans and fair representation, 134

agenda, control of, 38

alternation, 197–198

alternative minimum tax, 206

antidemocratic regimes, decline of, 1

Arab Spring, 191

Arrow, Kenneth, 193, 194

assembly democracy, 102–108. *See also* town meetings

associations, need for, 98

Athens: adoption of democratic government, 11; democracy in, 47; government of, 12; Pericles on, 39

Belgium, solutions to cultural divisions in, 193

bicameral *versus* unicameral legislatures, 121

bills of rights: in constitutions of democratic countries, 120

Bollen, Kenneth A., 222, 224, 225

Britain: electorate 1831–1931 (fig. 2), 24; growth of Parliament, 21–25

Buckley v. Valeo, 202, 203–204

campaign contributions, 202–204

capitalism. *See* market-capitalism

challenges to democracy: citizens' information and understanding, 185–188; cultural diversity, 183–184; the economic order, 181–182; internationalization, 183

citizen assemblies, 18–20

citizenship, inclusive. *See* suffrage, universal

Citizens United v. Federal Election Commission, 202, 203

competence of citizens. *See* political equality

compulsory voting, 205

conditions for democracy: adverse effects of foreign intervention, 147–148; control over military and police, 148–149; cultural conflicts, 149–156; democratic beliefs and culture, 156; economic growth and market economy, 158. *See also* market-capitalism

conflicts, cultural: Appendix B, 212; consociational democracy, 153, 212–214; as problem for democracies, 150; separation, 155; solutions for assimilation, 151–153

consociational democracies, 153, 212–214

consolidation (maintaining, survival) of democracy, 2, 193–199